W9-BKC-876

Getting
Better
Together

A DIRECTION DYNAMICS BOOK

GETTING BETTER TOGETHER

Bruce A. Baldwin, Ph.D.

DIRECTION DYNAMICS
Wilmington, NC
1993

Cover Design: Kaye Davis, Greensboro, NC

Printed by Carter Printing Company, Richmond, VA

Library of Congress Catalog Card Number: 93-090785

ISBN 0-933583-20-6

Published and distributed by: **DIRECTION DYNAMICS**
309 Honeycutt Drive
Wilmington, NC 28412
(910) 799-6544

Bulk order discounts on **DIRECTION DYNAMICS** books are available when ordering in quantities of six or more. Please contact **DIRECTION DYNAMICS** for details.

Manufactured in the United States of America

DEDICATION

To those many couples, including Joyce's parents and mine, who stayed together through thick and thin, good times and bad, growing closer and creating the good life for themselves.

ACKNOWLEDGEMENTS

By its very nature, writing a book is a difficult and time-consuming project. Further, any book of substance has many roots in the people who together helped bring it to fruition. Getting Better Together *is no different in that the author could not have done it alone. Without the wonderful support of my wife, Joyce, this project would simply not have been completed. Working out the many details, glitches, and frustrations of getting the manuscript ready for production was a daunting task for which I owe her an enduring debt. The suggestions and help of our children, Travis and Elissa, were also an important part of this book and they are therefore gratefully acknowledged. It is again my pleasure to salute the Editors and staff of* USAir Magazine *at Pace Communications (clearly the best in the business) who published as articles much of the material that appears in this book. Kaye Davis worked with us with great patience through many changes to get the book cover "just right." Mary Kay Dodson diligently edited the book and "cleaned up" the language to make it easy for the reader to understand. As in the past, Carter Printing Company has again put forth considerable effort to manufacture this book to the high standards that are required. Despite all our efforts, however,* Getting Better Together *will be a success only if the couples who read it find their way to the good life—together.*

CONTENTS

Introduction: Making the Good Life Come True

"Living today is like a grammar lesson; the past is perfect and the present is tense!"

"Every marriage is happy. It's living together afterwards that causes all the problems!"

"Life is what happens to you while you're busy making other plans!"

These three statements, made by astute observers of human behavior, unfortunately are too accurate. As the years roll by, life becomes ever more complicated as men, women, and couples pursue the goals of the American Dream. As life becomes busier and more intense, marriage relationships grow strained. Life together becomes less fulfilling unless couples maintain healthy priorities and take care to preserve all the good things in life. And, with the years, time begins to pass ever faster as busy husbands and wives focus on all they must get done each day rather than on their relationship and living the good life together. That's the bad news.

To make matters worse, with more complexity also come more stress and pressure on individuals, couples, and families. And, each day men and women are blitzed with seductive, but short-sighted "solutions" to problems: easy credit; the option to buy right now (no waiting); the "bigger, better, and more" mentality; the linking of self-esteem to material possessions. Millions of hard-working couples are now finding that these lifestyle patterns do not bring to their marriages deep contentment, emotional well-being, and personal happiness.

The good news is that this dissatisfaction is pushing these same men and women into looking beyond superficial values and the prevalent "commercial culture" to find deeper meanings within themselves and their families. They are both looking for and finding more potentially fulfilling avenues to create for themselves "the good life" they have always hoped for and dreamed about. And, to their credit, these adults are savvier and more motivated than any generation before them to pursue and find the personally satisfying lifestyles they want.

The answers to finding the path to the good life simply do not lie in more possessions, more debt, or more money. The thrust lies in simplifying life and going for the basics that have been left in the past. For example, taking pleasure in what you have rather than constantly striving for what you want. Putting a new priority on enjoying experiences with loved ones. Creating time to relax and rejuvenate and just have some fun. Finding fulfillment and meaning in day-to-day experiences. All this is the raw material from which the good life is constructed. And, indeed it can be done, but because life has become so complex, husbands and wives must now know more in order to create the good life for themselves.

Married couples who decide—together—to make these changes automatically have a bonus as they support one another overcoming bad habits and resolving conflicts that perpetuate problems. This support helps to resist external influences that keep these men and women physically and emotionally overloaded to the point where the good life slips away. More important, however, is that deciding to make these key changes together involves not only pursuit of the good life, but also a commitment to enjoying their relationship together.

Making such a commitment is a way of saying: "Let's do this for us. Over the years, we've neglected our relationship. We're important, and so is enjoying life as a couple." The result is that couples who have grown apart over the years begin to reverse that separation. They're more intimate and emotionally together. They enjoy life more. And, their relationship begins to blossom after years of inadvertent neglect. Ironically, the full extent of what has been lost in a marriage may only become apparent when the effects of positive changes are experienced.

While *Getting Better Together* is written primarily for couples who desire to work toward renewing their relationship, keep in mind that most of the necessary changes are individual ones. In other words, critical changes to create the good life together should not be motivated by a desire to please anyone else. Rather, such changes are made because they represent a healthier and more fulfilling way to live. The bottom line is simple. Because key lifestyle changes are made primarily for yourself, this book is pertinent not only for couples, but also for four kinds of presently single individuals.

1. MEN AND WOMEN WHO HAVE NEVER BEEN MARRIED. During courtship, solid relationship skills and healthy lifestyle values become a foundation for evaluating compatibility with a potential marriage partner. By developing a lifestyle balanced between working and achieving on the one hand and enjoying friendships, loved ones, and leisure activities on the other, many of the long-term pitfalls in a marriage can be prevented.

2. COUPLES WHO HAVE SEPARATED. Separations are often therapeutic because there is time for personal assessment and sorting out personal responsibility for problems. For men and women in troubled relationships, *Getting Better Together* pinpoints problems and helps develop new and more emotionally fulfilling ways of relating; these responses function as steps in resolving problems that separated the couple.

3. INDIVIDUALS WHO ARE NOW DIVORCED. After a marriage has ended, objectively examining what was right and what went wrong in that relationship is extremely important so the same mistakes will not be repeated in future relationships. Such personal assessment, along with its resultant changes, helps to rebuild a positive sense of self as a potential marriage partner.

4. MARRIED MEN AND WOMEN WITH UNCOOPERATIVE PARTNERS. Perhaps your spouse just isn't interested in or ready to enjoy the good life. In such marriages, which unfortunately are all too common these days, *Getting Better Together* can be extremely helpful. Don't waste time waiting for your partner to cooperate or get ready if you encounter strong resistance. Instead, begin to move forward living the good life for yourself.

The Themes of Fulfillment

Recent years have seen a growing backlash against many of the shallow, inappropriate, and amoral values that have become so socially dominant in the last two decades. Fortunately, those men, women, and couples involved in this backlash are striving in directions that reflect what is good, what is enduring, and what is deeply fulfilling in their lives together. Interestingly, this growing revolution is a quiet one. It is made up of men and women who dare to be different and who, without fanfare, decide to live by solid values despite what everyone else seems to be doing.

To help accelerate movement toward the good life, these trends have become themes in this book. It is certainly no coincidence that these same trends reflect changes that foster both emotional and physical health, as well as better marriages and family relationships. These trends do not reflect a naive desire to return to the past.

Rather, the focus is on creating solid personal and family values within the context of an often confusing contemporary culture. While difficult, this focus can be and is being successfully accomplished by growing numbers of involved couples.

The net result is that these men, women, and couples are "getting better together." As they do so, they grow personally and move far beyond the empty and superficial values of the past decades. A not inconsequential effect of these changes is that children growing up in these homes have healthier models for their own marriage relationships and better coping skills to deal with life's problems. Here are ten basic and interrelated themes of *Getting Better Together* that also reflect the wave of change now quietly sweeping the country.

THEME #1: MAKING A MARRIAGE LAST. Creating an enduring marriage relationship is perhaps the most fundamental reflection of a new way of thinking about the good life. In fact, several recent surveys have shown that divorce rates either have begun a slow downward trend or have stabilized. As men and women seek to make their marriage a lifetime commitment, they are more motivated to work out their problems. As a consequence, the "replaceable partner" attitude of the past seems to be fading. "We will make it work for us" is the new ethic.

THEME #2: A RETURN TO SPIRITUALITY. A need to find deeper meanings in life that transcend material wealth and possessions is rapidly developing. Couples are seeking personal fulfillment that the transient pleasures of "things" simply cannot fulfill. Church attendance has risen dramatically in recent years and seems to signal a need for a core of meaningful values around which life can be lived. Searching for this meaning and finding it in loving relationships, in good fellowship with friends, and in the simple things in life brings new dimensions of personal and marital contentment to couples.

THEME #3: STRIVING FOR DEBT CONTROL. It is virtually impossible to live the good life when more and more work is directed solely to satisfying creditors. Examining spending habits and reducing needless (or frivolous) debt through joint efforts counters the "spend now, pay later" philosophy of years past. Many families habitually live beyond their means and have pursued their wants, not their needs. These days, more couples are finding that deep fulfillment and personal satisfaction simply do not depend on income or possessions.

THEME #4: MAKING FAMILY AND FRIENDSHIPS PARA-MOUNT. With two career families now the norm, the demands of work and responsibilities (and making more money to pay debts!) have clearly taken precedence over family life. Many marriages have become hollow and unfulfilling as homes have literally become places to eat, sleep, and coordinate everyone's schedules. Once-close friends are not seen much anymore. But these days, many couples are feeling a strong need to bring back the positive experience of a rich family life. They are striving to make their home a place to relax and to share pleasant times together with family and good friends.

THEME #5: THE DESIRE FOR COMMUNITY. One of the most distressing feelings within men and women these days is a sense of not belonging. The world has become very impersonal with little sense of closeness to neighbors and to a community that was so much a part of life in years past. Such alienation produces loss of a sense of personal acceptance and affiliation that provides a source of personal strength and emotional stability. Because this sense of belonging does not occur naturally anymore, men and women are making efforts to create their own sense of belonging and commu-nity.

THEME #6: LOOKING FOR FUNCTIONALITY. As the decades of "glitter and greed" are left behind, couples are looking for practi-cality and lasting power in the products they buy. With costs of living continuing to escalate and income lagging behind, products defined solely by status value have become less attractive. Because this trend is closely associated with the need for debt control, resistance to purchasing expensive technological "gadgets" for their own sake is also growing. Instead, emphasis has shifted to products with proven functional value that serve well and last.

THEME #7: A NEED FOR SIMPLICITY. Lurking deep within many men and women is a recurring dream of running away from their present busy and pressured lifestyles. Life has become so complicated and pressured that it is barely tolerable. With family responsibilities added to home maintenance, community involve-ments, and a busy career, getting through each day becomes an overwhelming task. Deliberately setting out to simplify life in the midst of such complexity not only reduces stress, but sets the stage for finding personal fulfillment and living the good life.

THEME #8: A RETURN TO TRADITION AND ROOTS. As geographic mobility and social impersonality have grown side by side with materialistic values, a sense of rootlessness has developed.

Childhood memories often no longer reflect a close-knit family regularly sharing pleasant experiences together. Family traditions have also fallen by the wayside. As a result, those experiences that later give children a sense of security in adulthood have often been neglected. One result is that more couples are seeking their own personal and ethnic roots and creating family traditions for themselves.

THEME #9: LIVING BY ETHICAL AND MORAL MANDATES. Thank goodness, attitudes of the past such as "anything goes," "the ends justify the means," and the greedy "I'm going to get mine no matter what" seem to be passing. The related attitude, "If they can do it, so can I," is also being left by the wayside. Couples are beginning to closely examine the basic morality and ethics of the values they live by and hold deeply; often, they are found wanting. The result is couples deciding to live more ethically themselves and taking greater pains to instill sound moral values in their children.

THEME #10: STRIVING FOR PERSONAL HEALTH. Feeling good emotionally and physically has become a strong priority for many couples these days. With growing evidence of the mind-body link comes the realization that living the good life is sorely compromised by poor health or constant emotional turmoil. Armed with new information and fearing the consequences of highly stressful lifestyles, men and women are thinking about fitness in a more holistic sense. The result is that couples, expecting to live longer and feel better, are assuming more responsibility for developing healthier lifestyles.

Love Is Not Enough

Many books currently on the market focus exclusively on marital problems and how to overcome them. However, as the saying goes, love is not enough. Marriage requires skill and knowledge and the motivation to change in order to meet evolving needs over the years. To believe that love alone will overcome everything is a naive view found primarily among the young and inexperienced. Even with this understanding, though, focusing exclusively on a marital relationship is still too narrow. In fact, to accomplish what is required to have a fulfilling marital relationship and to enjoy the good life together, changes in three areas will be necessary.

FOCUS #1: RESOLVING IMPEDING PERSONAL ISSUES. All men and women have unresolved hurts, conflicts, and insecurities from the past that haunt them. For some, these are relatively minor problems. For others, whether married or not, these problems constitute major barriers to ever being happy and personally fulfilled. Making those changes necessary to help yourself become personally healthier and more emotionally complete will certainly accelerate your progress toward the good life.

FOCUS #2: MAKING POSITIVE LIFESTYLE CHANGES. With the years, life tends to slowly but surely become more complicated and difficult. In fact, most couples are molded by responsibilities in every part of their lives into lifestyles that reflect unhealthy values, resulting in endless pressure and personal distress. Confronting negative values directly and then, with your partner, deciding on positive lifestyle changes help immensely to simplify life and to enhance personal and marital fulfillment.

FOCUS #3: IMPROVING YOUR MARITAL RELATIONSHIP. Certainly, it is unwise to neglect making long-needed changes in your relationship with your partner. In combination with personal growth and positive lifestyle changes, directly improving your marital relationship becomes much easier. Why? Because you and your partner can move more compatibly toward enjoying life together unencumbered by personal insecurities and negative lifestyle values that have developed over the years.

Using This Book Effectively

As you now know, *Getting Better Together* has a much broader focus than a marriage manual written in the traditional manner. While every chapter is written as a separate unit that can stand alone, each chapter has also been written to dovetail with other sections of the book. In the book, there is a deliberate repetition of some concepts. This repetition is used to help the reader examine the same issue from different perspectives and to reinforce the importance of making specific suggested changes.

However, no self-help book (including this one!) can possibly provide the answers to every material and lifestyle problem. Nor should it. Giving a rote prescription for living the good life is not only impossible, but blatantly presumptuous. Rather, the emphasis here is on delineating basic concepts to help readers understand the forces and influences that have changed their lives in negative ways. Then, based on these understandings, specific suggestions for revolving these issues are provided.

In short, with this book as a guide, it is up to the reader to think out the issues and possible solutions to personal life problems. From that perspective, *Getting Better Together* is only a guide, and certainly no book can become a substitute for common sense and personal awareness. However, if successful, this guide to increased marital fulfillment and the good life can certainly aid readers immensely in defining and initiating needed changes. In fact, *Getting Better Together* can be used by couples in five interrelated ways.

SUGGESTION #1: USE THE BOOK TO CREATE A PERSONAL VISION OF THE FUTURE. In other words, it is difficult to define a path for yourself unless you know exactly where you are going. Many of the good things in life were there when you were young. Then they got lost. Now you and your life circumstances have changed. By reading *Getting Better Together* completely, a vision of what is possible and ultimately fulfilling in life *right now* can be created. This vision—your present definition of the good life—becomes a motivating force for both of you to focus and direct needed personal change.

SUGGESTION #2: READ *GETTING BETTER TOGETHER* FOR DIAGNOSTIC PURPOSES. Every marriage is different. So are the individuals who together make a couple. As you read through this book, you may find that some parts of your foundation for the good life together are in good order. On the other hand, there may be areas where considerable attention is needed to define healthier life priorities and to develop new skills. While some of these deficiencies are yours personally, both you and your spouse may need to work together on others if positive changes are to be achieved.

SUGGESTION #3: USE SPECIFIC TOPICS TO FOCUS DISCUSSION ABOUT CHANGE. There is a vast difference between thinking about change and using someone as a sounding board to refine awareness of needed changes. In the best of all possible worlds, the most important person to discuss meaningful changes with is your spouse. However, a good friend or colleague is also a possibility. Or several couples or an organized group can use *Getting Better Together* to guide and support positive change. By openly discussing needed changes with others, new understandings often develop as does encouragement for making those changes.

SUGGESTION #4: USE SPECIFIC STRATEGIES SUGGESTED IN THE BOOK. You will notice that in this book, specific problems that crop up time and again in marriages are defined, often with vignettes to help put these issues into realistic perspective. However, insight is simply not enough. Based on an understanding of defined problems, specific suggestions for positive change are provided in

Getting Better Together. While making specific changes, new responses in how the two of you relate each day will require practice to become natural; with time these changes will prove effective in bringing the good life within reach.

SUGGESTION #5: USE THIS BOOK AS A RESOURCE. With the years, couples change and so do their life circumstances. New issues may develop and, for many couples, their definition of the good life will also evolve. Once immediate and pressing changes have been made and life has become more fulfilling, *Getting Better Together* can be placed on your bookshelf or nightstand and used for reference. To counter backsliding or to find effective ways to respond to new life problems, an established familiarity with this book can quickly help locate specific and helpful strategies for change.

"Sculpting" the Good Life

Perhaps it's never crossed your mind to think of yourself as a sculptor. On the other hand, there just may be a very fitting relationship between creating the good life and the work of a sculptor. Many years ago, the famous artist Rodin was asked: "How do you sculpt an elephant?" His answer was right to the point: "I just chip away everything that isn't an elephant!" Now you see the relationship. It's your task to chip away all the superficial values, undue burdens, personal barriers, and unnecessary complications that have built up over the years until you have what is left: the good life for you and those you love the most.

It is a sad reality of contemporary life to see so many couples who, early on, enjoyed one another and lived life to the fullest. Then, over the years, mounting responsibilities pushed them apart. These days, this distressing state of affairs is almost the norm. Ironically, when the lives of these couples are examined, all the necessary ingredients for living the good life together are present. However, these men and women haven't been able to put the pieces together so the good life can be theirs. That's what *Getting Better Together* is all about. It's a guide for interested couples to begin chipping away until they regain the closeness and the personal fulfillment that they lost over the years.

The time to begin is right now. *Getting Better Together* is a "can do" book, but it requires a "can do" attitude on your part. The sooner you start making focused changes, the sooner you will experience the wonderful results. Keep firmly in mind that the good life if not defined by externals, but is found deep within yourself in the basic decisions about how you desire to live your life and what is important to you.

In the end, a fulfilling marriage and living the good life costs practically no money. In this sense, the process of getting better together is remarkably cost-effective. As the saying goes, "The best things in life are free." All the ingredients are there, right under your nose waiting for you to create the good life for yourselves. Go straight for what is deep and enduring and fulfilling. Remember, eliminating bad habits is not enough. Unless you build in the positives as well, you're left with a bland relationship.

Although it may initially appear to be a contradiction, it's actually sound advice that in order to get started, begin right away but don't rush it. It's best to make changes slowly and systematically, one step at a time. Look at it this way. Over time, many small focused changes function as chisels that will sculpt the good life for you. One last word. Always use the KISS method as a guide for creating the fulfilling life you have always wanted. Literally, Keep It Sweet and Simple. After all, every day, even this one, is a day when the good life can be yours—together. And, together, you deserve no less.

Chapter 1

Getting Established: The Progression to Problems

After finishing school, young men and women eagerly look forward to "making it" in the big, wide world waiting for them. Their whole lives lie ahead. Never mind that they are idealistic and green as the grass as far as the real world goes. They have their hopes and their dreams to carry them through any initial hardships. At their age, they have plenty of energy and are eternally optimistic. They're ready to go. After preparing themselves educationally for years, they can't wait to begin living "the good life."

Now, from these hopeful youngsters, let's fast forward for a moment to ten or fifteen years down the road. Boy, have things changed over the years. From this vantage point, these now established men and women are singing a different tune. The hopes and dreams and the unbridled optimism of youth have virtually disappeared. Because they are responsible and have a solid work ethic, in their workplaces, they are doing what needs to be done and they are doing it well. Fantasies, however, now intrude into their consciousness with ever more frequency.

Denny, always tired, sits at home virtually every evening in front of the television set, but he barely knows what's happening on the tube. He finds himself drifting away into his dream of buying a boat and sailing off into the sunset and never coming back to the daily grind that is now really getting to him. He rarely talks to his spouse. The kids miss their dad who used to laugh and do things with them.

Carla, usually very hard-working and dedicated, feels a deep anger within her. With grim humor, she vows that if anyone crosses her at work today she will quit and make four stops: 1) to the bank to withdraw all the money in her account, 2) to the real estate agent to sell her home, 3) to the orphanage to drop off the kids, and 4) to the nearest beach to live in a shack all by herself for the rest of her days.

Jeff, now living a hectic lifestyle as an accountant, frequently drifts off into dreamlike reveries while working. Virtually daily he fantasizes about a little cabin he will build in the woods so far from civilization that it will take years for telephone lines to come even close. He'll sit on the front porch and watch the sun go down every day. For food, he'll trap a rabbit now and then and grow a few potatoes.

Sound familiar? All of these individuals have several characteristics in common. First of all, they are established and successful in their careers. And, they are making a reasonable salary that pays expenses plus a bit extra. At the same time, however, all are unhappy. At work, they slip into a very responsible manner of relating and doing what needs to be done even though they aren't feeling good inside. Further, at home, life after work is simply not fulfilling anymore. There's no fun being with the family, and marriage relationships have become strained. And, because there seems to be no relief from the pressure they feel, each one has begun to fantasize about running away.

All three of these individuals are reacting to feelings that have been building inside for years. There are persistent nagging questions with no clear answers: Is this all there is? Is this what success is all about? Where is the good life I always thought I'd have by now? Is living the life of a dog what I've worked all my life to accomplish? Is there something wrong with me? Why don't I feel good about anything these days? Then comes the answer to these many questions and it's tinged with anger: "If this is really what success is all about, then I'm not sure that I even want it!"

Just what is success really about? It's a good question and, if not defined in ways that reflect healthy values, one that often causes many problems in later life. In a word, many couples confuse Quality of Life and Standard of Living. Perhaps at this point, defining each of these terms would be helpful.

STANDARD OF LIVING: *An economically-based measure of life success using materialistic criteria such as income, professional perks, size of home, and number and quality of possessions.*

QUALITY OF LIFE: *A measure of life success using emotionally based criteria such as satisfying work, having adequate time for leisure, enjoying positive family relationships, feeling healthy and fit, and experiencing personal contentment.*

When it comes to being successful, it is deceptively easy to inadvertently strive solely for an enhanced Standard of Living and completely forget about preserving Quality of Life. Many marital and other life problems then ensue. Fortunately, the answer to this common dilemma is reasonably straightforward. It comes with the recognition that there is more to life than work and then more work. Striving to balance living each day in the direction of an enhanced Quality of Life together is the answer. Before that's possible, however, you must first clearly understand what has happened as you and your spouse have spent many years working hard and struggling to establish yourselves.

Lifestyles of the Young

To gain perspective on the negative lifestyle changes that occur during adulthood, it is necessary to contrast two age groups and how they live. First, there is young adulthood. These are young men and women who are twenty-two to twenty-five years of age. They have completed their education, whether it is technical school, community college, or a four-year degree. Some go on to post-graduate or professional degrees. When they approach their mid-twenties, most have been on their own out in the world for a year or two.

Once they have graduated, young adults in this age group tend to flounder for a year or so. Many are not sure of themselves or their personal directions quite yet. As a result, changes in locale or in employment are common. Perhaps the job they really wanted wasn't available. Maybe they didn't like the city or town. For some, the position they thought they wanted just didn't turn out to be so great. However, most settle into a community and down to a specific career path within a year or two of graduation.

It is at this point that young men and women begin the process of establishing themselves. That is, they strive to gain all the basics necessary for a middle-class lifestyle. For most, accomplishing this requires a decade or more of hard work. However, for the first few years, the lifestyles of these young men and women are characterized by three qualities: simple, well-balanced, and fulfilling. An examination of life at this age reveals why.

1. CAREER. These young men and women have been hired into entry level positions at work. As such, they have not yet been overwhelmed by responsibility and the burden of work that comes with promotions and career advancements. In these early years, work is usually an eight-hour day. Income is adequate but limited.

2. FAMILY. More often than not, in the early twenties, no family is in the picture yet. Young men and women are waiting longer to marry and have families. These days, the average age of marriage for both sexes is about twenty-five, and children may not come until several years later.

3. HOME MAINTENANCE. Because young adults have not accumulated an economic base yet, they tend to rent apartments, duplexes, or condominiums. Often, the cost is shared with roommates. When there is a problem, the maintenance department is called immediately to come and fix it.

4. COMMUNITY INVOLVEMENT. Very minimal. Young adults in their early to mid-twenties tend to live primarily as free agents, and as such are relatively aloof from the community at large. They are not found heavily involved in volunteer work, civic organizations, or their churches.

5. LEISURE. These young men and women have plenty of friends who they see regularly. Time is readily available for fishing, golf, going to the beach, or other recreational activities. Socializing is important and is arranged at every opportunity. Overnighters or weekends out of town for fun and relaxation are a regular part of life.

6. LIFE PRIORITIES. If raised with a solid work ethic, these young men and women push hard to "make it" economically and to advance in their careers while at work. However, when they come home from work, another life priority is quite evident: "How am I going to enjoy myself today?" They follow through and do just that.

In a nutshell, life for the first few years of establishing themselves is relatively simple for these young men and women. And, it is a healthy lifestyle because it is nicely balanced between work, achievement, and the pursuit of success on one hand, and friends, leisure activities, and good times on the other. This is done on a shoestring because there isn't an abundance of money at this age. These young men, women, and couples are actually living "the good life." The problem is that they won't realize how good they had it until ten to fifteen years later! Then these early years are fondly remembered as "the good old days."

The Established Couple

From this nicely balanced and personally fulfilling lifestyle of the mid-twenties, a solidly middle-class lifestyle begins to emerge with the passing years. Changes, almost imperceptible on a day-to-day basis, slowly but surely take place in every facet of life. And, for the most part, these changes are not positive. To see the changes wrought by the years, a comparison of a couple in their mid-thirties or forties with the young adults they used to be is very enlightening.

To put it bluntly, these men and women, now well-established in their communities and in their careers, are living in a very different way than they were in the early years just after school. "The good life" they had expected, and were in fact living early on, has completely disappeared. Instead, these couples now are experiencing incessant pressure and high levels of daily stress as they attempt to keep everything in their lives together. No wonder. Look at what has taken place.

1. CAREER. By now, this hard-working young man or woman has advanced several steps up a career ladder. Promotions have brought a better income, but also more responsibilities at the office. Work boundaries have disappeared. Not only does the office demand greater productivity and longer hours, but work is often taken home for evenings and/or weekends. The pressure of meeting a myriad of work responsibilities has steadily mounted with the years.

2. FAMILY. The free and single young adult who socialized a lot has met someone and fallen in love. After marrying, within just a few years, the children begin to come along. The individual is now a family man or woman who must expend constant energy to meet the needs of a spouse and children. Husbands and wives begin to live separate lives under the same roof and communication between them is breaking down. Life at home is steadily becoming more tense and intense as the years pass.

3. HOME MAINTENANCE. An essential part of the Great American Dream is home ownership. As young men and women marry, they almost immediately begin to save for their own home and eventually purchase it. Now they own a home, but when something goes wrong, the maintenance department isn't called; the owners are the maintenance department! In the average house, at any given time, there are four to six "fix-it" jobs waiting in the wings for someone to have an hour or two to deal with them.

4. COMMUNITY INVOLVEMENT. The husband and wife and their children, now living in their own home, have become part of a neighborhood. When their first child is born, couples become re-involved in their churches. Daily, they are taking the kids all over town to after-school activities. They stay in touch with the schools and teachers and go to P.T.O. or P.T.A. meetings. And, they belong to civic organizations or volunteer their time to the community.

5. LEISURE. Enjoying life has diminished dramatically over the last decade or so because there is no time. Once-good friends are hardly seen anymore. Fishing rods, tennis racquets, and golf clubs now gather dust in the closet or basement. By Friday night, only enough energy remains to get a bite to eat and go to bed. Husbands and wives may get out for a little while on the weekend—if there's not too much to do at home! Getting away for an overnighter or a weekend has become extremely complicated. At twenty-four or five, it could be done on an hour's notice on a Friday afternoon. At thirty-five plus, it usually takes four to six weeks of very careful planning and tremendous work. Often, it's not worth the effort.

6. LIFE PRIORITIES. The healthy life priorities of the young have become completely inverted over a decade or more of striving to become established. From that healthy and fulfilling lifestyle of the young where enjoying life after work was a top priority, another orientation has taken over. These men and women in their thirties and forties are obsessed twenty-four hours a day with one thought: "How in the name of heaven am I going to get everything done that needs to be done today so I can get up tomorrow morning and do the same thing again?" Enjoying life has dropped to the absolute bottom of the priority list. A couple gets what's left over, but there is rarely anything left over. They have nothing to give to themselves or to one another.

The Shattered Dream

The changes that take place between young adulthood and established adulthood are both profound and very destructive to a marriage and family life. However, to truly understand what has happened psychologically, another reality of adult lifestyles as they are lived today must also be understood. Once adulthood is reached, each man or woman daily encounters a *minimum* of ten to fifteen minor aggravations or frustrations. These are not great events in the great scheme of life; rather they are all the little problems and glitches that accumulate as the day wears on. Some typical examples:

- an unexpected detour that makes you ten minutes late for a meeting
- the neighbor's dog chewed up your newspaper this morning
- you can't find your checkbook or car keys anywhere
- working on a computer, you delete thirty minutes of work by accident

- you missed a meeting because the memo went to the wrong desk
- your child will not let you have a three minute conversation with your spouse
- you need to go somewhere and there is absolutely no gas in the car.

Day in and day out, at work and at home, life's frustrations and minor problems pile up without cease. As each day wears on, internal pressure builds. However, in young adults who have regular leisure activities, relaxation time, and interesting diversions in their lives, the internal tension these problems create is regularly diffused. As pressures build up, they are reduced to healthy levels through relaxing activities that enable them to "get away from it all."

However, as young adults move toward their late twenties and thirties (and beyond), three realities collide in slow motion over the years. This collision sets the stage for the creation of many marital problems and the slow destruction of the once-anticipated good life that was to be lived together. Here's what creates the crunch.

1. THE INDIVIDUAL'S STRONG SENSE OF RESPONSIBILITY. When young men and women are raised well, their work ethic becomes manifest in a strong commitment to meeting all personal responsibilities. Their code: "I'm a responsible person. I have responsibilities in every part of my life. And, I *will* meet those responsibilities and meet them well!"

2. EACH YEAR THERE ARE MORE THINGS TO GET DONE. With an ever-busier career, marriage, children, home maintenance, and community responsibilities, there are more demands on time and energy in every sector of life. As the years pass, it becomes increasingly difficult to keep up with all that needs to be done each day.

3. THE FACT THAT THERE ARE JUST TWENTY-FOUR HOURS IN A DAY. This is certainly the harshest reality of all. For each and every person, there is not a second more or less than twenty-four hours in each day. And, the individual's energy level permits only a given number of hours that can be worked each day without negatively affecting emotional (and sometimes physical) well-being.

The core question that this lifestyle "crunch" creates is very simple: "In order to get done all that needs to be done each day, guess what slowly but surely gets cut out of your once-satisfying lifestyle?" If your answer is, "All the leisure activities, the nice times we used to have together, and the interesting diversions in my life," you would be absolutely right on target. And, unfortunately, you would be right with the crowd. Unfortunately, the slow but sure elimination of these activities has an extremely destructive effect on individuals and on their marriage relationships.

Feelings of DREAD

By this time, typically by age thirty and beyond, the dream of the good life has virtually disappeared. Because there is a deep commitment to meeting all life responsibilities, a couple begins to focus solely on doing what needs to be done at work and at home each day. And, as can be seen, while being very responsible, couples lose much over the years that heavily contributes to emotional health, personal fulfillment, and a satisfying marital relationship.

To be more specific, the reason why husbands and wives begin feeling bad is that extremely important personal needs have been systematically neglected in lieu of being ever more responsible and getting more done. Typically, when this happens, not only is a marital relationship diminished, but a number of negative feelings that well up within and grow stronger with time are also generated. Five of these negatives feelings in particular can be described by the acronym DREAD.

"D" STANDS FOR DEFENSIVENESS. With lowered self-esteem, this husband or wife is extremely sensitive to any kind of criticism, especially from a spouse. With deepening personal distress, even innocuous feedback or attempts at discussion cause an emotional overreaction and sometimes a counterattack. This sensitivity tends to shut down communication and diminish closeness.

"R" STANDS FOR RESENTMENT. Deep inside, a growing anger typically manifests itself as high levels of irritability toward loved ones. There is often a belief that "I'm giving and giving, but no one is giving back or cares about me." The basic reason for this resentment, however, is that very important and critical emotional needs are not being met in this marriage partner.

"E" STANDS FOR ESCAPE. More often than not, spouses daydream and fantasize about leaving and never coming back. Deep down, they believe that life has become too difficult and too complex. Life has also become much less personally fulfilling. This generates that dream of escape to live "the good life" elsewhere because it doesn't seem possible in the here and now.

"A" STANDS FOR ANXIETY. Internal tension and pressure just don't seem to go away. Sometimes because of so much anxiety, the individual feels ready to explode inside. Or, the anxiety may be transformed into impatience with everyone and everything. Physical problems include tight muscles, sleeplessness, and other manifestations of chronic stress.

"D" STANDS FOR DEPRESSION. Mixed in with all the other feelings is a low-level depression. It does not interfere with work, but rather creates persistent feelings of pessimism, disillusionment, dissatisfaction, and discouragement. Sometimes mates express these to one another; but whether they do or not, the down feelings are always there.

Danger: You're Falling Out of Love

You know that you're not feeling good inside as you struggle to get done all that needs to be done each day and to keep up with your responsibilities. Along with the feelings of DREAD that have been building for some years, a deep and insidious fear has begun to grow. You've become so disconnected from one another that you're not even sure that you're in love with your husband or wife anymore. Those close feelings you once shared regularly have become more fleeting with widening intervals between them. You're worried because if these patterns continue, you see disastrous implications in the years to come.

In fact, your thoughts reflect some of the danger signs that may-be you're both falling out of love with one another. You're becoming increasingly afraid of what you're thinking and feeling these days.

1. YOU'RE NOT SURE OF YOUR SPOUSE'S FEELINGS TOWARD YOU. There has been so much irritability and overreaction that emerges when you're together that you just don't know if your spouse really loves you anymore. And, because of the growing distance between you, it's become steadily more difficult to talk openly and intimately to affirm your commitment to one another.

2. RECENTLY YOU'VE STARTED TO FEEL VERY LONELY INSIDE. When you were young, you would have never believed that a marriage could be lonely, but you do now. You go about your work each day, but there's a lack of connection with your husband or wife that you miss acutely. The lack of support and caring that you are experiencing now has led to lonely feelings that are hard to shake.

3. YOU LOVE YOUR SPOUSE, BUT YOU DON'T LIKE THAT PARTNER MUCH THESE DAYS. Deep down, you know that there are still positive feelings for your husband or wife, but they seem to be buried and becoming weaker. At a surface level, you have come to dislike your spouse because of the emotional distance that has developed and the unpleasant responses that are directed toward you.

4. YOU DON'T SEEM TO BE A HIGH PRIORITY FOR ONE ANOTHER ANYMORE. In other words, as you look at how you both live each day, it seems that everything else takes precedence over your marriage relationship. In short, you've both started to take your relationship for granted. The assumption seems to be that the relationship will continue without emotional nourishment.

5. YOU WOULDN'T CALL YOUR SPOUSE YOUR BEST FRIEND THESE DAYS. Way back when, you and your spouse were the best of friends. Now, you don't even seem to be casual friends, or even friends at all. You function more like roommates who share expenses, but little else. In fact, it worries you that you both have been living increasingly separate lives under the same roof.

6. IN BED, YOU ARE HAVING SEX BUT NOT MAKING LOVE. Your declining physical relationship is signaled by the lack of emotional connectedness, even in bed. Your sexual relationship has become filled with ambivalence and doubts. At best, it gives you physical release, but the deeper level of emotional intimacy that is the core of making love just isn't there anymore.

7. YOU'RE NOT SURE YOUR MARRIAGE IS GOING TO MAKE IT. For the first time in your life, you're wondering if there is enough left in your marriage to sustain it for the long haul, or whether the distance that has grown between you will eventually doom it. And, worst of all, you can't express your insecurity because you're afraid of what your partner will say.

You've found yourself wondering: "Is this the way all couples feel after they've been married for a number of years?" What you're really asking is: "Is this normal? Does this have to happen?" While these kinds of doubts and fears are very common, the fact is that they do not have to happen at all. So, the answer is a simple "no," not all couples feel this way. Further, those who find themselves with a growing sense of estrangement from a spouse can reverse these feelings. With some focused effort, most can reestablish their commitment to one another and become close again.

To set the stage for doing something about these destructive changes, the only realistic starting point is to begin loving one another once again. Many naive men and women believe that being in love is defined by subtle chemistry that either exists or doesn't exist between two people. Not so. At a mature level, to love and to be in love is a decision that is made personally by each partner. When both partners make such a decision, it then becomes a commitment to one another that is experienced each and every day. And, this kind of deep love is so obvious that even an outsider can readily see it.

Now, you ask: "What is love, really?" Certainly, there are many superficial ways to define love. However, for a husband and wife who want to recover the closeness they once shared together, here's an excellent definition to use as a starting point to begin getting better together. It reflects the deep commitment that is the core of love between a man and a woman who have become partners in life.

LOVE: *A deep personal decision to remain emotionally close to a husband or wife, combined with a willingness to consistently give of oneself to that partner even when the desire to do so isn't present.*

At this point, a very prevalent myth about love must be addressed. It is that the opposite of love for your spouse is intense anger or even hatred. That is, when you begin to hate your spouse, the marital relationship has been irreparably damaged. Not so. Anger, even intense anger, reflects existing feelings between a husband and wife that can be used as a foundation to rebuild that relationship. Typically, positive feelings do remain, but they exist below the anger which is on the surface. As already mentioned, such anger stems not only from hurt, but also from personal emotional needs that have been systematically neglected for years. This unfortunate situation can certainly be rectified with effort by both partners.

However, your feelings of love are in very deep jeopardy when you become permanently indifferent to your spouse. That is, you just don't care one way or the other anymore and you can't make yourself care. Often, either a husband or wife begins to experience such frightening absence of feeling for short periods of time and then it disappears. It is only when indifference, an emotional disconnect toward a spouse, is there all day every day that love—that deep feeling of caring and the desire to give of oneself to a partner—has withered and is almost dead. As time passes, if no effort is made to improve that marital relationship, indifference becomes extremely difficult—even impossible—to reverse.

The Road to Recovery

The erosion of marital relationships and with it the ability to live "the good life" is virtually par for the course in couples once they have established themselves as part of the Great American Middle Class. The negative inner feelings, the distance between the husband and wife, and the lack of shared time lead many couples to just live together while steadily drifting farther apart. Without realizing it, they begin to live separate lives under the same roof. Many others, unfortunately, separate and divorce in an attempt to find a more fulfilling life elsewhere.

Ironically, these personal and marital crises tend to occur just when couples are established and the good life is within their grasp. Mutually improving your relationship is entirely possible, but as a couple you've got to know how to go about it. For marriage partners intent on moving toward renewed closeness and sharing good times, here are some excellent ways to begin.

1. CONFRONT THE CHILDHOOD MYTH THAT THE GOOD LIFE HAPPENS AUTOMATICALLY. Children are told constantly by parents and teachers that if they do everything society mandates, there will eventually come a day when, magically, it will all somehow fall together and they will live happily ever after. Hogwash! That's a sure prescription for unhappiness. If you are beyond your thirtieth year and reasonably established, the future is not later, it's today. Don't sit around waiting for it all to fall together. It won't. Instead, begin to make the good life happen for you right now—no more waiting!

2. REALIZE AND ACCEPT THAT YOU ALWAYS HAVE CHOICES. One of the most common complaints of couples experiencing personal or marital crises is that their lives are out of control. Because of the perception that there are no real choices, you experience a trapped feeling that breeds all the DREAD emotions. The reality is that you always have choices, but they're not always easy. Don't forget that your present unhappiness developed through many choices you've made over the years without thinking them out. Now begin to take active control of your life by making better choices that reflect a commitment to taking care of yourself emotionally and meeting the needs of your marital relationship.

3. IMMEDIATELY STOP TAKING YOUR CUES FROM WHAT OTHERS ARE DOING. In this society, it is very sad to see just how many men, women, and couples subscribe to life values that are shallow, unfulfilling, and highly materialistic, all of which ultimately erode personal contentment. These same couples, instead of thinking through what they want from life and from one another, begin to take their cues from what they see everyone else doing. They become trapped by peer values that are superficial and simply not healthy. Instead, begin to adopt life values that are deeper, more enduring, and more personally fulfilling. Then, together, commit yourselves to those values even if you must stand separately from your peers.

4. DEFINE A JOINT VISION OF THE GOOD LIFE FOR YOU AS A COUPLE. This takes time spent together and ongoing discussion. Start by talking about the "the good old days" when you were both young and just starting out. You had less materially, but you were happier and more personally fulfilled because you had time to share together and to sit back and relax regularly. Now, shift to how you are living these days and the changes you must make to meet these same needs. Begin to define together specific ways to meet those basic emotional needs within your marriage. As you redefine your priorities, begin to implement those changes one at a time to bring back emotional closeness and good times shared.

5. MOVE BEYOND A MATERIALISTIC ORIENTATION TO LIFE. The fact is that you are already established in terms of an adequate income, a successful career, a home, your family, and your community. It's far past time to begin to think in terms of meeting your *emotional needs* instead of being driven by *materialistic wants*. The "bigger and more and the best of everything" ethic is not only shallow, but its pursuit is one of the royal roads to personal unhappiness. Strive to get your finances in order. Reduce your debt load. Resist the temptation to buy more and more. Learn to value life's simple pleasures and to enjoy what you already have.

For too many hard-working men and women in their thirties and beyond, it is a sad irony that as their standard of living rises, quality of life in terms of personal enjoyment steadily falls. In the heady days of youth, young men and women striving to "make it" in the real world prove their progress by materialistically raising their standard of living. The trap is that as the years pass, standard of living and quality of life cease to rise together. As they diverge, standard of living may continue to go up as happiness and personal contentment diminish and a once-good marriage begins to feel the strain.

There is no time like right now to rectify this too-common couple's condition. Keep in mind that real success in life can be defined by moving steadily in the direction of experiencing together what is truly fulfilling for you and your loved ones. As you begin using this definition to guide your choices as a couple, you will also be striving for an enhanced quality of life—together. You can begin caring and sharing with one another in different ways right now. As the saying goes, "You've got only one life to live and it's definitely *not* a dress rehearsal!"

Chapter 2

Confronting Myths About Marriage: Developing a Realistic Perspective on the Good Life

As a couple works hard to become established, their standard of living steadily rises. However, when the quality of their life together is examined, it is often found wanting. Inside the home of that couple, trouble is brewing because the marriage relationship is stagnating. Two people once deeply in love are now living together, but growing steadily apart. Ironically, they spend more time at home than ever before because there's so much to get done. However, the quality of that time is the pits. They don't talk much anymore except about problems at work, issues with the kids, who's spending the money on what, and schedules for today and tomorrow. They are making a good living, but they're not very fulfilled nor even happy anymore.

Both partners find themselves wondering: "Where did the good life go? This just isn't the way it was supposed to be!" Indeed they are right; this isn't the way it's supposed to be. On the other hand, it's exactly the scenario in millions of homes these days. A marital relationship that was to last forever has become shallow, strained, and unfulfilling for both partners. Deep down, neither spouse wants the relationship to end, but the thought has sure crossed each one's mind. Both husband and wife are feeling the strain, and one or the other is beginning to react. Why? Because the marriage has reached an emotional crisis point.

How a couple handles this kind of very common but serious problem will determine whether the relationship will be renewed or continue to deteriorate. On the negative side, the options range from affairs, burying yourself in more work, excessive drinking or drug use, physical separation and divorce, or just continuing the *status quo* in a relationship that has little substance. Most of the time, however, these choices just create more interpersonal problems and deepening dissatisfaction.

To complicate returning a once-good relationship back to the "good old days" of emotional closeness and to the fun times they shared together, a husband or wife (sometimes both) may encounter barriers produced by myths about marriage. However, changes (or lack of change) based on these erroneous assumptions about marriage often backfire to make a marital relationship even more tenuous and distant. However, before various myths about marriage are discussed, it will prove helpful to define their origins. In fact, four points of origin are often found. For couples to get better together, not only must marital myths be eliminated, but the effects of past experiences and the influence of specific individuals who produced these myths must also be resolved.

ORIGIN #1: PARENTS. *Example:* Jana came from a home in which an alcoholic father and a strong-willed mother viciously battled it out in front of the kids. Little ever got resolved, and over the years, Jane concluded that in a good marriage, conflict is virtually absent and everyone gets along beautifully.

Children observe their parents for many years before finishing school and leaving home. From those experiences, children develop their own ideas about what marital relationships are like. When parental modeling is healthy, children are often spared problems when they become adults. However, if parents have a problem marriage, children may either inadvertently recreate the same kind of marriage relationship for themselves, or they may rebel and go to the opposite extreme. In addition, naive parents may even directly teach children erroneous ideas about marriage and the good life (*e.g.,* marry for money and position).

ORIGIN #2: PEERS. *Example:* Bert, a small businessman in his hometown, had a circle of lifelong friends there. Spending regular time with them reinforced the idea that all a wife really needed to be satisfied was a regular paycheck and good sex. He came to believe that this was the basis of a good marriage.

Beginning in adolescence, cliques of adolescent boys and girls form and talk about their feelings and experiences. Frequently, these discussions include misconceptions about the opposite sex that are regularly reinforced. Too often, these perceptions are based on immature adolescent perceptions of reality, instead of adult experience or perspective. Most adults eventually move beyond these immature ideas about relationships to the solid values required to sustain a good marriage. However, significant numbers of men and women never grow up emotionally. They move into adulthood and marriage believing the same naive ideas about relationships that they had in high school.

ORIGIN #3: A PARTNER. *Example:* Eleanor always wanted to be affluent and so did Jim, her husband. As successful professionals, they make an excellent income, but they're not really happy. As a couple, they believe that eventually, when they make enough money, they will then find happiness together.

Time and again, one or both partners in a marriage have misconceptions about what the good life is and how to be happy together. Then, these erroneous ideas become the foundation for directing their energies toward goals that they think will bring contentment and the good life closer. Not infrequently, these preexisting ideas are reinforced by observations of other similar couples. When this happens, it is a case of the blind leading the blind. To get better together first of all requires a very mature perspective on what the good life is all about. Then, marital and lifestyle decisions reflecting solid relationship values must be made despite what others are doing.

ORIGIN #4: PERSONAL PRESSURE. *Example:* Rob has been under intense pressure in his work for some time. Every day he comes home exhausted and irritable. Good times with Sally have virtually disappeared. Rob doubts she loves him anymore and blames her for all the marital problems they are experiencing.

There is no question that constant pressure and stress eventually begin to distort perceptions. It follows, then, that when a husband or wife (or both) are under the gun constantly, how they see one another and their relationship together may be distorted as well. Further, it is a basic human proclivity to blame others for personal unhappiness or problems. And, who is easier to blame than a husband or wife who is there every day? When marital problems develop, nine times out of ten both partners bear some responsibility. However, the solution is not to try to change others, but rather to look inward to personal contributions to marital discord and to strive to eliminate them.

The bottom line is simple. A couple can reverse the negative changes that have occurred in a marriage by changing the choices they make each day. The first choice is very simple: to eliminate erroneous ideas about what constitutes a good relationship and to build a partnership with your husband or wife to create the good life together. Most of the time, when naive ideas that sabotage the good life are removed, a healthier perspective on life values that are deep, enduring, and emotionally fulfilling begins to grow. As these new values are applied to your relationship together, you will feel the difference almost immediately.

Marital Crises Develop Slowly

As you decide to move your marriage relationship from the bottom of the priority list to the very top, you will be well positioned to make the necessary changes that will enable you both to get better together. Make no mistake about it. It will take time to make the positive changes necessary that will enable you both to grow closer and to begin enjoying life again. To understand the process of how your relationship deteriorated, you must recognize a set sequence of events that occurs over the years. Often, the destructive effects of this process develop so slowly and insidiously that they are not perceived until serious marital problems develop. To answer the question, "What happened to our relationship?" here are four points that reiterate how marital crises develop.

REALITY #1: MOST MARITAL PROBLEMS GROW SLOWLY OVER LONG PERIODS OF TIME. By almost imperceptible increments, a marital relationship erodes over the years. Typically, it takes from five to fifteen years for the emotional distance to become acutely felt and for the lack of personal fulfillment to create a painful void within. The root cause is those thousands of little daily decisions that slowly but surely diminish the importance of the marital relationship.

REALITY #2: MARITAL PROBLEMS ARE OFTEN CLOSELY CORRELATED WITH AN INCREASE IN RESPONSIBILITY. Early in a marriage, there is one precious commodity that helps insure closeness and good times together. This same commodity slowly but surely disappears with the years. It is time for one another. With the years come responsibilities: children, busy careers, home maintenance, and community involvement, not to mention taking the kids all over town virtually daily for their practices, games, and other activities.

REALITY #3: THE RESULT IS THAT ONCE-HEALTHY LIFE PRIORITIES BECOME INVERTED. Most marriages begin with the highest priority placed on being together and enjoying one another. As the years pass, two destructive priorities slowly take precedence:

1) to make more money so there can be more and more "things" and 2) to spend all available time getting things done that need to be done. The net result is that a marital relationship slips to the absolute bottom of the priority list.

REALITY #4: A "MAKE OR BREAK" MARITAL CRISIS DEVELOPS. If couples who have been happily married for many years are questioned, the majority will mention a time when the marriage was in serious jeopardy. Perhaps there was even a separation or serious talk of it. Most of the time, these marital crises reflected priority problems that had developed. In these good marriages, a couple worked together to resolve the issues separating them and went on to live compatibly and happily for many years. Where problems could not be resolved, the marriage usually did not survive.

Index of Marital Impoverishment

To help each couple seeking the good life together to clearly define what has been lost through the years, read through this Index of Marital Impoverishment. Note that this checklist has nothing to do with income. In fact, it is ironic that many couples who have attained a very adequate standard of living find that quality of life has steadily declined. They may be making good money, but emotionally they have become poverty-stricken. Check those areas of life satisfaction that have been lost. Then, as a couple, make a joint commitment to begin enjoying life and one another again by together bringing back those qualities of life that were once enjoyed.

_____ 1. My spouse and I have slipped into monotonous routines at home; it's no fun to be around the house anymore.

_____ 2. When we were first married, we were always polite and considerate of one another; now all that has changed for the worse.

_____ 3. As a couple, we now stay at home a lot, but we basically do our own thing and live what seems to be separate lives under the same roof.

_____ 4. Too many evenings and weekends are spent passively watching television (or working while watching).

_____ 5. Because we've purchased so many things, financial pressure is great, and it is more and more difficult to make ends meet each month.

_____ 6. Nowadays, we rarely look into one another's eyes and say "I love you" with feeling.

_____ 7. My partner and I used to share stimulating recreational activities, but now we seldom have fun together.

_____ 8. When I need to talk about a problem, my spouse never seems to want to listen anymore.

_____ 9. There are few interesting surprises that my husband or wife creates for me these days.

_____ 10. Our physical relationship isn't as frequent nor as fulfilling as it was in the past because it seems that we're having sex, not making love.

_____ 11. As a couple, we don't have many good friends these days because there just doesn't seem to be enough time to keep up the relationships.

_____ 12. No matter what I do, nothing really seems to be fun anymore because it seems like I'm just going through the motions.

_____ 13. Right now, there seem to be few smiles and very little joking around with one another like when we were young.

_____ 14. For some reason, we rarely get away together these days without the kids for an evening or weekend just for us.

_____ 15. We fight more now than in the past (or withdraw into stony silence) and say hurtful things to one another.

_____ 16. While I'm not literally alone, I have been feeling lonely because my partner doesn't seem to be there for me anymore.

_____ 17. Sincere, spontaneous, from-the-heart compliments and upbeat comments from my spouse have virtually disappeared.

_____ 18. I'm dragging these days because I'm getting out of shape and not taking care of my health the way I should.

_____ 19. There now seems to be a constant irritability just below the surface that seems to pop out whenever we spend time together.

_____ 20. When we're together, all my spouse and I talk about are kids, money, work problems, and schedules; when we're done, we don't seem to have anything more to say to one another.

The Beginning: Removing Myths About Marriage

Deep within most couples whose relationship drifts into trouble is a desire to make it good once again. And, you're both now more aware of just how much you've lost since you were first married. In recent years, the popularity of "if it doesn't work, find someone else" throwaway mentality has been eroding as far as marriage is concerned. Thankfully, the "me" generation is evolving into the "we" decade seen at present. In its place is a deeper and stronger commitment to making the relationship work. And, along with this underlying commitment are more realistic expectations of what it takes to keep a marriage viable and strong.

While it is certainly not uncommon to see marriages in trouble these days, sadly, many erroneous beliefs either perpetuate the problems or even make them worse. Eliminating these myths about marriage is actually the first big step in the process of renewing it! It's a good idea for both partners to discuss each one of these myths and then to each take the necessary steps to reorient priorities in healthier directions.

MYTH #1: THE MORE YOU LOVE SOMEONE, THE BETTER YOU TREAT THEM. Early in a relationship, couples are extremely responsive to one another. As the years roll by and life becomes pressured, an ironic situation develops. At work, an individual must be a kind, caring, courteous, and responsive individual. At home, however, in the private part of life, positive attention once given to a spouse is replaced by constant irritability, avoidance, negative communication, and outright rejection.

REVERSAL: Your first step is to recognize this sad state of affairs and then to begin to modify how you respond to one another. Don't say those three or four negative things you'd love to say to your partner each day. And, while you're chatting, completely eliminate children, chores, money, schedules, and work as topics. Good eye contact and taking the time to really listen to one another is mandatory. And, remember that a compliment a day keeps marital trouble away!

MYTH #2: COUPLES WHO SPEND A LOT OF TIME TOGETHER USUALLY HAVE A GOOD RELATIONSHIP. Early in a marriage, couples in love spend every spare moment together. And they really enjoy one another. Years later, however, overworked, chronically pressured, and burned-out couples still spend a lot of time together. It's usually at home, though, because there is no time to go out and besides, they're too tired to do much else. The quality of such time together is not high. Pressed a bit, these same men and women often admit to being painfully lonely while living together.

REVERSAL: Making time for one another *at home* is an absolute key to a successful marriage. Begin by legitimizing this time together. To do so, you must both break two bad habits. The first one is looking around, seeing so much to be done, and deciding to do chores instead of spending time with your partner. Second, at all costs, turn off the television set. Spend some time sitting and talking on the back porch or take a slow, leisurely walk together instead.

MYTH #3: IF WE ONLY LOVE ONE ANOTHER ENOUGH, EVERYTHING WILL FALL INTO PLACE. This is a perception of marital bliss seen through rose-colored glasses by the young and naive. That love *is* a good relationship is its magical essence. The idea that love conquers all (with no work) is easy to believe early in a marriage, but it's not true. Rather, love only forms the bond between a man and a woman that is the foundation for a fulfilling life together. And, love can easily die if other healthy relationship and lifestyle values that affirm that bond of love are not present.

REVERSAL: The good life and a loving relationship based on healthy life priorities rarely happen automatically. They are created. In fact, any good relationship requires constant attention, energy, and personal change to make it work. As life becomes busier and more complex with the years, giving attention to your marriage and mate becomes steadily more difficult, but necessary. Emotionally nourishing your relationship is the only way to deepen the love that exists between husband and wife.

MYTH #4: IT'S MY SPOUSE'S ROLE TO MAKE ME HAPPY. Rarely stated out loud, this is a common misperception. In fact, couples must meet some basic needs in one another for a relationship to be good. In broader form, though, this idea reflects an avoidance of responsibility for personal contentment. The deep belief is that it is up to someone else to make you happy and that person is your spouse. And, when a spouse doesn't do just that, that partner becomes the object of blame.

REVERSAL: Accepting responsibility for personal happiness is the first step when dealing with this myth. Making positive moves toward personal growth is the second one. It's up to you to break out of the rut. For yourself. Bring back some variety to your life by taking time for things you enjoy. Begin an interesting new hobby. Start a project you'd really enjoy. Take a short course. Or start seeing friends you've neglected for years.

MYTH #5: IF WE HAVE A GOOD SEXUAL RELATIONSHIP, EVERYTHING ELSE WILL FALL INTO PLACE. Early in a relationship, relating physically is extremely important. The chemistry is intense and couples find this part of their relationship very fulfilling. With the years, though, relating sexually, while remaining important, typically drops from a top priority to third or fourth. Other things become more important in the relationship. As a result, focusing only on renewal of a sexual relationship when there are marital problems is like hitching an extra cart to the horse before you fix the broken wheel.

REVERSAL: To reestablish a healthy marital relationship, one key change is an absolute must. That is to bring back into your marriage regular, spontaneous, sincere, *nonsexual* affection that has disappeared as responsibilities have grown. The fact is that sitting close, holding hands, snuggling on the couch, even horsing around in the kitchen are essential prerequisites for a healthy relationship. Paradoxically, bringing back nonsexual affection is one of the very best ways possible to rejuvenate a stagnating sexual relationship. Often, this is all it takes!

MYTH #6: OUR RELATIONSHIP WOULD BE WONDERFUL IF THERE WAS NEVER ANY CONFLICT BETWEEN US. This is a belief often held in marriages where there is too much emotionally destructive conflict. Complete absence of conflict is definitely not a sign of a good relationship. The difference between a good relationship and one that is not isn't the absence of conflict, *but how that conflict is handled.* Two mature individuals living together have differences and as they change with age, new differences are created. Learning to resolve those conflicts in mutually compatible ways is a major key to a good marriage.

REVERSAL: Given that there will be conflict in a marriage, the trick is to learn to fight fairly. A few simple rules help immensely. First, strive for two winners, not a winner and a loser. Second, no name-calling or low blows to your partner's vulnerabilities. Third, stay with one issue to be resolved now (instead of going to the past or other current problems). Fourth, agree to disengage and resume discussion later if relating becomes too heated or emotional. Finally, be willing to personally change to make things better for both of you.

MYTH #7: WE'RE SO DIFFERENT FROM ONE ANOTHER, IT'S NO WONDER WE'RE HAVING TROUBLE. Early in a relationship, couples are prone to say that opposites attract. Later on, these same couples cite differences as a major source of their problems. The fact is that most couples have differences: in values, interests, recreational outlets, sociability, and backgrounds, just to name a few. As with conflict, what separates good relationships from unfulfilling ones is not the absence of differences, but how those differences are handled.

REVERSAL: In good relationships, three qualities are almost always present. First, differences are accepted and accommodated between partners. There is no pressure for one to be a mirror image of the other. Second, the strengths of one are used to complement weaker areas of the other. For example, one who is good handling finances assumes responsibility in that area; the other may be better at dealing with household repairs and takes over that area. Finally, the couple has at least one activity that they regularly enjoy experiencing together.

MYTH #8: IF THE KIDS WEREN'T AROUND, WE COULD BE VERY HAPPY TOGETHER. There is no question that children require time and attention. However, when a husband or wife subscribes to this myth, there may be several undesirable offshoots. First, resentment toward the kids may build because they are seen to be the cause of problems. The real problem is failure to nurture the marriage after the kids come. The second undesirable offshoot is that all will be well in a marriage when the kids finally leave. In fact, the year after the last child leaves is a very high risk time for a couple to divorce.

REVERSAL: Seen in the long term, a husband and wife will be together much longer than the children will be in the house. Until that day comes, it is a dire mistake to take your spouse and your marriage for granted. Spending regular time alone, without the kids, is absolutely necessary in order to keep a marriage relationship strong and emotionally fulfilling. Then, when you become "empty nesters," you will be a together couple ready to enjoy life to the fullest, not strangers living under the same roof.

MYTH #9: IF WE WERE ONLY MORE ECONOMICALLY SUCCESSFUL, THEN WE'D BE HAPPY. This is the old "money will bring you happiness" argument. Most men and women, now economically successful, define the "good old days" as their youth when they had little money, but plenty of time to enjoy life and one another. As demands mount and responsibilities increase, life becomes extremely complicated although they have a much better income. It then becomes seductively easy to strive toward making even more money to bring happiness because financial resources available now just aren't doing it!

REVERSAL: To opt out of this easy myth, first stop defining yourself by how much you make and what you own because you already have the basics. Don't let your ego drive you further into debt. Instead, for deeper personal fulfillment begin to define yourself in terms of your key relationship: husband, wife, friend, companion, lover. Put energy into being together and experiencing together. A bit of romance just like in the "good old days" when you were young wouldn't hurt a bit, either.

MYTH #10: IF ONLY OUR RESPONSIBILITIES WERE FEWER, WE'D HAVE MORE TIME FOR ONE ANOTHER. The parenting years are extremely busy, but at any age you can tie up your time getting things done instead of nurturing your marriage. It's easy to convince yourself that there is so much to do that you have no choice in the matter. And, because you have no choice, you put your marriage on the back burner. The result is that you take your marriage for granted, slipping into the belief that your partner will always be there even though the relationship is being emotionally neglected. You may find yourself sadly mistaken.

REVERSAL: The choice to do the lawn, wash the dishes, or stay overtime at work are actually personal choices to put time together aside in lieu of chores. Start now to put your partner and time spent together *first*. Stop harassing one another at home for daring to sit down instead of doing things. Then, at all costs, grit your teeth and overcome the tendency to look around the house, see things that need to be done, and feel guilty about relaxing together. These healthy choices will help you reduce stress and increase your marital satisfaction.

MYTH #11: IF ONLY MY HUSBAND/WIFE WOULD CHANGE, THEN WE COULD REALLY LIVE THE GOOD LIFE. An old adage states that when men and women talk about change in a marriage, they are usually talking about changing their partner! This projection of responsibility for renewing a marriage has within it a severe flaw: "I want you to be just what I think you should be!" As this way of thinking about a partner grows, true acceptance of your partner diminishes and resentment builds. A related facet of this thinking is also extremely negative: "There is nothing I need to change. My spouse needs to do it all!"

REVERSAL: The first rule of thumb is to change yourself, not your partner. Look deep within yourself for *your* contributions to a stagnating marriage. Then, you take the initiative to make key changes in your priorities and choices simply because they are the right and healthy thing to do. You will become a positive model for your partner, and reciprocation will be easier. You will feel more in control, and more than likely your marriage relationship will become more personally fulfilling as a result.

MYTH #12: WE HAVE TO WORK HARD NOW, BUT THERE WILL BE PLENTY OF TIME FOR US LATER. Children are promised "the good life" if only they will study hard and sacrifice now. Young couples striving to become established sacrifice so they can enjoy life "later." To put aside personal pleasure to work for long-term goals is an essential skill for economic success. However, sacrificing a marriage relationship definitely isn't part of success. Daily, negative choices are implicitly made and the underlying message is clear: "Just be patient and wait. Someday, I'll have time for you and then we'll be good to one another." It doesn't happen.

REVERSAL: For any couple who has reached "thirty-something," the future must be now, not later! Work hard, but make it a point to enjoy the present instead of habitually waiting for "the future." To do so, you will have to face guilt for slowing down a bit, but you'll last longer. You will have to overcome your ego need to build a personal empire. What you gain will be personal satisfaction, emotional closeness, fun times together, and all the deeper fulfillments of "the good life" that elude so many.

Other Marital Aids

Let's face it. Like virtually every other relationship, the strength of a marriage is gauged by what happens when things go wrong. It's easy to have a good relationship when all is right with the world. It is when the crunch comes with personal unhappiness, stress, pressures, and lack of emotional fulfillment that couples either rise to the challenge or the relationship dies. And, a relationship can die whether you separate and divorce or whether you just continue to live together in lonely disharmony.

When you're unhappy, you find temptation everywhere. Other relationships are available. You can run away and start all over again elsewhere. And, the grass is always greener where you are not. However, one of the basic truths in life is that the easy way is usually not the right way. Such moves tend to give temporary relief, but seldom bring long-term satisfaction. A corollary to this principle is that what seems to be the easy way often turns out in the long run to be harder and more difficult than the alternative.

The message here is simple, and it reflects the guiding ethic of the "we" decade. Hang in there. Take a good hard look at your priorities. Do some changing. Put energy into that relationship. Find the good life together. It's worth it. A contemporary adage with a marital addendum is worth repeating here: "When the going gets tough, the tough get going . . . together." When this happens, a couple gets better . . . together. Literally and figuratively.

It's togetherness that makes a good marriage personally fulfilling and a strength for both. If you are ready to renew your marriage, first of all take responsibility for yourself. Stop blaming and making excuses. Then, as you make those key changes that really count, use as guidelines the four C's of marital communication. Keep in mind that communication is reflected in both what you say and in your actions.

THE FIRST "C" IS COMMITMENT. Commitment is a basic — the antithesis of the "throwaway" mentality of past decades. At its root, commitment is a solid underlying belief that marital problems *can* and *will* be worked out *together*. If at present, you can't quite believe this, then assume it. With this underlying foundation, you never threaten to leave or divorce when the going gets rough. You think only in terms of we, the two of us, a partnership, together.

THE SECOND "C" IS CARING. Most men and women verbally profess to care about their spouses, but you'd never know it from their actions. Begin by communicating the most basic caring of all: "I love you." Then follow it up with little (and not necessarily expensive) expressions of these feelings. Take the initiative to help out. Make a call to say "Hi" in the middle of the day. Plan a surprise lunch out. Take a walk hand in hand. The possibilities are myriad and they all count.

THE THIRD "C" IS COMPLIMENTS. It's easy to become so preoccupied with all you have to do that you don't say nice things to one another anymore. The fact is that everyone needs to hear nice things regularly. And, there are many opportunities each day to do just that. Comments on a bright smile, how good clothes look, and the wonderful dinner are just a few. It bolsters self-esteem and invites the same in return. A bonus is that thinking in upbeat terms keeps you upbeat!

THE FOURTH "C" IS CREATIVITY. "Variety is the spice of life," and creativity is the essence of variety! That means keep your marriage interesting. Routines become monotonous, so break them at all costs for yourself and for your marriage. It takes a little planning, but only when you're out of the "routine rut" will you realize how deep it was! It's as simple as trying a new recipe or planning an afternoon alone together.

In the end, there's a fifth "C" in a good marriage and that's Courage. The courage to live in a better way without being controlled by materialistic values or a distorted need to define yourself by what you own. It is reflected in an ability to see the deeper and more enduring values in life and to create relationships that reflect them. Courage is an ability to do what is right, not what is easy. It means thinking out the issues and living in positive ways without blindly doing what everyone around you is doing. Why? Because what everyone else is doing may not be right!

There can be no doubt about it. Making a marriage work takes understanding, maturity, and persistence. But, as the key relationship in a family, the satisfactions and fulfillments gained from a healthy and fulfilling marriage relationship far outweigh the inevitable problems that every husband and wife will encounter. In a fast-paced, hurry-up, I-want-it-right-now world, the real payoffs in a good marriage take many years to accrue. Infatuation doesn't last, but commitment, companionship, and quality communication will build deeper and more fulfilling bonds between you. Perhaps Mark Twain put it best: "Love seems the swiftest, but it is the slowest of all growths. No man or woman really knows what perfect love is until they have been married a quarter of a century."

True, but keep in mind that you must both work at it. Just living together and going through the motions while immersed in marital mythology doesn't count!

Chapter 3

Values Programming: The Work Ethic Strikes Back

The vast majority of husbands and wives work very hard these days. In fact, they have so much to get done each day that they have little hope of ever getting on top of their responsibilities. And, with the years, these incessant demands on time take a toll on emotional and physical well-being. It could easily be argued that the basic problem is that there is simply too much work to get done. However, making such an assumption would be a serious error. While there are many demands on time and energy these days, the fundamental problem lies in a deeply internalized work ethic and an overdeveloped sense of responsibility.

In order to relax and enjoy the good life, work values must be closely examined. It's certainly true that most parents want their children to grow to adulthood with a solid and well-developed work ethic. Why? Because they want their children to grow up to become emotionally mature, personally responsible, and economically self-sufficient adults. What many parents do not realize is that during the parenting years, the push to develop the work ethic in children is often inadvertently overdone.

In fact, for children, socialization designed to develop a solid work ethic begins very early in life and never ceases. To illustrate how this social programming works, let's look at the Dumores, a highly responsible husband and wife who are also greatly stressed. They tackle head-on the daunting task of being effective parents for their three children. Telling interactions with the kids take place practically every day.

Tommy, age 7, is told in no uncertain terms that he is not to go outside to play until every bit of his homework is done. He really would like to play, but he reluctantly does his work only because his parents are keeping a close watch on him.

Donna has to be reminded time and again to anticipate and plan for tests and school projects. A fourth grader, she finds this difficult because there's always something she'd rather do that's more fun.

She is habitually unprepared and is frequently scolded by her teachers.

In the seventh grade, Mike was supposed to do the lawn and his other chores, but he "forgot"—again. He goofed around with his friends instead. His parents were angry and restricted him for three days, certainly not for the first time.

What do all parents who respond in these ways have in common? That's easy. It's a shared interest in promoting the development of responsibility, personal accountability, and achievement motivation in their children. They want the kids to grow to take their places in society as successful adults. Through modeling, mandates, discussions, encouragement, and discipline, they systematically reinforce the values of a solid work ethic. As the noted economist, John Kenneth Galbraith once commented: "There is no ethic as ethical as the work ethic." As achievers themselves, parents like the Dumores really believe it.

However, at a personal level, Mr. and Mrs. Dumore don't feel that great these days. They are successful because they're constantly striving to meet all their work responsibilities at the office and at home. They've worked hard for years and now own their own home. They earn an adequate and stable income, and they've even saved a bit for unexpected expenses. At an economic level, they've made it to middle-class America.

The only problem is that the Dumores are about as miserable as they've ever been in their lives! Not only do they suffer personally, but their marriage relationship is suffering as well. All they do from the moment the sun cracks the horizon in the morning until long after it goes down at night is hurry and rush to meet their responsibilities. They run to get everything done that needs to be done so they can go to bed, get up tomorrow, and do it all over again. They both live each day in a deep rut.

Both of these good parents with solid values are really feeling the pressure these days. On one hand, it's true that life is certainly more intense and complex than it has ever been. On the other hand, daily routines should include a bit more time to relax and enjoy life. As they look back on the last ten years or so, they see the changes. The good times have slowly been pushed aside. Replacing them have been increasing expectations and now demands on their time. More and more, they wistfully look back to the early years of their marriage. In the good old days, they weren't making much money, but they sure did have a good time. Now it's just the reverse. The

Dumores make a good living, but the good times have become but a bittersweet memory of how they once lived and loved.

Understanding the Work Ethic

Unbeknownst to them, the Dumores are actually in the same paradoxical situation with their children as their parents were with them. They are systematically training each of their children in the values of the work ethic. Through their teaching, the message to the children is simple: "Be like us! Work hard and you'll make it." They are only dimly aware of the unstated part of their teaching: "Grow up and be achievers like us. We're miserable because our work ethic is so strong that we've lost all perspective on healthy priorities and enjoying life together!"

For busy men, women, and couples like the Dumores to reach the good life, they must, in fact, learn to regularly shift away from the strong work orientation which has come to dominate their lives. Before this can be done, however, several aspects of the work ethic must first be clearly understood.

1. A WELL-DEVELOPED WORK ETHIC IS A FUNCTIONAL NECESSITY. It's tough and competitive in the marketplace these days. And the bottom line is that a highly-developed sense of personal responsibility, along with effective work skills, is necessary for building a career, maintaining a household, and being a good parent. To give up the work ethic entirely is to court personal and economic disaster.

2. THE WORK ETHIC IS NOT A SINGLE VALUE. When asked, men and women often define the work ethic very simply: "It means you work very hard," or "You just keep pushing to get everything done." While not entirely erroneous, the fact is that the work ethic is actually a whole constellation of interrelated values and attitudes. To effectively understand the negative implications of this value system, each component part must be defined.

3. CHILDREN RESIST, BUT MOST OF THEM SLOWLY INTERNALIZE GOOD WORK VALUES. Small children have a pleasure-seeking, impulsive, and self-centered orientation. Seeking to turn these immature youngsters into responsible adults, parents become frustrated because teaching the kids good work values doesn't seem to "take." However, even though children overtly resist work, parents need to consistently guide them toward the development of a work ethic which children will gradually internalize.

4. THIS VALUE SYSTEM IS MASSIVELY REINFORCED OVER DECADES. Rewards are given to children who are responsible and who work hard: good grades, complimentary feedback, and honors. Later in life, the rewards for such behaviors increase: career advancement, perks, material wealth, status, power, respect, and many others. These rewards, accruing over decades, cause such work responses to be even more deeply internalized and repeated.

5. INDIVIDUALS LOSE CONTROL WHEN RESPONSIBILITIES GROW. Work demands at the office and on the home front begin to grow with the years. Life slowly but surely becomes more demanding and complex. The net result is that individuals gradually lose so much control that, over a period of time, needed relaxation becomes virtually impossible because there is so much to be done.

6. THE RESULT IS PERSONAL STRESS, MARITAL DISCORD, AND FAMILY FRAGMENTATION. The net result of overwork driven by a highly developed sense of responsibility is loss of the good life. Everyone begins to suffer. Personally, chronic stress and pressure create emotional turmoil. Marital relationships become strained as time together disappears and intimacy wanes. Children live in homes with little affection and nurturance among family members.

A New Reality: Emotional Fatigue

Any discussion of the detrimental effects of an overdeveloped work ethic must focus on an increasingly common complaint. It's heard from men and women, husbands and wives, and couples of all ages. Interestingly, just a decade or so ago, this complaint was not heard much at all. With many minor variations, here's what is heard in middle-class homes all across the nation.

"I just don't know what's wrong with me. I'm tired all the time and I can't seem to get rid of it. No matter what I do and how much I sleep, it doesn't go away. It's there in the morning, at noon and at night, even on weekends. Last summer we went on vacation and I was still tired. I'm so tired of feeling tired that I can't stand it anymore. I just hope there's nothing seriously wrong with me because I've never felt this way before."

This common lament brings with it two assumptions about this new prevalent type of fatigue. Both sound logical on the surface, but when examined in more depth, both prove to be erroneous. The first misconception is that this chronic fatigue is due to the aging process. Men and women believe that they are now "over the hill" and on the "downhill slide" because they're tired all the time. Subscribing to this belief, they believe that their tiredness is only going to get worse with the years. And, to make this erroneous assumption even more absurd, many husbands and wives who make such comments are not yet even out of their thirties!

The facts are clear that this deep fatigue has very little to do with age. In virtually every city, town, and hamlet across the nation, many men and women well into their seventies have plenty of energy to get through the day. In fact, many of these energetic senior citizens run rings around those tired men and women in their thirties and forties! The bottom line is as simple as it is optimistic. If care is taken to remain physically and mentally healthy, energy levels should remain entirely adequate at least into the early seventies and often beyond that age.

To understand the second erroneous belief about this chronic fatigue that sets in takes a bit more explanation. The problem has its roots in how men and women think about fatigue. They see it correctly in one sense, as they always have—in physical terms. The sequence is very simple (see Figure 1). First, physical or muscular exertion as in cleaning the attic or working out in the gym depletes physical energy. This then leads to physical or muscular fatigue. Of course, as everyone knows, the remedy for this kind of physical tiredness is to sleep or rest. With rest or sleep, tired muscles rejuvenate and are ready to work again.

So far so good. The catch is that technological development has changed the nature of work in every facet of life. As you may already realize, mental labor has steadily replaced physical labor at home and at work. Problem solving, making decisions, dealing with unpreventable glitches, overseeing the kids's homework, programming your VCR, and balancing the checkbook, along with getting the bills paid and saving all financial records for tax purposes, require constant mental labor at work and at home.

This kind of constant mental work, the basis of which is active thinking, requires tremendous energy (see Figure 1 again). However, the catch is that mental labor, while stressful, does not require physical or muscular energy. Rather, mental labor depletes reserves of emotional energy. The result is the development of an emotionally-based fatigue that is qualitatively different from physical fatigue. However, at a superficial level, emotional fatigue may feel somewhat like physical fatigue, especially to those who do not understand the difference.

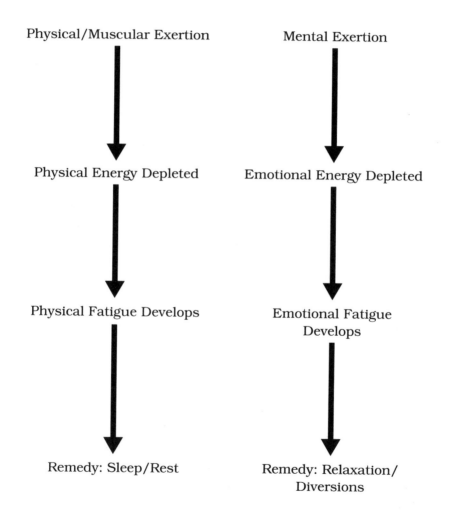

DEVELOPING
PHYSICAL FATIGUE

DEVELOPING
EMOTIONAL FATIGUE

Physical/Muscular Exertion

Mental Exertion

Physical Energy Depleted

Emotional Energy Depleted

Physical Fatigue Develops

Emotional Fatigue
Develops

Remedy: Sleep/Rest

Remedy: Relaxation/
Diversions

Figure 1: Differences Between Physical and Emotional Fatigue

At this juncture, another serious problem emerges. Without realizing they are suffering from emotional fatigue, many overworked husbands and wives assume they are physically tired and use the appropriate remedy: to sleep or rest more. The error here, although simple, is serious in its consequences. Emotional fatigue cannot be resolved using the remedy for physical fatigue. In fact, the more sedentary one becomes, the worse this growing emotional fatigue stemming from mental overwork seems to get. The remedy for emotional fatigue is not sleep or rest; rather it lies in taking regular time for relaxation and creating interesting diversions in your life.

The basic reality that must be accepted by those men and women who want to feel physically and emotionally energetic these days is simple: Because of the growing shift to mental labor as a mode of functioning at work and at home, men and women who want to function well must cope with *two different kinds* of fatigue every day. Of course, these two kinds of fatigue are the physical and the emotional. Basically, these two types of fatigue are like apples and oranges. They are two very different processes without much overlap that require two entirely different remedies.

Further, many husbands and wives ask a very legitimate question: "How can I tell whether I'm suffering from physical or emotional fatigue?" Be assured that these two types of fatigue can be distinguished from one another. The first cue is that emotional fatigue typically does not respond to sleep. You may be emotionally tired (but physically rested) before getting out of bed in the morning! The fatigue stays no matter where you are or what your are doing. Second, emotional fatigue has a deep quality; it seems to have its origins in the very core of your being. When you begin to actively try to distinguish physical from emotional fatigue, you will soon learn to tell the difference.

One more point is worth making. If it happened to be true that mental work was confined to the office, the problem would certainly not be as severe or as prevalent as it is today. However, mental work is rampant at home too. Take a moment to review all the things that you must constantly be thinking about to keep your home running smoothly. And, if you let it happen, even recreational activities can be filled with "technological advances" that require mental work (and frustration).

The end result of this lifestyle reality is a most pertinent question that must be effectively answered if emotional health and happy marriages are to be maintained: "If it is true that more and more of the work that I do these days is done in my head, then how do I get away from it?" Because stressful work now occurs between your ears, you can take it anywhere with you and do it in any locale. For example, you can take it with you to bed, on a walk, on vacation, or on a car ride. It is no longer feasible, or even possible, to gain physical distance from mental exertion.

The bottom line is that if you cannot learn to shut it down between your ears, then you can't get away from it; the resultant mental stress and fatigue will eventually take its toll both on you personally and on your marriage relationship. As already stated, for emotional rejuvenation to take place, you must make time for quality relaxation or diversions in your life. The nature of relaxation is quite simple to define:

> **RELAXATION:** *Your ability to allow yourself to become deeply and pleasantly absorbed in any activity that is valued primarily for the pleasure of the experience.*

In other words, in order to emotionally rejuvenate, you must regularly shift into another mode. That is, true relaxation requires that you become so absorbed in an activity that is so interesting and stimulating for itself that you completely forget about worries, work, schedules, and destinations. This kind of experience provides mental relief, thus facilitating emotional recovery from chronic fatigue. Interestingly, because of the differences between emotional and physical fatigue, it is entirely possible to become physically tired through active recreation (*e.g.*, a game of tennis), yet emotionally rejuvenated at the same time!

The Values of the Work Ethic

Now back to the increasingly unhappy Dumores. The reality is that while there will always be a great deal of work for couples like the Dumores to get done each day, the major barriers to the good life exist within themselves. The key lies in understanding the problematic side of each of the values that collectively make up the "work ethic." As a responsible man or woman, you may also be feeling the negative effects of overlearning the values of the work ethic both on a personal level and in your marriage.

Here is an overview of each of the eight interrelated work values, all of them learned during childhood and quite valuable to "making it" economically. Each of these values later backfires to erode the good life you wanted and surely deserve after years of hard work and sacrifice.

WORK VALUE #1: YOU CAN MAKE THINGS HAPPEN BECAUSE YOU'RE IN CONTROL. Parents consistently try to instill this value in children: "You can be anything you want to be. You can make it happen." "Just believe you can do it. Hang in there and develop all your potential." These kinds of statements are meant to be encouraging to a child. The intent is to communicate that despite barriers, problems, and setbacks, ultimate goals are attainable if there is a sense of personal control and an inner determination to get there. And, to a great extent, this philosophy works—at least in some aspects of life.

The problem here is so simple that it's easy to miss. It's simply the fact that no one is in rational control of everything. For example, you can't "make" yourself go to sleep because you don't directly control it. Instead, you must relax and let sleep come. That requires a very different approach. Similarly, did you ever try to "make" yourself be spontaneous? Many circumstances in life simply cannot be rationally controlled by any individual. And, when attempts are made to impose conscious control on such activities, they are sabotaged.

SUGGESTION: In selected areas of life—sexual functioning, going to sleep, relaxing, being open and spontaneous—give up trying to direct and control the experiences. Instead, learn to relax and let your body and mind respond naturally. It's easier, and furthermore, a delightful part of you that has been long suppressed will begin to emerge.

WORK VALUE #2: THERE IS A DIRECT RELATIONSHIP BETWEEN EFFORT AND REWARD. "The harder you try, the better the outcome" is the ethic here. "Study more and you'll get better grades." "Push a bit more in your job and you'll get promoted." "If you don't mow the lawn and do it right, you won't get paid." This certainly isn't a bad value to instill in children, and parents go to great lengths to teach it. They do this through their communication with children and by structuring experiences at home that create this critical effort-reward linkage.

Related to the need for rational control, the problem here is that with some activities, the harder you try the *worse* the outcome. For example, pushing ever harder to make something happen at times undermines getting what you want. For instance, trying hard to get to sleep sabotages it. And, consciously putting great effort into trying to relax is a surefire way to short-circuit the experience. Pushing too hard to be creative often blocks the creative process. The trick here is to understand when the effort-reward value is functional and when it isn't helpful.

SUGGESTION: The best approach to overcoming this problem is to selectively turn off the "try harder" value. Don't try at all in those kinds of activities where the effort-reward relationship doesn't work. Instead, surrender to the experience (which takes no effort at all) and try adopting the "whatever will be, will be" philosophy. When you do, what you want to happen probably will.

WORK VALUE #3: DENY YOURSELF NOW AND GREAT REWARDS WILL COME LATER. The ability to choose self-denial over immediate pleasure is absolutely crucial to the attainment of long-term goals. "Save your money now so you can buy that new bicycle next summer." "Do your homework (instead of playing) and you won't regret it because it will help you get a good job later on." There is no doubt that the capacity for personal sacrifice and self-denial is absolutely necessary these days to attain career success and to insure economic self-sufficiency.

The downside of this highly desirable value comes when habitual self-denial becomes a lifestyle. Typically, men and women do sacrifice tremendously during the first part of their careers. They do so to get through school, to save money for a home, and to otherwise get started in life. However, there comes a point at which they are reasonably well-established and economically comfortable. Within, though, is a tendency to continue the learned pattern of personal denial. As a result, with well-meaning rationalizations, they consistently put off enjoying life or doing things for themselves to some vague point in the future.

SUGGESTION: To solve this problem, you must decide that the future begins right now! Yes, you must provide for your future security, but at the same time you can begin *today* to enjoy life and break the self-denial habit. Take that vacation. Indulge yourself just a bit now and then. After all, you've worked all your life to get where you are and you deserve to enjoy it now.

WORK VALUE #4: YOU MUST ALWAYS HAVE SOMETHING TO SHOW TO JUSTIFY THE TIME YOU SPENT. This value is a parent's best defense against a child perceived to be too pleasure-oriented or prone to "goofing off." "You mean that you spent an entire afternoon together and didn't get a thing done?" "How can you lie there and watch television when you have all that work to do?" In their efforts to train a child to be responsible, parents want time to be spent meaningfully. As a result, in direct and indirect ways, they communicate that if there is nothing tangible to show to justify how time was spent, it is time wasted; therefore a child is being irresponsible and should feel bad.

This particular part of the work ethic begins to backfire when this value is extended to relaxation time as an adult. Men and women with this internalized value sometimes can't sit down to enjoy themselves even for a few moments, especially at home. Before ten minutes have elapsed, they experience a rising tension which is then transformed into guilt. Without even thinking about it, that individual will get up and find something to do that is defined as "productive" to relieve the guilt. As the result of this overlearned work value, many adults can no longer relax without feeling intensely guilty.

SUGGESTION: First, recognize that true relaxation and quality leisure time are best achieved by enjoying an experience moment by moment, not by reaching goals or by pushing to have tangible products to show. Make such time for yourself a priority. The "products" that result are intangible but real: emotional well-being, renewed energy, and enhanced personal health.

WORK VALUE #5: YOU MUST GET ALL OF YOUR WORK DONE BEFORE YOU CAN RELAX AND ENJOY YOURSELF. A child's orientation is very simple: that is, to minimize pain and maximize pleasure. Parents want their children to have the commitment to meet their responsibilities even if it isn't much fun. As a result, they mandate the "work first" way of doing things: "There's no way you're going outside until every bit of your homework is done." "Don't even look at that dessert until there isn't a green bean left on your plate!" These kinds of messages communicate parents' expectations that directly counter a child's pleasure-oriented "fun-first" motivation.

The problem is that with these kinds of messages communicated hundreds, even thousands, of times during the course of development, the work value internalized by the kids is slightly different from the one parents intended. Parents want children to balance work and play. The kids pick up the messages literally: "You can't justify having fun or doing anything for yourself until all your work is completely done." Later in life, when there is a busy career, home maintenance, parenting responsibilities, and community involvements, this deeply-held belief acts to prevent you from doing anything for yourself because all your work isn't done!

SUGGESTION: First, modify this value by recognizing that right now you will probably never be completely on top of things. Then, begin taking regular time for yourself and justify it on a dual basis: to improve your physical and emotional health and because you deserve a little time and pleasure for yourself. Conversely, those who do not take some time for themselves typically become resentful and angry.

WORK VALUE #6: ALWAYS ANTICIPATE THE CONSEQUENCES OF YOUR ACTIONS AND PLAN AHEAD. Contemporary realities are such that if you don't anticipate and plan ahead, there will be unnecessary difficulties. The messages from early in life are quite clear and consistent: "Think about what you'll need before you go camping. If you don't, you're going to forget something important and have problems." "Don't forget to study for that test that's coming up on Friday. Prepare for it now and don't wait until the last minute." This kind of anticipatory thought process is drilled into children as a means to help them more adequately meet their responsibilities and function in a mature fashion. There is no question that it's a valuable skill.

The flip side of this value is worth noting, however. It's simply that there is often a negative value (subtly communicated, but often well-learned) placed on living too much in the present and not anticipating the future. The fact is that it's very difficult to relax completely when your well-trained mind is always thinking ahead, anticipating what's coming next, and planning ways to get done all that needs to be done. Individuals who do this too much, particularly during relaxation time, often lose the ability to psychologically "let go" and enjoy the moment. They may be in the right setting to relax, but their minds won't let them do it.

SUGGESTION: The trick here is practice. Find an activity that you enjoy, and involve yourself in it regularly. Remove as many distractions as possible and give yourself enough time. You'll know you've relearned how to really "let go" if you can get so deeply involved in something you enjoy that you lose track of time. (*Note:* All children can do this naturally until they are systematically trained by conscientious adults to be "responsible.")

WORK VALUE #7: BIGGER AND MORE IS ALWAYS BETTER THAN WHAT YOU HAVE RIGHT NOW. This work-related value is communicated to children in many direct and indirect ways. It leads to an "upward and onward" empire-building motivation. Parents may often say to a child: "If we only had more money, think of all the things we'd have and how much better off we'd be." "People who live in big houses are obviously more successful than those who live in smaller ones." Certainly, there is nothing wrong with wanting to make an adequate living and to live in a comfortable home. As such "bigger and more" work-oriented goals are consistently reinforced; however, they become ends in themselves and often result in personal problems instead.

In short, if this motivational orientation is not kept in perspective and balanced with common sense and healthy life values, empire-building begins to create unnecessary stresses and conflicts that impair a couple's relationship and erode the good life. For example, striving for a bigger home may lend itself to more prestige and status, but is it worth it if the consequences are being "house poor" because of an extremely high mortgage payment and working even harder on upkeep and maintenance? Or, is accepting a promotion simply for more money really going to be fulfilling if you are not emotionally suited for (or trained in) that kind of work, with the result being chronic stress and emotional turmoil? An unbridled drive upward and onward, always pushing toward "bigger and better and more," is often not the road to the good life.

SUGGESTION: When a major decision about a move, career advancement, or home purchase is confronted, look at all the issues involved, including the potentially negative effects on you and your family. It takes a strong and emotionally secure person to see beyond ego and status needs to decline a move that would adversely affect personal well-being, a marriage, and living the good life.

WORKING VALUE #8: THE ROAD TO SUCCESS IS TO SET GOALS FOR YOURSELF AND THEN TO ATTAIN THEM. No doubt about it. Setting personal goals and then pushing constantly to attain them is the royal road to making it these days. And, the payoffs for setting and reaching personal goals are both tangible and emotional: "Focus on making the team. Train every day and you'll make it." "Winning that science fair contest will be great. Everyone will see just how smart you are!" Working toward and attaining goals despite challenges, setbacks, and problems also builds character and perseverance—qualities that are greatly in demand these days.

On the other hand, an overdeveloped orientation toward goal attainment has a flaw that often does not show up until later in life. It's the learned expectation that all rewards come at the end of an activity when goals have been reached. If you focus exclusively on endpoints, that is, the *product* of your efforts, you may neglect the fulfillment that comes from enjoying the *process*. Imposing such a focused goal orientation on leisure activities, vacations, and relationships distorts them and often transforms them into psychological work instead of enjoyable and relaxing experiences.

SUGGESTION: In social and leisure activities in particular, make it a point to set no goals for the experiences. Take out negative competitiveness, ego needs, and the requirement to have a product in order to justify the experience. Instead, learn to value such activities for the moment-by-moment pleasure they can bring. You'll expend much less energy and enjoy yourself more.

The Pattern Principle

As life gets busier and an overdeveloped work ethic begins to drive a lifestyle characterized by overwork, emotional exhaustion, and increasing marital distance, several other destructive effects of this value system must also be understood. First, motivation to get everything done that needs to be done each day begins to change how a husband or wife becomes oriented to life each day. The work ethic, which emphasizes meeting responsibilities, slowly trains a husband or wife to perceive life only in terms of those responsibilities. A characteristic way of thinking about each day begins to grow: what needs to be done, what didn't I get done, what is coming next, have I forgotten anything important? In effect, an overdeveloped work ethic begins to orient a husband and wife exclusively toward external priorities, that is, responsibilities.

With the years, it becomes more and more difficult to stop thinking about work and what needs to be done. In settings like your home, where there is always work undone, the sight of such unmet responsibilities triggers even more such thoughts. As this process takes place, internal life priorities that reflect emotional well-being, a fulfilling marriage relationship, and living the good life together are systematically neglected. The end result is a work-driven, emotionally exhausted man or woman who has lost all perspective on what is deep, enduring, and, ultimately, fulfilling in life. Unhappily, they begin to just plod through life, feeling trapped and discouraged that the good life they had always hoped for has become so elusive.

With the years, the negative consequences of this strong external orientation toward responsibilities are felt acutely as a marital relationship, even a family, slowly fragments inside a reasonably nice home with an adequate income. The root of the problem lies in what might be called the Pattern Principle.

THE PATTERN PRINCIPLE: *Consistent daily decisions to*

complete tasks and to be highly responsible become, over time, long-term patterns of emotional neglect of loved ones and oneself.

In other words, tasks (such as mowing the lawn, spending an extra hour at the office, cleaning the living room, washing the dishes, making telephone calls in the evening, or preparing for tomorrow's work) are undertaken every day without even thinking about them because they reflect the motivation to be a highly responsible man or woman. While these tasks reflect a need to be responsible, they also convey an unspoken, but powerfully negative message, particularly to a spouse, and often to children: "You aren't really important to me. I'll spend some time with you when I finish everything else I need to get done."

The catch is that usually no time is left over. Or, when there is time, both partners are emotionally and physically exhausted and in no mood to spend quality time with a spouse. The unfortunate end result is that a husband and wife, once close and loving, begin to take their relationship for granted. And, as they do so, they begin to grow further apart while living under the same roof because their relationship together is not being nourished. It is at this point that many personal insecurities, along with doubts about whether a marriage will make it much further, begin to grow because once-healthy life priorities shared by a couple have now become completely inverted.

Reversing Inverted Priorities

To make coping with the overlearned values of the work ethic even more difficult as an adult, another unrealistic expectation is inadvertently communicated by parents. This expectation is completely untrue. Defined, it's the idea that if you do everything that parents and society say you should do—study hard, get good grades, sacrifice and deny yourself, do your best to meet every one of your responsibilities—then, at some point, everything will *automatically* fall into place and you will live happily ever after. Needless to say, this expectation is a blatant fantasy.

The reality is that if you are going to create the good life for you and your loved ones, initially there will be some hard work to shift the way you go about doing things. Again, it's not going to happen automatically. You must be ready to make key changes in your life that will set the stage to bring more happiness and personal fulfillment your way. Here are seven steps to help you do just that.

1. REALIZE THAT YOU LEARNED TO BE WORK DRIVEN. No child comes into the world with all the values of the work ethic already developed. Those values and ways of relating are learned through decades of direct teaching and constant reinforcement. That's the bad news. The good news is that because these ways of living and relating are learned, they can also be unlearned.

2. MAKE A COMMITMENT TO YOURSELF AND TO YOUR SPOUSE. To live the good life together, you and your spouse must decide that you are ready to involve yourselves in getting better together. By making this decision jointly, you are also making a commitment to your marriage and to a fulfilling future. As you assume control of your lives, you make each day enjoyable for you both.

3. FOCUS ON MAKING KEY CHANGES AT HOME. Learning to enjoy life at home is the very best place to begin making the key changes that will bring the good life within reach. However, because tension and irritability are all more easily expressed at home, it is also one of the most difficult places to make necessary changes. Making key changes together makes it easier.

4. "DIET" WITH YOUR WORK ETHIC. You can't give up work values entirely because you must support yourself and your family. Bringing your work ethic under control is not like smoking cessation; that is, by stopping completely you will be healthier. It's much more like dieting; you must continue to eat (and work) daily, but you must make different choices and do so in moderation.

5. CONFRONT IRRATIONAL GUILT AND ANXIETY. To resolve the overwork trap, you must confront uncomfortable emotions. When you stop working, internal tension and guilt build swiftly. This emotional discomfort will then drive you back to work to get rid of it. Instead, begin to relax at home, confronting this kind of irrational guilt and tension directly and consistently; it will dissipate over time.

6. STOP GUILT-TRIPPING ONE ANOTHER. "There you sit . . . again. You don't even care how this place looks." Or, "Those dishes have been in the sink for an hour now. This place is going downhill fast. What's going on around here?" This kind of harassment and guilt-tripping make it even more difficult for a couple to relax at home. Completely eliminate it as it only creates anger in your partner that drives you further apart.

7. PROTECT THE POSITIVE CHANGES YOU HAVE MADE. Positive lifestyle changes can't be made and then forgotten. Your own bad habits and external influences will pull you both back into old patterns. Instead, carefully guard those positive changes through encouragement and complimentary remarks. Gently and supportively help your partner get back on track when there is slippage.

There are many reasons to put some effort and energy into recovering the good life for you both. You want more than work out of life. Your children need to share experiences with you and to see you as a good parental model. And, perhaps most important, you desperately need a bit of time and satisfaction for yourself. Over the years, you've slowly gained depth in your understanding of what life is *really* all about.

These days, you're much more aware of what is enduring and deeply fulfilling and what is not. And, you know that economic success alone doesn't necessarily bring happiness. But there is also another reason to begin now to translate these understandings into practice. As the man said, "The future just ain't what it used to be." That's certainly true. But, the fact is that there just isn't as much of it left as there used to be, either!

Chapter 4

Having the Time of Your Life: Humane Time Management for Couples

For busy couples, time is a very precious commodity because there is never enough of it. Most men and women know from experiences when they were just starting out in life that, used wisely, time can bring emotional fulfillment, personal satisfaction, and just plain fun. With age and growing responsibilities, one's time priorities often become distorted as an overdeveloped work ethic takes over and begins to drive men and women all day each day. Then, these same men and women find their use of time brings only constant pressure, internal tension, and persistent negative feelings that eventually erode their relationship together.

Perhaps a pertinent question to address is the nature of the choices you make regarding use of your time each day. This examination is particularly relevant for busy husbands and wives who, given the harsh reality that there are only twenty-four hours in each day, find to their chagrin that they have twenty-six hours of work to do! When you think about it, you may find yourself repeating contradictory statements to yourself and to others. During busy moments, you find yourself saying:

"I have so much to do. I just wish there were more hours in the day so I could get it all done!"

Just as frequently, you make a wish:

I wish I had more time for myself. I know I need to slow down and relax. I'm burned out and feel terrible."

With your current busy lifestyle, both of these statements are undoubtedly valid. However, it is a stark reality that there are only 24 hours in each day, 168 hours in each week. You already know that there is simply not enough time for you to do everything. With all your responsibilities bearing down on you each day, it is difficult to take time for yourself to insure emotional well-being, a loving marital relationship, and a solid family life. Yet, if you don't take this time, the price tag may be very high. Some of the best years of your life may slip by while you work yourself to the bone for highly suspect and not well-thought-out reasons.

Your lifestyle, and the decisions and values that underlie it, are closely related to your philosophy of time management. You might argue that you have no philosophy of time management, but you would be wrong. Your beliefs about time priorities are reflected in the decisions you make each day about how to use this precious, but limited, commodity. Over the years, you have developed your own ways to deal with time problems. Some of your strategies are undoubtedly quite helpful and some less so. A few may be downright unhealthy! When you get right down to it, there are two diametrically opposed approaches to time management. Which one best fits *your* lifestyle these days?

TRADITIONAL TIME MANAGEMENT: *A philosophy of organizing oneself more tightly and enhancing personal efficiency to increase productive output from a given amount of time.*

Whether learned directly or adopted by trial and error, the basic techniques of this productivity-oriented approach are probably quite familiar.

• Always do two or more things at once so you can increase your output.

• By doing everything faster, your productivity increases.

• If you think about what you need to do next before you're done with what you're doing now, you get a head start on it.

• By blending work with relaxation (or a vacation), it's much easier to keep up.

• Whenever there are a few spare moments (*e.g.*, waiting in line in a grocery store), make sure you have something with you to do to avoid wasting time.

This "output" philosophy of time management may have some virtues, but it also has many liabilities. In short, over time this approach becomes skewed in the direction of ever more productivity at the expense of personal well-being. Most often, this way of using time is adopted by highly conscientious men and women who have simply not thought out the consequences. For more than a few, being highly productive at all times becomes virtually mindless. You just keep on doing things because they're there to be done! For contrast, here's a healthier time management philosophy.

HUMANE TIME MANAGEMENT: *The process of creativity balancing personal organization and productivity with the* *skills required to insure emotional well-being and to preserve quality of life.*

This is a much more sensible approach to time management in these days when middle-class lifestyles have become very intense and complex. In fact, you may be square in the middle of that time of life when you have more work to do each day than you can possibly get done. The big question is whether you have lost control of your time. That is, are your responsibilities controlling your life or are you still in charge? If you're feeling excessively stressed and pressured, you may have inadvertently lost not only control but perspective on what you are doing with the time of your life—*and why.*

The first step in your recovery from this unhealthy way of living is to accept that no matter what your life circumstances, you always have the power of personal choice in how you use your time. Second, you must realize that you will never get completely caught up with all you have to do and get done. The third important step is to start being kinder to yourself by meeting important emotional needs that will help you enjoy life a bit more and "hang in there" over the long run.

You certainly don't want to be approaching retirement with the lament: "I certainly got a lot done, but I never did have a chance to enjoy myself along the way." But many do. Or, as someone once astutely commented: "I never met anyone approaching the end of life who wished that more time had been spent at the office." That's true whether your "office" is at your workplace, your home—or both!

"Timeless" Issues

To begin moving in the direction of having the time of your life— literally and figuratively—obstacles of many kinds must be surmounted. It will also become apparent that these barriers to living well together, loving deeply, and taking care of yourself are very powerful. Look at it this way. If the impediments to having a bit of time for yourself and living the good life together were not significant, you would have dealt with them long ago. And, you would not be feeling all the negative feelings inside, including increasing marital distance and personal insecurities that have been growing within you for years.

The process of making time for the good life together is actually a way of redefining yourself in a healthier and more psychologically mature fashion. Do understand that while taking time for yourself and getting better together with your mate will not be easy, nonetheless it is a task that is eminently worthwhile. The first step is to understand the nature of the various barriers to the good life. They tend to have their origins in four areas. However, regardless of origin, it is up to you, and you alone, to confront and resolve each one of them. That task is accomplished by making personal decisions not to allow these issues, now clearly conceptualized, to impede your progress toward the good life for you and your mate. Because these problems are interrelated, dealing with one may help erode the power of several others.

I. PERSONAL BARRIERS

These personal issues lie primarily in a man or woman's perceptions of responsibility and how such responsibilities should be met. Often, these values and beliefs have never before been clearly articulated and examined for their validity in daily life. Instead, they become motivating forces that begin to drive a husband or wife, even though the basis for such work behavior is irrational or based on unhealthy beliefs.

A. AN OVERDEVELOPED WORK ETHIC. You already know the various values of the work ethic. However, you may not have realized how powerful they have been in shaping how you lived life each day, particularly as life has become busier. At this point, you may be seeing life only in terms of work, work, and more work because these values have been internalized too deeply.

B. EXCESSIVELY HIGH STANDARDS. Many men and women derive great personal satisfaction from doing very well what they set out to accomplish. In narrow perspective, there certainly isn't a problem with high standards. However, when life becomes very hectic and busy, and this need for extremely high standards remains intact, quality of life often erodes.

C. BAD PRECEDENTS. Many men and women, at the office and at home, strive to be highly responsible; however, they begin to set bad precedents with others. That is, they often do for others what those other individuals should be doing for themselves. The end result is predictable. One individual is overworked, and the recipients are permitted to remain irresponsible.

II. EMOTIONAL OBSTACLES

These problems come in the form of negative feelings that arise whenever perceptions of strict responsibility are not met. Over time, these questionable feelings come to psychologically represent being irresponsible, immature, and somehow "bad." To prevent them from arising, all available time is spent being "responsible," which is defined primarily in terms of tasks completed. Three feelings must be dealt with.

A. GUILT. Feelings of personal guilt for not doing everything that "should" be done is a powerful motivator. In fact, without thinking it out, husbands and wives consistently avoid the buildup of guilt by always staying busy with one task or another. This guilt is not moral guilt; it is nothing more than a pathological by-product of an overlearned work ethic.

B. ANXIETY/FEAR. These irrational feelings stem from the consequences of discovery by others that a man or woman has not been adequately meeting personal responsibilities. By deciding to take care of oneself in lieu of getting more work done and tasks completed, you arouse anxiety or fear. It's akin to a child's fear that parents will discover uncompleted homework.

C. FAILURE. When there is a conscious decision, unattended by good excuses or viable rationalizations, not to do work that needs to be done, feelings of personal failure set in. These are often accompanied by guilt for not meeting personal standards. This guilt becomes a powerful reinforcer for not taking time for oneself or spending quality time with one's mate.

III. PROBLEMS FROM THE PAST

Many of the issues that arise to complicate and cause problems in adulthood have their origin during personal development in the family. Often, parents inadvertently teach values and ways of living that they don't intend to. Or, just as frequently, children perceive reality in immature ways that reflect their ages. However, these lessons clearly lead to dysfunctional behavior once busy adulthood has been reached.

A. PARENTAL MODELING. It is not infrequent to find that over-work and neglect of loved ones and oneself is passed from generation to generation through modeling. Children observe their parents for many years before reaching adulthood themselves. What they observe their parents doing often becomes internalized as values that negatively influence their lifestyles when the kids reach adulthood.

B. PARENTAL LABELING. Early in life, parents are the most important adults in the world to children. What parents say is the truth—reality. When parents label children—lazy, unmotivated, selfish—it often creates a drive to overcome the label in adulthood. Or, parents can relate to a child in ways that reflect acceptance only when there is success and achievement.

C. PERSONAL VULNERABILITIES. Often a child develops personal vulnerabilities that create overcommitment when these "soft spots" are used by others—by adults and children inside and outside the family. Many different unresolved personal issues permit manipulation to take place: guilt for saying "no," avoidance of conflict, saying "yes" to flattery, fear of disapproval.

IV. INTERPERSONAL BLOCKS

Often, irrational amounts of time are given away as a response to other individuals. Most of the time, the closer those individuals are, the more powerful their influence on a husband or wife who is in the position of constantly giving to others. It is indeed ironic that when responses to others are inappropriate, the net result is often a deterioration in the quality of those relationships that are the most important of all.

A. CHILDREN'S NEEDS. Many parents feel irrationally guilty about not spending more time with children, especially in two-career families. In lieu of spending quality time with the kids, such parents work ever harder to give material things. In either case, their personal energies are expended with no time left over for a husband or wife or to relax oneself.

B. A SPOUSE'S REMARKS. When life becomes very busy, relaxing together is often made virtually impossible because of a spouse's guilt-inducing remarks. "Why aren't you fixing that door like you promised?" or, "That living room is a mess every time I see it." Such comments, often backed by a spouse's workaholic style, imply that it is inappropriate to relax at home.

C. OBSERVATION OF FRIENDS. Friends' homes are immaculate. Everything is tidy; no dust is visible anywhere. At work, colleagues seem to get everything done on time. However, these observations do not reflect reality. Friends' homes are not as tidy when company isn't coming. And, friends who are on top of work do it at home, often while sacrificing quality time with a spouse.

Save Some Time for Peace of Mind

In other words, save a bit of time for yourself (not to get more done) so you don't go stark raving crazy or shuffle through life each day a burned-out, semidepressed man or woman who doesn't enjoy anything anymore. If you've been feeling too pressured and you're ready to commit yourself to a healthier and more satisfying lifestyle, a number of specific changes can start the process. These are survival skills. By adopting them, you move beyond a mindless productivity orientation to really enjoying life. Because you deserve it. Because it is necessary for "making it" in the long term. Because now is the time of your life. Because living the good life with those you love is important.

If your commitment is strong, you will not be driven back to work by the initial discomfort you will experience when you begin to take time for yourself. Soon you will begin to feel better. Here are some starting suggestions.

SKILL #1: FIND A "NONPRODUCTIVE" LEISURE ACTIVITY. It is imperative that you find a leisure outlet you enjoy just because it is pleasurable. Neither products nor goals need be involved. The core of relaxation and rejuvenation is simply your ability to let yourself become deeply and pleasantly involved in an activity that is valued primarily for the experience itself. Literally, it may be "product-less" time and therefore wasteful from a traditional time management perspective. Realistically, however, such time may be the most personally valuable of all. Because it's time for you, it makes all that you do seem easier. An added bonus is that you also become more efficient.

SKILL #2: BREAK THE POLYPHASIC ACTIVITY HABIT. One way to cope with a busy life is to do two or three things at once. However, habitual polyphasic activity has subtle, but very destructive effects. First, doing two or three things at once is inherently stressful. Second, as this habit becomes a normal way of functioning, it creates anxiety when it is stopped (*e.g.*, watching a movie on TV without working creates tension). Third, it becomes very difficult to "let go" and relax when your mind is going a mile a minute all the time. Break this habit by taking time to enjoy yourself and make it a point never to do two (much less three) things at once during this time.

SKILL #3: TEACH OTHERS TO RESPECT YOUR TIME. When it comes to the time of your life, it is easy to be taken for granted by others if you let it happen: people dropping in unexpectedly, calls to chat (or calling with business concerns after hours), a spouse or children invading time you set aside for yourself at home. It is entirely up to you to teach others to respect your time. Otherwise, you and your time will easily be abused. It will probably be difficult at first because you have set too many bad precedents over the years in the guise of being a good person. On the other hand, it is quite possible to be both assertive about teaching others to respect your time and well-liked, too.

SKILL #4: ELIMINATE UNFULFILLING OBLIGATIONS FROM YOUR SCHEDULE. At this point in your life, you have probably picked up a number of outside obligations that have little to do with the necessities of home life or work. These may involve committee work of various types, an officership in a civic organization, or volunteer time. Examine these time-consuming extras carefully. If any of them are not fun or fulfilling anymore, phase them out. Keep only the ones that you really find enjoyable. By doing so, you will be spending less time on extra obligations in total, but enjoying the remaining ones even more. A bonus is that you have a bit of extra time left for you.

SKILL #5: LEARN TO DELEGATE AT HOME AND AT WORK. In short, spread some of the work around. Far too many people fall into an old trap: "If you want it done the right way, you have to do it yourself." Hogwash! Quality work requires that you take a little time and endure a little frustration to teach someone else the right way to do something. Then you won't feel so burdened and resentful that others aren't pulling their fair share of the load. A second mistake is to look at delegation only in terms of your work. Make no mistake about it—delegation on the home front is equally important. In addition to marriage partners sharing the load at home, children should be consistently given chores to help out around the house.

SKILL #6: KNOW WHEN TO STOP. With strong work ethics, marriage partners set up agendas for what must be accomplished each day. Some people feel that these agendas are set in stone. It must be done today; after all, it's on the list, isn't it? Then, with the list as a report card, anything not done that "should be done" brings a sense of failure. To avoid "failing," men and women ignore physical and emotional limits by not taking time to eat adequately, to get enough sleep, or to spend time relaxing. For better health and peace of mind, keep your lists in perspective. They're only reminders. Stop at a reasonable time, regardless what has been accomplished. You'll feel better.

SKILL #7: RESIGN FROM AT LEAST ONE LEADERSHIP POSITION. Many men and women are natural leaders; others sense this quickly. To reveal the problem, first review all the outside activities you are currently involved in. Then, list how many of those activities are leadership positions replete with responsibilities, paperwork, and deadlines. If virtually all your outside activities involve leadership tasks, it's past time to make some changes. Choose at least one outside activity you still enjoy. Then make it a point to never, ever allow yourself to be given leadership obligations. Instead, spend time in that activity as just one of the crowd and enjoy yourself.

SKILL #8: LEARN TO SAY "NO" BY REDUCING YOUR VULNERABILITIES. Everyone has emotional vulnerabilities. If you are consistently being "talked into" accepting obligations and responsibilities that you later resent, you must ask yourself why. The answer usually turns out to be an emotional vulnerability to persuasion or outright manipulation. Common vulnerabilities are apprehension about rejection or disapproval, guilt, fear of conflict or anger, flattery, or a hard luck story, just to mention a few. You must first define your specific vulnerabilities. Then, seek to reduce your sensitivity to them if at all possible. If they can't be totally eliminated, use key feelings as a signal. "If I'm being made to feel guilty, I am probably in the process of being manipulated into something I don't really want to do." Then, your best strategy is to buy time: "Let me think about it. Give me twenty-four hours, and I'll let you know tomorrow."

SKILL #9: ADJUST YOUR EFFORTS TO THE IMPORTANCE OF THE TASK. This is a skill especially helpful to those prone to perfectionism or overplanning. The facts are that some things are important and some are not. It's silly to take the time to make a routine memo into a literary work of art or to transform a pile of laundry into symmetrical perfection. Instead, spend time on what is really important (objectively) and lower your standards for other tasks that realistically don't matter much. This sounds very simple, but to a dyed-in-the-wool perfectionist, it requires transforming a lesser standard into a positive time management strategy rather than a signal of personal failure. However, while difficult, this shift is entirely possible and, timewise, well worth the effort.

SKILL #10: PLAN FOR AN IMPERFECT WORLD. In other words, make your schedule realistic. The fact is that people don't always arrive for appointments on time. Or, they may run over. There are detours on the road and mechanical failures with office equipment. All of these realities necessitate that individuals learn to add "glitch-time" to their schedules. Leave yourself at least a few minutes between appointments. Be generous with your travel time. At home or at the office, an excellent technique is to schedule about 15–20 minutes of "accordion time" midmorning and midafternoon. This will help compensate for unavoidable delays that throw your schedule off. And, if things go just the way they should, you have a bit of free time to relax a bit or catch up on other things.

Priority Shifts and Personal Tips

Humane time management helps you blend health maintenance strategies with the skills you have already developed to remain reasonably productive and efficient. However, to adopt this philosophy of living requires that you be a bit different from many of your friends and contemporaries as you treat your personal well-being as the high priority in your life that it once was. As you begin to use your time in ways that reflect a more humane perspective on life and living, you are at the same time restructuring the value system that underlies your lifestyle.

To get started in making the necessary changes that will enable you both to get better together, here are shifts that form the foundation of humane time management. These shifts, made between your ears, set the stage for a new way of relating to that most precious commodity of all—the time of your life.

SHIFT #1: FROM AN EXTERNAL TO AN INTERNAL ORIENTATION. Your strong work ethic has required that you respond to both completed and uncompleted tasks around you. In so doing, you have neglected or put aside what is really important in your life. This shift requires you to regularly look inside to determine if your emotional needs are being adequately met and if you are oriented toward what is personally fulfilling and emotionally enduring.

SHIFT #2: FROM TANGIBLE TO INTANGIBLE GOALS. Preserving your health, spending time with loved ones, and living the good life for yourself are intangible goals. They're not the same as the tangible goals of a strong product-orientation. You can't hold living the good life in your hands, but it's still extremely important. To shift to humane time management, intangible goals must be placed at a much higher priority than in the past.

SHIFT #3: FROM ACHIEVEMENTS TO EXPERIENCES. In the past, payoffs came at the point of tangible goal attainment. You could see, even revel in, what you've achieved. In fact, you may have defined your self-esteem by what you accomplished each day. Now you must shift to valuing experiences, particularly those that embody the good life with loved ones. After all, experiences with loved ones are the core of most fond memories.

To reinforce these necessary shifts, it is helpful to just sit down, by yourself, for a few moments each day. Contemplate the good life and what it means to you. Muse about the kind of lifestyle that will bring you fulfillment and deep personal meaning. As you do so, you will see the value in making these three shifts. You will also begin to see how you have let the time of your life slip away so easily. As you make a personal decision to use your time more wisely, here are a number of tips that will help you do just that.

TIP #1: LEGITIMIZE BEING "RESPONSIBLY SELFISH." In other words, it is critical that you begin to place taking care of yourself and nurturing your marriage at the top of the priority list, not at the bottom. Taking some time for yourself lets you continue to give to others without resentment or anger. And, making sure that your marriage relationship isn't being taken for granted insures that you will be together now and also when the kids leave home and you become an "empty nester."

TIP #2: OBTAIN SUPPORT. It is much easier to resolve the blocks to living the good life with someone you love if you have support. Preferably, that support should come from your mate. Then, shifting your time priorities and life goals is not only easier, but with joint goals comes the opportunity to grow back together again. If your spouse just isn't interested, a good friend who will support positive changes and who will tactfully tell you when you're slipping into bad habits again is essential.

TIP #3: TAKE IT ONE STEP AT A TIME. As life has become busier, one bad habit after another has developed as a means to keep up with all your responsibilities. Because these habits have been part of how you've lived for years, trying to undo them all at once becomes an overwhelming task. Instead, in a planned and systematic way, tackle one time management problem at a time and resolve it. After one habit is broken and the new way of responding feels natural, then go on to a second issue and so on.

TIP #4: USE SELF-AFFIRMATIONS CONSTANTLY. Personal affirmations are self-talk, that is, positive statements you make to yourself about yourself. These motivational statements, made out loud or silently, reinforce your self-concept and resolve. Keep your commitment to the good life strong by making a series of positive affirmations to yourself, every day: "I'm a good person and I deserve time for myself and my mate. Living the good life and keeping my marriage strong are my top priorities."

TIP #5: SMALL BLOCKS OF TIME ARE BEST. Busy men and women work long and stressful hours every day. Waiting until "next weekend" or a vacation to relax just isn't enough. Instead, try taking little bits of time, perhaps in 30–40 minute segments, on as close to a daily basis as possible. Spend this time doing something you enjoy, or better yet, spend it with your husband or wife. These pleasant times just to relax and enjoy one another help you stay close and make the hard work worthwhile.

TIP #6: THINK ABOUT WHAT YOU WANT YOUR CHILDREN TO REMEMBER. Think back to what you remember most fondly about your mother and father. The fact that they were never available probably didn't make much of a positive impression. Do you want your children to remember only that you were busy and irritable all the time? What children remember most in adulthood are the times spent sharing pleasant moments and experiences. These same shared experiences, even moments spent daily, are also what keep a marriage strong.

TIP #7: BE PREPARED FOR SOME STATIC. As you begin to take a bit of time for yourself, to delegate more, and to say "no" to external demands, don't expect others to especially like it, particularly in the beginning. They won't be on the receiving end of your victim-oriented giving. As you reestablish personal control over your time, others—your spouse, children, and friends—will get used to your new priorities. As these others take more responsibility, you can give more openly with positive feelings.

TIPS #8: DON'T STOP AT SURVIVAL LEVEL. If you're going to live the good life together, go "all the way." Both men and women have a strong tendency to make a few changes and then stop because they feel a bit better. However, such changes may bring you back only to minimum survival level. And, just surviving isn't the good life. Keep making changes until the good life is yours, but make it a point to take it one step at a time. Remember, too many changes at once can be overwhelming.

From "Timelessness" to the Good Life

Practicing humane time management simply isn't easy. In fact, the traditional time management orientation ("Get more done in a given amount of time") fits only too well with the intensity of contemporary lifestyles. However, that doesn't make this approach right or healthy or good. In fact, it's just plain unhealthy. The unremitting pressure that you create for yourself is simply not conducive to either your physical or emotional well-being in the long run. The process is insidious because with the years you are gradually molded into a lifestyle defined by productivity for productivity's sake. Slowly you lose control and become a "timeless" automaton.

As you let this happen, you lose the time of your life as you work and work and then work some more to avoid that guilt that builds every time you slow down. Work becomes stressful because you're doing so much of it. Leisure triggers guilt because you are (heaven forbid!) trying to relax and enjoy yourself when there is still work to be done. How do you spell relief under these conditions? You don't. It's a no-win situation.

To make matters worse, don't forget that in your drive to get everything done, you may also be living on the edge of your human endurance. In short, you are not taking care of yourself emotionally or physically. Daily, you may push yourself to the limit without getting adequate sleep, eating nutritious and well-balanced meals, and finding enough time for exercise. Keep in mind that as you age, your body will simply not take the punishment it did when you were in your teens and twenties. Certainly there are significant health hazards to such physical neglect. Moreover, it also contributes heavily to stress overload, emotional exhaustion, depressive states, and high levels of anger.

On the other hand, there's a tremendous bonus in taking time to enjoy yourself and loved ones. In the process of restructuring your time priorities, you may discover long-lost parts of yourself—lost as life became busier and priorities became distorted. Delightful and creative parts of yourself may have been long suppressed beneath a heavy burden of responsibilities. Now is a good time to take time for yourself, so that deeper parts of yourself can once again emerge. The reason is simple. Like it or not, the future is now. But, only you can balance all the necessary hard work with good times and enjoyable experiences. That's really what humane time management is all about.

There has been an interesting evolution in recent years in terms of how the use of time is perceived. In fact, the perception of time use seems to reflect the ethic of the times, the soul of the men and women of a particular generation. And, those trends are becoming increasingly healthy, reflecting a growing need for what has been lost over the years. From another perspective, these changing values also reflect phases in the lives of husbands, wives, and couples as they mature and develop more perspective on what is deep and enduring in life. In a slightly whimsical but very real way, here is the trend.

INITIAL ETHIC: *"He who dies with the most toys wins."* This value system reflects a strong materialistic orientation in which the accumulation of possessions is used to define personal adequacy and success in life. However, this soon becomes an unfulfilling motivation if you have lots of toys, but no time to play with them. Unfortunately, many couples never mature beyond this naive orientation to life.

SECOND ETHIC: *"He who has the most time to play with toys wins."* As life becomes busier, time for oneself becomes a higher priority. There is a shift away from materialistic accumulation in the direction of trading more income and success for more discretionary time. While certainly healthier, this motivation can nonetheless become excessively self-centered as relief is sought from excessive and incessant responsibilities.

MATURE ETHIC: *"He who has the most time to play with loved ones wins."* With this belief, a personal value system has matured and a healthy perspective on what life is really about is gained. There is the realization that simply owning toys and spending time selfishly are not ultimately fulfilling. While some personal time is required to rejuvenate, what brings contentment and deep satisfaction is playing and having good times with loved ones.

Keep in mind that your use of time reflects your true value system. If you want to determine your real life priorities (and not be misled by your rationalizations), take a good hard look at how you spend your time. You may find that you're giving nothing more than lip service to taking care of yourself and living the good life. As a wit once said: "We are all in this together—by ourselves." The solution? While everyone else around you may be mismanaging time, you must choose to be good to yourself—for yourself and for those you care most about—so you can *all* enjoy the time of *your* life! Together.

Chapter 5

Creating "Home Base": Making Your House a Home

The young, almost by definition, are idealistic. They envision themselves as adults making a good living, residing in a beautiful home with plenty of time for one another and enough left over for fun activities. And, that's not too far-fetched considering that early in adult life, there *is* plenty of time for friendships and romance. Regular recreation or time to just goof off is a given. These pleasant diversions from work are a very high priority. Good times can be had on a shoestring. Life is good because life is simple.

Then it begins. The simple life begins to become more complicated with every passing year. And, the home, once a refuge from the stresses of the world for an emotionally close couple, starts to change. The change is as slow as it is distressing. The good life begins to inexorably slip away as does the vision of fulfillment in the future. Hardworking couples who have been married for years voice complaints fast and furiously. Witness these veterans:

Darren, married fifteen years: "At home, we just don't have much to say to one another any more. We used to talk all the time. These days, it seems like we're living completely separate lives under the same roof."

Ellen, married twelve years: "Our love life has steadily gone downhill for the past seven or eight years. Al and I are so tired all the time that making love just doesn't seem worth the energy anymore."

Terri, married 5 years: "I just don't know where we are as a couple now. All we do is work. I work at the office, come home, and start the 'second shift' the moment I hit the front porch."

Joel, married 8 years: "Barbara and I used to enjoy weekends together. We'd do all kinds of fun things. Now, weekends are spent just trying to get everything done that didn't get done during the week."

Keisha, married 19 years: "I remember the way it used to be. We really cared about one another and it showed. These days, what we share with one another at home is mostly our irritability. We both wish it was different."

This is definitely not the way it should be. Further, no couple sets out to live this way. Unfortunately, these very typical and destructive changes take place as a couple gets established and achieves at least the basics of the American Dream. As their standard of living rises, quality of life, defined by closeness with one another and time for relaxation, slowly diminishes. This has been defined as the Ironic Cross (see Figure 2). That is, when you're young and poor and just starting out, you have little money, but plenty of good times. Later, as the result of hard work and career success, you have a reasonably good income, but your good times have vanished!

The bottom line is that for these couples, marital relationships have deteriorated as husbands and wives have become busier. Life priorities have become negatively skewed. And, to their chagrin, the quality of their life together has been diminished. Perhaps the best way to characterize the change is to state that for them, they don't have a home anymore. They did once, in the beginning, but now, without physically leaving, they have inadvertently moved from a home to a house. Perhaps it would be instructive to define these terms.

HOME: *An emotionally comfortable and fulfilling living environment where family members and friends regularly relax, enjoy one another, and share positive experiences.*

HOUSE: *An emotionally barren domicile filled with personal possessions where family members eat, sleep, work, and coordinate their schedules.*

Looking at this change from a developmental perspective, most young couples begin their lives together by creating a home to share with one another. No matter how humble it might be, it's still home and a refuge from the world where life can be enjoyed. As the years pass and life becomes more complicated, two major changes occur. First, stresses and frustrations that have built up at work are discharged toward loved ones at home. Second, from an early priority emphasizing the enjoyment of life and one another each day, a personal obsession develops that reflects a dramatic change in what is important in life: "How in the name of heaven am I going to get everything done today that I need to get done?" Life just isn't much fun anymore.

Perhaps you've never given serious thought to the many negative changes that have occurred over the years at home. You're probably not enjoying one another now like you used to do. Like many others around you, home has become a pressure-cooker filled with frustration

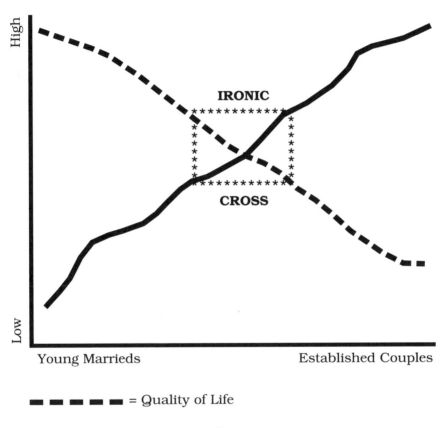

Figure 2: Illustration of the *Ironic Cross* Where Quality of Life and Standard of Living Meet and Diverge to Create Marital Problems.

rather than fulfillment. There's a very basic reality here. If you're ever going to live the good life together, you must take time at home to relax, to enjoy your husband and wife and children, and to spend quality time with good friends. To do so, making some strategic "in house" changes to create an emotionally warm and loving home once again is the very best way possible to begin the process.

The House or Home Scale

Before any specific changes at home are attempted, however, it may be helpful to assess the status of your present living environment. The House or Home Scale will help you do just that. As you read the following statements, check each one that describes your life at home with your spouse and children these days. The more statements that are checked, the more likely it is that you and your loved ones are living together in a house, but not enjoying an emotionally fulfilling and loving home anymore.

_____ 1. There is virtually no time for relaxed and interesting conversations among family members these days.

_____ 2. Lately, it has become quite unusual for all family members to be present for a meal together.

_____ 3. There is never a time when there isn't at least one television set on in the house, even at mealtime.

_____ 4. At home, you have withdrawn and isolated yourself from your mate and you tell your spouse and children to "leave me alone" often.

_____ 5. Fishing rods, golf clubs, picnic baskets, bicycles, and other leisure equipment haven't been used recently.

_____ 6. Weekends have become very hectic and are usually spent "catching up" on everything that didn't get done during the week.

_____ 7. Holding hands, big hugs, and sitting close at home have virtually disappeared in lieu of an occasional peck on the cheek.

_____ 8. These days, contact with once-good friends is maintained primarily by telephone, because finding even a little time for them to "drop in" is almost impossible.

_____ 9. Whenever you sit down to rest at home, you and your spouse tend to "guilt-trip" one another for relaxing when there's so much work to be done.

_____ 10. You have built amenities for the house (pool, deck, jacuzzi), but you hardly ever take the time to enjoy using them.

_____ 11. These days, there is little contact with neighbors beyond waving and saying "Hi" as you depart or return home.

_____ 12. Recently, it seems that entertaining at home requires such a tremendous amount of work that you'd rather not do it.

_____ 13. Relaxed, romantic interludes for the two of you that you used to enjoy at home have virtually disappeared.

_____ 14. You're both so busy and so tired that you stay at home more than ever, but inside the house you don't do much together to have fun.

_____ 15. Things are so tense at the house that almost anything can happen when you and your spouse first meet at home after work.

Creating a Marital Support System

To live in a house where there is little emotional fulfillment of any kind, with just work and more work facing you, is simply not the exception these days. Unfortunately, it is virtually the norm, particularly during the hectic parenting years. However, when these destructive changes on the home front are allowed to happen, and they do, everyone loses. You don't feel good anymore. Within, deep dissatisfaction and discouragement grow, along with intense frustration and stress that begin to further damage your relationships with your spouse and children.

It's deceptively easy to blindly just keep putting one foot in front of the other and keep pushing along, doing nothing to address these problems. When this unfortunate situation and its root causes are examined closely, however, some good news and some bad news emerge. By doing nothing, not only do you feel overwhelmed and discouraged, but it is quite apparent that you will never quite achieve that vine-covered cottage, filled to the brim with love and devotion, where husband and wife live happily ever after. To make matters worse, it's a fact that with every passing year, the demands and expectations placed on middle-class couples and families are slowly increasing—with no end in sight. That's the down side.

The good news is that there are clear and effective ways to make your lifestyle much more satisfying for you and your partner. But, you've got to know how to go about it. Your very first step must be to sit down with your spouse and make five key decisions. When these choices are consciously made, then you'll be ready to begin tackling the specific changes needed to make your house an emotionally comfortable home once again.

1. DECIDE THAT IT'S RIDICULOUS NOT TO BE ABLE TO ENJOY YOUR OWN HOME. If you step back from your home and examine it, you may realize that your home life nowadays is little short of absurd. And, it's very different from the "good old days" when you were young, and "home," as humble as it was then, was a place to relax, have some fun, and shut the whole world out just to have time for the two of you. Little by little an enjoyable home life has been replaced by "home work." Now the results are clear. You live together under the same roof, but you're living more or less separate lives and your marriage relationship has suffered more than you'd like to admit. Your first decision, for the two of you, is to arrest this process right now by recognizing the sheer absurdity of what has happened.

2. DECIDE THAT YOU CAN'T DO EVERYTHING. As the years have rolled by, every single part of your life has filled up with responsibilities, demands, and expectations. Because you have a solid work ethic and because you have made a personal commitment to meet your responsibilities and meet them well, you have slowly evolved into a superman or superwoman. The fact is that there is more to get done each day than is humanly possible to accomplish. You've also finally realized that you will never get caught up and be on top of everything. Begin to overcome this distressing state of affairs by setting your personal limits at a level you can comfortably manage each day, not at the absolute edge of human endurance as you've been doing. When this decision is made, you'll feel better when you do work. Further, you'll be more upbeat and emotionally you'll have a bit left over to give to your marriage relationship.

3. DECIDE THAT YOU DO HAVE SOME CONTROL. One of the most serious barriers to living the good life is the belief that "I have no control." Translated, this means that "I have no choices and I must continue to live the way I've been living." Not true at all. Further, this destructive attitude contributes to depression in many men and women. The fact is that you always have choices. However, the nature of choice dictates that you must give something up to get something better. Perhaps you and your spouse would benefit from discussing the choices available to you both. For example, you may have to sacrifice some elements of your present standard of living to gain quality of life. Or, you may have to lower your standards just a bit. When you make an active choice to make life better for you and for your loved ones, you are asserting the personal control to make good things happen for you both and, as a consequence, you will begin to feel better about yourself.

4. DECIDE THAT BEING EMOTIONALLY FULFILLED AND ENJOYING LOVED ONES IS WHAT IS IMPORTANT IN LIFE. When you take control of your life and begin to make healthy lifestyle choices, you quickly begin to realize that once you have the basics, material wealth and possessions really don't count for much when it comes to real fulfillment. What really matters is the renewed closeness to your partner and your improved relationships with the kids, not to mention the emotional well-being you experience each day. Only after you begin to make key changes will you become fully aware of how marginally you have both been living in terms of everything that is really important in life. In your retirement years, what do you want to remember about your life? That you worked like a dog all day every day? That you gave everything you had at the office? That you had no time for anyone because you had too much to do? That your home was filled with lots of things, but little love? It's to your benefit to begin creating the "good old days" right now.

5. FORGE A PARTNERSHIP TO BEGIN LIVING THE GOOD LIFE AND TO "GETTING BETTER TOGETHER." It is important for the two of you to be very supportive and encouraging of one another in making the healthy changes needed at home. Do recognize that you are vulnerable to negative external influences as well as your own bad habits that you've picked up over the years. When you decide to sit on your deck and enjoy some time together, do you only see what must be done in the back yard to get it into shape? Can you say no to requests by others because it would take away from time needed together? Encouraging positive changes and gently, tactfully pointing out bad habits help immensely to develop the teamwork necessary if the good life is going to be brought within reach for you both.

Specific "Home-Making" Changes

Now that key decisions have been made, you're ready to begin to work together to put into practice the specific changes necessary that will help make your house the warm and loving home you've always wanted. And, in so doing, you will be taking a giant step toward not only developing healthy life priorities, but also making the good life come true for you and your loved ones.

Here are seventeen possibilities for change to be considered. Don't try to change everything at once. Rather, choose one or two and put them into practice. Then, when these changes are comfortable, talk together about your next step and then start doing it. Don't be afraid to be creative and try some interesting variations that you've thought about yourselves. Interestingly, because many of these suggestions are interrelated, mastering one may help accomplish several others.

1. SPEND 30–40 MINUTE TIME PERIODS TOGETHER OUTSIDE THE HOUSE. This is the very best first step possible for couples who are living together in a house, but who have grown apart. The positive changes that accrue just from these short interludes spent together three or four times a week are remarkable. It is necessary to get outside the four walls of your house because of inside distractions like the kids or television. Further, when you're outside, you remove a major problem: that is, seeing work that must be done that will trigger you to go and do it or to make you feel guilty if you don't. Do note that for these times spent together, you need not get in your car and drive; in fact, you should not as it is very time consuming.

SUGGESTIONS: Take a leisurely walk together around your neighborhood; go out on that deck you've built (but haven't previously enjoyed) and read a bit; get a cup of coffee or an iced tea and watch the sun go down; ride your bicycles down to the corner store to enjoy an ice cream cone or a soft drink together.

2. ELIMINATE THE "DEADLY FOUR" TOPICS FROM YOUR MARITAL COMMUNICATION. Very busy couples are asked what's left after they eliminate these four topics from their interaction with their marriage partners: 1) all the hassles encountered at work today; 2) the concerns and problems the kids created today; 3) who's spending the money on what; and 4) what are our schedules tonight and tomorrow. What's left? The answer is simple: "Nothing." Except, perhaps, irritable remarks that serve to push your partner away. During time spent together, make it a point to talk about anything other than these four topics. In the beginning, the silence will be deafening, but that's part of the rut. If you keep at it, interesting conversations will soon evolve.

SUGGESTIONS: Tactfully remind your partner or change the subject when conversation slips toward these overused topics; take turns talking about interesting subjects chosen at random; play word games with one another (*e.g.*, how many different ways can you say the same thing in different words).

3. BEGIN REGULAR "TV FREE" NIGHTS AT HOME. It is amazing how powerful a television set that is on all the time can be in terms of fragmenting a family and eroding the relationship between a husband and wife. It's not that TV is bad; it's simply that it's watched too much and too indiscriminately by adults *and* children. When it begins to dominate all time spent together at home, that time is very low quality. You can't talk because you're watching TV and in the middle of a program. Or, you separate to watch your own shows in different rooms. Perhaps the kids have the TV on loudly, contributing even more to the noise pollution in your home.

SUGGESTIONS: Regularly turn off the TV set for one night at a time for you and the kids; sit together regularly for some time to just read or chat; set aside some regular "quiet time" (at least one hour) each evening for the kids and begin to enforce it.

4. TEACH CHILDREN TO RESPECT YOUR NEED FOR TIME ALONE WITH ONE ANOTHER. Many couples, busy with their careers, begin to feel guilty for not spending every minute of all available time after work with the kids. Unfortunately, this same priority does not extend to a spouse, especially at home. Certainly regular quality time with your children is important, but it's gone too far when it means that your entire focus at home is on the kids to the detriment of your marital relationship. Children naturally tend to force parents to respond to them. To preserve the marriage that will last longer than the kids will be at home, teach your children that at certain times they are not to intrude on your time together as a couple.

SUGGESTIONS: Insist that children not interrupt when parents are talking to one another (it's only courtesy); create specific alone time in the home or put one room "off limits" to the kids when adults are there; hang a "Do not disturb" sign on your bedroom door and teach your children to respect it.

5. START TO DO FUN THINGS TOGETHER AT HOME. Couples can share many pleasurable experiences at home. However, you already know they won't happen if you've fallen into the television rut. Find a few things that you and your mate can enjoy together and then do them. You may have to experiment a bit. The specifics of what you do together are not as important as making time to be together in a relaxed and comfortable way. Practice shutting out thoughts of what you "should" be doing in terms of work. This is difficult, but you'll both get better with time and repetition. What you really should be doing is enjoying one another every day at home and getting better together.

SUGGESTIONS: Try cooking a special meal together; sit down together to play a board game or a card game; make a date to meet in the living room to enjoy listening to your favorite music while sharing your favorite snack.

6. STRIVE TO MAKE YOUR COMMUNICATION MORE POSITIVE. One of the major forces that drives couples apart is constant negative communication. It's hard to feel close if you are always on the receiving end of negative comments, never ending discussions of problems, and perennial criticism when you are at home. The natural tendency is to avoid your partner by withdrawing and shutting down on communication. Or, you might just get fed up and counterattack. Then the hurtful things you say to one another widen the distance between you. Furthermore, keep in mind that saying negative things only reinforces within you a negative view of the world and a perception that you are a victim. This, then, makes it even harder to become an upbeat and cheerful spouse.

SUGGESTIONS: Catch yourself and cut out negative self-talk that keeps you down; make it a point not to make three or four critical comments to family members each day; compliment your spouse and comment on the positive at every opportunity; choose not to add martyristic or guilt-inducing endings to what you say.

7. BEGIN TO ENTERTAIN INFORMALLY AT HOME. It's time to begin to invite friends and neighbors back into your home. In retrospect, perhaps you've realized how much you've neglected once-good friends. To do this should not require a great deal of preparation, nor does it necessitate much expense. These kinds of social activities, often impromptu and shared together in your home, bring friends closer together again. In addition, if your neighbors are included, you also get to know them. Informality is the byword. And, forget about whether your home is "white glove" clean. That's not what's really important, and most people really don't care. Just tidy up a bit. A bonus is that there is often reciprocity if one couple takes the initiative to create good times for a circle of friends.

Note: When a couple makes entertaining in their home a major social event, there are at least two backfire effects, one obvious and one subtle. First, by spending inordinate amounts of time preparing for such social occasions (*e.g.*, preparing a big dinner), the host and hostess are often tired and frustrated by the time company arrives.

Or, they may have argued or experienced uncomfortable conflict during the preparations because they are so long and arduous. Under these conditions, it then becomes difficult to enjoy themselves and their company.

More subtle, however, is the fact that by making a big production of entertaining in their home, there is indirect pressure on those invited to reciprocate in kind. Often, rather than try to do the same, they opt out of socializing with that couple because of the time, expense, and frustration involved. Paradoxically, the net effect is that by making a big production out of entertaining in your home, you may actually be inhibiting future invitations to socialize in friends' homes! Conversely, by making socializing in your home easy and informal, it becomes correspondingly easy for other busy couples to reciprocate in the same fashion.

SUGGESTIONS: Have a few friends over to cook hot dogs and hamburgers in the backyard; ask a neighbor to drop by for a leisurely cup of coffee and a chat; on the spur of the moment, have a good friend come home with you from work for dinner.

8. DISCONNECT COMPLETELY FROM YOUR WORK AT THE OFFICE. Staff cutbacks at the office usually burden those who remain with more work. And, using information processing technology, work can more easily be taken out of the office to be done at home. However, letting work from the office intrude into your home life will surely destroy the rejuvenation time you need. Often, this "spillover" is not necessary; frequently an individual allows others to erode away family time. The bottom line is that others must be trained to respect your time at home, and only you can train them. It's far past time to put your foot down and stop allowing others to take advantage of you this way.

Note: In many families, the other side of this problem must also be addressed. A husband or wife comes home in the evening and, after dinner, picks up the telephone and talks for hours "staying in touch" with others. Maintaining relationships via the telephone is fine in moderation. However, when telephone time begins to eliminate time with your spouse night after night, then it becomes another reinforcement of the distance between you. To have quality time together, you must begin to limit your telephone conversations in the evening.

SUGGESTIONS: Make it a point to leave work at a reasonable time each day; train others *not* to call you during evening hours or weekends; turn on your answering machine during mealtimes; if you must work at home, set aside special time to do it and then put it away again (out of sight!).

9. CREATE SPECIAL SENSORY EXPERIENCES FOR YOU BOTH TO ENJOY. Perhaps, over the years, you've neglected to provide the sensory richness at home that is very important to keep things interesting. Without some effort, home life can be reduced to nothing more than monotonous and boring routines that are deadening to a marital relationship. Variety is the spice of both life and love. Creating special sensory pleasures for yourselves at home helps to counter the routines that often develop. The possibilities for sensory pleasures certainly need not be limited to romance nor should they be. Use your imagination. Be creative. Create sensory stimulation for you both as a way to be good to yourself and your partner.

SUGGESTIONS: Make a date and dress up for your spouse even if you stay at home; try a backrub using scented oils; bring out that special cologne or perfume again; try a candlelit dinner with soft music in the background; run a warm, scented bubble bath for yourself (or for the two of you!).

10. BEGIN A SERIES OF VALUE-ORIENTED DISCUSSIONS. In other words, begin to involve yourselves as a husband and wife in personal growth as a couple. Whenever possible, it's helpful to include the kids as well. Taking just a bit of time each day to talk about values and what is really important in life is a good way to reinforce positive lifestyle changes. These discussions not only bring a couple together regularly to talk, but these times also become a forum to focus on "us" and "how we are living." Such conversations become the foundation for lifestyle decisions and strategies for carrying them out. Then, the forward momentum to create the good life for you both and to get better together is easier because it is a team effort.

SUGGESTIONS: Go to your bookstore to find a value-oriented book and read a short passage to one another each day and then talk about it; get together regularly with another couple or two to have coffee and discuss family and parenting issues; pick one word (*e.g.*, love, intimacy) and talk about what that word means to each one of you.

11. DEVELOP A HOME-BASED PERSONAL INTEREST. By definition, true relaxation is something that you do for yourself. It is time spent just for you, just for the pleasure of the experience. And, preferably, it should be an activity that is regularly experienced in the comfort of your own home. No pressure, no task-oriented goals, no ego-involvement. To heighten your satisfaction at home, choose a relaxing activity that you enjoy and then do it. Remember, trying to make money with a "relaxation" activity or engaging in intense competitiveness often kills the fun in such experiences. In the best of all possible worlds, you and your spouse can be involved together. The time necessary may vary from individual to individual. At a bare minimum, what is needed is thirty to forty minutes at a time several times each week.

SUGGESTIONS: Clear out the garage for a workshop or crafts room; start a neighborhood hobby group to work on projects in a different home each week; go back to your childhood to a hobby you once enjoyed and try it again as an adult; join a hobby group or club and invite those with similar interests to meet in your home.

12. CONTAIN YOUR HOME OFFICE. With the advent of sophisticated information-processing technology, the necessity to have an office at home has correspondingly increased. More and more men and women have an area set aside at home that is used as an office work area. This home office may be either a primary workplace or a support work area for one's job. In either case, to a responsible individual, a home office area represents work that needs to be done. With a personal computer, modem, fax machine, and telephone, all manner of (usually mental) work can be completed right at home. Uncompleted work visually looming in front of you triggers anxiety and guilt that make it extremely difficult to relax and enjoy down time at home.

SUGGESTIONS: Create an office area where the door can be shut and keep it shut; keep all work in your home office out of sight and not spread around the house; create set hours when you will be working in your home office and then leave; if financially feasible, have a separate phone line and answering machine for your home office.

13. BEGIN SPENDING UNSTRUCTURED TIME TOGETHER. As life becomes busier and more hectic, deadlines develop along with the need to plan all activities and to structure time carefully. On the other hand, one of the true joys of adulthood is to once again begin to spend time with no structure, that is, no appointments, no deadlines, and no schedules. You used to immensely enjoy time like this just "goofing off" when you were young, remember? It was fulfilling and you had nothing but good memories to show for it. As an adult, such time is tremendously rejuvenating, but you haven't had any practice for awhile. Relearning this value skill around the house not only frees you from work, but also frees you to share good experiences together again.

SUGGESTIONS: Never create "do" lists or schedules of any kind for your weekend (or at least one part of it); on evenings and weekends, do not carry or wear a watch; one night a week, make it "your night" to be together and then be completely spontaneous and follow your feelings.

14. BRING LOVE BACK INTO YOUR HOME. There's a vital difference between living in a loving home and existing in an emotionally sterile house. Perhaps you have both lost "that lovin' feelin'" for one another over the years. Or, you've become so stressed out and irritable that you just don't feel like being that caring person you once were. Most likely, those deeper feelings of caring and affection are still there, just buried beneath a layer of uncomfortable emotions stemming from negative lifestyle changes. Only you, and you alone, can bring that closeness back with small acts of kindness and caring each day. Remember, these caring gestures are an important part of the emotional "cement" that keeps your relationship close and strong.

SUGGESTIONS: Come into the house with a cheery hello to your mate; bring back spontaneous hugs and sitting close or a pat on the back (but don't sexualize that affection); give your spouse a "chit" good for one big hug or a neck rub within the next twenty-four hours; pick some wildflowers for your mate on the way home from work.

15. BEGIN MARITAL/FAMILY TRADITIONS IN YOUR HOME. Home-based traditions or rituals are not only enjoyable, but help create a sense of togetherness for couples and families. A ritual or tradition is simply defined; it is something that "we always did" in a particular way or on a specific date or time. With repetition of such activities over the years, traditions or rituals become a bonding process that helps keep couples close to one another. Some of these traditions can be for the kids, some just for the couple, and some for an extended or blended family. These traditions additionally provide a base of positive memories for the kids that contributes heavily to a sense of personal security when they reach adulthood.

SUGGESTIONS: Make spiced cider and have a few friends in on the weekend after Thanksgiving; make very Friday "spaghetti night" at home; on your wedding anniversary every year, share a favorite memory with the family at dinner; give Mom a breakfast in bed on

Mother's Day; have a "Doldrums Party" the last weekend of January each year.

16. BEGIN A HOME-BASED GIVING PROJECT. Every community has many individuals and families with unmet needs and no resources. Taking just a bit of time to create a giving project focused on meeting just one need brings with it many positive feelings. The entire family can join in such activities, as can neighbors, if willing. The possibilities are as broad as the many needs found in every community. These giving projects are a way of caring about others and building community awareness. Not only can it bring a couple, as well as the kids, together, but it brings with it good feelings that only giving of oneself to others can bring. Often, starting to give to others represents a new stage in your maturity; you have enough and are secure enough to meet the needs of others who are less fortunate.

SUGGESTIONS: Make your home the center for collecting complimentary hotel shampoo and conditioner from friends who travel to benefit local agencies for the homeless; during the year buy used toys at yard sales to repair and donate to needy children; from your plants, grow starts and take them to brighten up nursing homes.

17. TRY VACATIONING AT HOME. When they were young, most couples lived a simple life. They could get away for either day trips or a weekend outing on very short notice. At that time in their lives, such getaways cost very little and took little planning time. Then, life became increasingly complicated. With responsibilities looming in every part of their lives, getting away together to relax and enjoy themselves became virtually impossible. Not only did a weekend away become very expensive, but getting ready to go was stressful and it took immense planning time and skill to get everything set just right. For such couples in the midst of the busy years, taking regular vacation weekends at home may be an ideal solution.

SUGGESTIONS: Make a commitment to do no work of any kind on that vacation weekend; leave the house to enjoy nature or community activities; eat out as much as possible; do not answer the telephone because you are on vacation that weekend; have the kids stay with friends or with a babysitter at least part of the time; be creatively romantic with one another right at home.

Beyond Parallel Lives

A wit once wryly commented that "Marriage is like stepping into a bath. It's not so hot once you get used to it!" You smile with understanding—and no wonder. Look what has happened to you both over the years. In the name of getting more done each day, family life in our society has virtually disappeared. Divorce rates are higher here than in virtually any other industrialized nation. Stress-related diseases are rising dramatically. Children from middle-class homes are growing up emotionally deprived because of the pressured living environments created by their overwhelmed parents. And, last but certainly not least, living the good life that is the dream of every young couple slowly disappears with the years.

There is no question that our society is hard-working and dedicated to getting things done. The many highly pressured and constantly stressed couples can attest to that. But, life is more than getting more and more done in a given amount of time. And, real success in life cannot be defined by possessions or in other materialistic terms. Examined within the context of the daily life of middle-class America, the work ethic has been carried to near ridiculous extremes. There comes a point in every couple's life where mindlessly getting things done begins to create serious problems in preserving healthy family relationships, maintaining emotional health, and certainly, living the good life.

Centuries ago, the Chinese philosopher Confucius (c. 551–479 BC) made this astute observation: "The strength of a nation is derived from the integrity of its homes." That notion cannot be disputed even today. And, if that's the case, as a nation we may be heading for big trouble. Now is the time to begin the process of getting better . . . together. Since home is where couples spend most of their time together (quality time or not!), taking a close hard look at how they live life together there is most certainly the best place to start.

Make a commitment—together—to make positive changes at home for yourselves and, by extension, to do your part to build a better society. Remember, the longer you wait, the more difficult it is to recover what you once had together. It's very late to begin when there is so much bitterness and hurt built up over the years that it's exceedingly difficult to trust one another anymore. It's very late when all of your needs are being met through activities and involvements outside the home. It's very late to start after an affair begins. And, it's often too late when one partner finally gives up and walks out the door.

These unfortunate realities at home are even more distressing when you realize that these negative changes do not have to happen at all! They can be prevented or, even reversed. What it takes is understanding, commitment, and teamwork. But, to reestablish the good life at home will require taking a hard look at the totality of your relationship with one another. For example:

1. LOOK AT YOUR PRIORITIES AS A COUPLE. Examine these from the perspective of what is important as reflected in what you do each day, not what you tell yourselves (or one another). Compared to early in your life together, you may see changes in how you are living as a couple that are startling in their magnitude. Ask yourselves if these priorities are healthy and fulfilling.

2. CLOSELY EXAMINE YOUR PERSONAL VALUES. Your values reflect the code of conduct by which you live. Deep down, your values define what is really important to you. Is it really how much money you make? Or what you possess? Your status in the community? Or do your values reflect deeper and more enduring qualities in your relationships with loved ones at home?

3. ASSESS YOUR GENERAL ATTITUDES TOWARD ONE ANOTHER. Along this dimension, the years may have wrought many changes. It's entirely possible that you have taken your partner completely for granted. Or, your attitudes may reflect cynicism and negativism. Just how do you perceive your partner these days? Is your partner a companion, a friend and lover, or a workhorse just like you?

4. DEFINE THE MANY LITTLE DECISIONS YOU MAKE EACH DAY. Every day, your decisions reflect how you spend your time at home. Do you decide to get more done rather than spend time with your partner? Do you let the kids consistently interfere with keeping your marriage relationship emotionally deep and strong? Your daily decisions may be inadvertent, but they are still important.

Make the Healthy-Happy Commitment

To make the house where you now eat, sleep, and work into a loving home where relaxation, togetherness, and quality time spent together is legitimized, you must balance how you spend your time at home. Yes, there are things that must be done each day. On the other hand, there are many small tasks that can really be dropped. To create this balance, make a basic commitment to one another as husband and wife and to yourself. Here's the commitment; write it out and put it in a conspicuous place so it will remind you daily. Repeat it over and over to yourself, especially in the beginning. It's just a little tongue-in-cheek, but it contains great wisdom.

THE HEALTHY-HAPPY COMMITMENT

*I commit myself to maintaining this home
in such a way that it is clean enough to be healthy
and dirty enough to be happy!*

In the end, what goes on at home will either make or break a marriage. And, the quality of your home life will either create or destroy the good life together. Put simply, the tasks facing couples who have lived under the same roof, but who have grown apart over the years are easily defined. Such couples must once again begin to deeply CARE about their relationship in all the truly important ways. Then, they must begin to emotionally SHARE with one another to recreate the fulfillment they once had together. And, in so doing, they will REPAIR the damage that they have done to themselves and to their relationship over the years. As the saying goes, "A house is not a home . . . until you make it so."

Chapter 6

Married and Best Friends: It's the Way It Should Be

It is unfortunate that the days when men and women grew up in the same town and had lifelong friends have virtually disappeared. In an era of great geographic mobility, men, women, couples, and families now move away from their childhood homes to begin new lives elsewhere. Economically, there are often great benefits to such moves. Indeed, many such moves to new locales are absolutely necessary to find and keep work. However, the price of such moves is often a sense of rootlessness and isolation from the communities in which these men and women live.

An increasingly common problem directly related to this geographic mobility lies in the difficulty of maintaining close friendships. The hard reality is that it is much more difficult these days to establish and keep friendships that are close and fulfilling. On the other hand, it can certainly be done. Witness the following men and women who were observed. . . .

ON A PLANE: Two obviously good friends are flying together to a resort destination for a few days of fun and golf. They are laughing, telling jokes, talking about mundane things in their lives, and periodically slapping one another on the back. Regularly having such good times together, they are having a whale of a time and don't seem to have a care in the world.

IN A RESTAURANT: At a table near a window, two good friends are lunching together. Overheard is one talking about a current problem with one of the kids. The other is listening intently with empathic nods and many supportive responses. Along with good eye contact, at one point one gently touches the other's hand with obvious caring.

ON A BEACH: Stretched out on reclining beach chairs, two good friends are leisurely surf fishing in the early evening. While casually keeping an eye on their rods, they are also enjoying a beautiful sunset gathering all across the horizon. Obviously enjoying just being there together, they understand one another so well that they don't have to say much.

Now here's the question: "Do you think that these friends, spending these kinds of quality time together, are married?" To this question, the answer is "Yes." In fact, all are married. However, the catch is that they are not married to one another! Now another question: "Should these men and women be spending such quality time with their spouses?" Again, the answer is a resounding, "Yes." However, are they doing so? For too many couples these days, the answer is, "Probably not." And, as a result, their marital relationship is diminished. Such couples suffer because they are married, but no longer good friends . . . or even friends at all!

Ironically, most young couples begin their relationship together by becoming best friends. And, as the friendship blossoms, they become friends *and* lovers and decide to marry. Unfortunately, with the years, many factors in their lives begin to collectively undermine their once-close friendship. As their lives together become more complicated and pressured, many couples slowly drift into a lifestyle so hectic that they gradually begin growing apart while living under the same roof.

This unfortunate state of affairs, combined with the unrelenting demands on their time and energy every day, often leaves each marriage partner feeling very alone and without emotional support. This lonely feeling often occurs in the midst of a family. Ironically, these feelings grow despite the fact that the couple is "making it" economically. The consequence is that serious questions begin to cross each partner's mind: "What am I doing here? I don't feel good and my marriage has become nothing more than an empty shell." The remedy for such men and women is that they need a good friend, indeed a best friend. And, to begin living the good life together, that best friend must be your spouse.

Facets of Friendship

It is ironic that in the most important relationship in your life—your marriage—friendship is at once easily neglected and most difficult to maintain. Furthermore, there seem to be many complaints these days about the deterioration of friendships outside a marriage. It is almost as if many men and women have completely forgotten not only the vital importance of becoming friends with a spouse, but also how to be a true friend to someone else. At this point, a working definition of a best friend is in order.

BEST FRIEND: *An individual with whom regular positive*

*experiences are shared and in whom emotional trust is so deep
that anything can be discussed without fear of abandonment or
retribution.*

Placing the framework of this definition over many relationships, it can be seen that many friendships, including far too many marital ones, fall short. Some do not even come close and might be termed "friendships" only in the most superficial sense of the word. In a marriage in particular, when there is no core friendship between a husband and wife, there is not much left. As an antidote to this distressing situation, recognize these seven major facets of friendship with specific suggestions on how to create each one.

I. GOOD FRIENDS STAY IN TOUCH WITH ONE ANOTHER

At one level, to say that friends maintain contact with one another seems almost absurd, but it is absolutely necessary. Friendship always implies an ongoing relationship in which both parties involved make consistent efforts to keep it strong and viable. With a friend who is not a spouse, these efforts might involve regular good times spent together, telephone calls, cards on special occasions, and just dropping in to say "Hi." Neglecting to make these special efforts is to risk allowing the relationship to wither and to possibly disappear entirely. In fact, this is exactly what often happens with many once-good friends who lament that: "We just grew apart over the years." The fact is that such relationships were allowed to die of sheer neglect.

Unfortunately, this is also exactly what can happen with a best-friend spouse over the years. It is deceptively easy for a couple, once very close and deeply in love, to drift far apart emotionally while living together. One of the most critical aspects of a marital friendship is that your spouse is frequently in your thoughts in positive ways. With hectic lifestyles and inadvertent negative changes in life priorities, daily focus shifts to accomplishing tasks rather than staying in touch with your best friend—your spouse. The eventual consequence is that your marital friendship begins to wither and will eventually die unless direct efforts are made to nurture it.

This unfortunate chain of events often occurs by such slow increments that couples often don't realize it is happening until it is nearly too late. To counter this problem, begin to communicate that you care and that you are emotionally aware of your marriage partner. Keep in mind that the more water in the form of neglect that is under the bridge, the more difficult it may be to recreate an emotionally strong and healthy marital relationship. Here are three specific suggestions to put into practice right away.

A. VERBALLY EXPRESS INTEREST IN YOUR SPOUSE. To remain best friends with your marriage partner, it is necessary to communicate directly and indirectly that "I am interested in you as a person." Make it a point to regularly ask your spouse about his or her day, inquire about the other person's experiences, and engage in other forms of small talk that transcend career and parental roles.

B. TOUCH BASE EVERY DAY. This is the coordination function that is a necessary part of busy lifestyles these days. It is not only very helpful, but it also affirms a marital friendship to take a few moments every day to get signals straight about schedules and activities. Taking these few moments to coordinate also prevents conflict and frustration.

C. LET YOUR SPOUSE KNOW WHERE YOU ARE. Far too many spouses don't take the time to let their spouses know where they are going and when they will return. Make it part of your routine to do so. And, it's only courteous to let your husband or wife know when you will be late. A cheerful hello coming in, a caring goodbye when going out also help keep that important friendship alive.

II. GOOD FRIENDS SHARE OF THEMSELVES AND THEIR LIFE EXPERIENCES

In other words, good friends let one another be part of their lives, that is, share their inner lives and personal experiences both good and bad. Such sharing is the intimacy part of any good relationship. Sharing at levels beyond the superficial is not only a defining characteristic, but it is also one of the deepest and potentially most rewarding aspects of any friendship. In other words, without this kind of personal sharing, you may have an acquaintance, but you certainly don't have a good friend, much less a best friend. By sharing their thoughts, feelings, and experiences, good friends not only get to know one another at deeper levels, but also create an openness that strengthens the bond between them.

It is unfortunate that in many marriages the husband-wife relationship deteriorates so that when feelings are shared (if at all), they tend to be negative ones which are often communicated in hurtful ways. Comments become unduly critical or cynical, focusing only on problems and frustrations. Or, sometimes couples withdraw from one another, sharing little at all because of perceptions that a partner doesn't really care, and besides, "It's just more of the same." To keep a marital friendship alive, consistent efforts must be made to present yourself as a competent and well-rounded man or woman who has not succumbed to the mutually-shared and characteristic "victim" posture seen so often in husbands and wives who have drifted apart.

To begin bringing back the many benefits of openness and positive sharing in your marital friendship, you must first of all *want* to share yourself with your partner. That may be hard to do in the beginning because the trust you once had in a partner to respect your personal feelings may have dissipated. With time and a little effort, however, relating openly with your partner at all levels slowly becomes easier. Here are three relatively nonthreatening ways to begin recultivating marital sharing.

A. BANTER WITH YOUR SPOUSE. This is basically nothing more than verbally expressing interesting thoughts or feelings. It may involve telling your spouse the latest joke you heard. Or, make it a point to verbalize a thought you had about something that is important to you. When a fond childhood memory crosses your mind, take a moment to share it.

B. CREATE INTERESTING THINGS TO TALK ABOUT AND SHARE. Men and women who are doing interesting things come alive and have stimulating ideas and feelings to share. If your lifestyle has become excessively routine, create new and stimulating experiences for yourself or with your partner. Doing so gives you something to get excited about and to share with your partner.

C. KEEP YOUR VISION OF THE FUTURE ALIVE. In the early years of their relationship, young couples talk often about their future and what they want together. Often, this vision dies of neglect with the years. To keep your marital future alive, talk often about what "we want" and how "we" are going to get there together. Such sharing helps to solidify the partnership in your marriage.

III. GOOD FRIENDS ARE THERE DURING TROUBLED TIMES

This characteristic defines one of the most striking differences between a true friend and a "fair weather" friend. Almost everyone has had an unfortunate experience in which a so-called friend just wasn't there at a time of great emotional need. Under such circumstances, the relationship either ends outright or becomes much more superficial. The lesson that must be learned is that friends must always be there for one another, not only during the good times, but also during times of emotional turmoil or personal crisis. To have such a friend in times of need is a wonderful source of strength; not to have such support during troubled times brings painful feelings of aloneness and great vulnerability.

It's sometimes easy to forget that in marriages this same need to be there for a spousal best friend is equally important, if not even more critical. Typically, couples experience many small problems along with some major crises during their years together. Little frustrations can often be handled on one's own. However, it is absolutely necessary to be there as a true friend to your partner when personal crises occur. Spouses need to provide emotional strength when a loved one dies or when a serious health problem develops or when a job is lost. No doubt about it, to be a source of support when such crises occur takes time, energy, and commitment. But, when this support is present, it is strengthening because each partner knows that "Together we can get through virtually anything."

The bottom line is that far too many men and women simply don't know how to be there emotionally for their partner. Or, once very supportive of one another, a husband and wife have grown apart and have forgotten how to share their emotional strength. Sometimes, the spouses are so tied up with personal problems that they cop out at critical times. To be that source of strength and emotional support for your spouse is just not that difficult. Here are three key suggestions to begin putting into practice right away.

A. MAKE YOURSELF AVAILABLE TO LISTEN. Notice that this suggestion does not necessarily include much talking. When there is a problem, let your partner take the initiative and then do lots of listening. Make it a point to be immediately available no matter what else is going on. Don't try to give advice or solve problems unless asked; it's enough just being there and being attentive.

B. TOUCH IN SUPPORTIVE WAYS. A gentle hug, holding hands, a caring neck rub, or sitting close are all important aspects of being there for your spouse during times of great emotional need. Often it is not necessary to say anything at all; your actions communicate your caring. As you emotionally share in physically supportive ways, keep sex entirely out of the picture.

C. TAKE INITIATIVE TO SHOW YOU CARE. When there's a

crisis, communicate to your spouse that you empathize with the other's emotional turmoil. In small ways, show that you care enough to make life a bit easier because of it. For example, cook a special dinner, do more to keep the kids occupied, or arrange time alone. All these help immensely during times of crisis. Don't wait to be asked.

IV. FRIENDS CONSISTENTLY VALIDATE ONE ANOTHER

In a word, good friends communicate a very simple message in very different ways: "I like you and being with you makes me feel good." In a true friendship, these feelings become reciprocal as each individual communicates good feelings about the other during their time together. It is this "liking" dimension that makes a friendship literally attractive. The experience of enjoying time spent together is the cement that is absolutely critical in maintaining a strong day-to-day friendship. Such feelings are easy to share because good friends are quite comfortable (*i.e.*, not guarded or defensive) and have memories of many positive experiences with one another.

In a marriage, this kind of positive reciprocal validation is just as necessary, but more difficult to maintain over years as life becomes more complicated. The fact is that you're with your spouse every day. There's more than a little truth in the saying that if you're not very careful, "Familiarity breeds contempt." As stresses and pressures build, family members express their inner negative feelings most freely to other family members; as a result your previous upbeat way of relating begins to disappear. Quality time spent together outside the home may also begin to disappear. The cautiousness or outright defensiveness that often develops impedes open communication. The net result is that couples don't enjoy each other any more. Happy memories of times spent together recede into the distant past.

This unintended but rather sad state of affairs is best exemplified by a marital partner who states: "I still love my spouse, but I'm not sure that I like him/her much anymore." If you've had such feelings, it's past time to reestablish the reciprocally validating part of your friendship that used to be there. Way back then, it was so natural that you didn't even think about doing it. Now, you may have to consciously do it until it again becomes easy and natural. Start the process by making these three suggestions part of your daily routine.

A. CHEERFULLY ACKNOWLEDGE YOUR PARTNER WHEN YOU COME HOME. Seek out your partner right away when you first get home after work. Approach your spouse with a cheery acknowledgment: "Hi hon, I'm home." Proceed with a smile to make small talk for just two or three minutes. A hug at this time of day doesn't hurt a bit, either. Your greeting sets the tone for the whole evening.

B. COMPLIMENT YOUR SPOUSE EVERY DAY. Directly bolstering your partner through sincere compliments gives a wonderful feeling. Make such positive remarks an important part of your day together. When compliments become a priority, you begin to notice positive things about your partner. This self training counters the bad habit of "seeing" only the negative.

C. FLIRT AND "HORSE AROUND" WITH YOUR SPOUSE. Flirting is a wonderful way to relate. Young lovers do it all the time. And, flirting certainly needn't end in the bedroom. It's an important message that simply says: "You're still attractive to me as a man/woman." Playing around flirtatiously is not only great fun, but also makes both partners feel good inside.

V. TRUST IS DEEP BETWEEN FRIENDS

In short, the core of this important principle of friendship is twofold. Good friends not only have a deep loyalty to one another, but they are also very careful never to betray one another either. As a friendship deepens, almost by definition, a corresponding willingness to share personal experiences and feelings develops. To be open in this way also requires vulnerability—that is, letting a friend know about personal doubts, sensitivities, and unlikable traits. While it is very healthy to share these parts of oneself with a best friend, such information must always be respected. And, the vulnerability it entails must never be violated. If such trust is not strictly kept or if it is betrayed, the friendship usually ends quickly. If the relationship survives at all, without trust it simply becomes a shell of what it once was.

The same kind of trust that exists between any good friends must also be present between marriage partners. In one important sense, such trust is the bedrock on which deep emotional intimacy between husband and wife is built. There is no question that over time marriage partners become very aware of one another's vulnerabilities. Then, as life becomes more pressured and the marital relationship becomes strained, two critical questions arise. First, do two marriage partners keep their relationship open enough to share their innermost thoughts and feelings? Second, do these same spouses deeply respect their partner's vulnerabilities, and not use them in hurtful ways? If the answers to both of these questions are not a truthful "Yes," then it is likely that trust in that relationship has been severely impaired, perhaps even completely destroyed.

Repeated marital betrayal significantly damages the entire relationship, not to mention the intimacy between a man and wife. As a result, while they may continue to live together, their marital relationship becomes much more superficial. Both husband and wife suffer because they cannot risk being hurt by being too open with their partner. To rebuild the trust necessary for intimacy, consider these three suggestions.

A. NEVER HIT "BELOW THE BELT" DURING A FIGHT. One of the surest ways to shut down intimate communication in a relationship is to use a personal sensitivity to hurt your partner when you get mad. The only remedy for this extremely destructive habit is to resist temptation. Always respond in mature, nonpunitive ways when there is conflict, even if your partner doesn't do so.

B. DO NOT GOSSIP ABOUT YOUR PARTNER. Far too many husbands and wives talk in indiscreet ways about their spouses to friends, relatives, and acquaintances, even strangers. When such exchanges are positive and upbeat, "bragging" on your partner reinforces good feelings. However, when you divulge disparaging or intimate information, it betrays marital trust.

C. DO NOT BE JUDGMENTAL WITH YOUR PARTNER. "I can say anything to my best friend and know I will not be rejected" is clearly one of the best qualities of any friendship. By reinforcing acceptance of your spouse, even if you don't agree, trust is retained. Harsh or premature judgments or outright rejection damages marital relationships the most.

VI. FRIENDS CAN "LET GO" AND HAVE FUN TOGETHER

No good friendship can exist over long periods if it focuses exclusively on discussion of problems. Nor can it if it consists of constant and deep emotionally intimate discussions that are draining to both parties involved. While openness to deeper relating must be present, it is also important that good friends have fun together. This may involve many different kinds of experiences: playing a stimulating game of tennis, sitting quietly enjoying small talk, laughing together over lunch, or dancing the night away. Good friends can "let go" to enjoy good times spent together knowing that they mutually accept and rely on one another.

Certainly, the ability to "let go" and enjoy pleasant time together is even more crucial to maintaining a best friends' marital relationship. But, as life becomes busier and daily pressures mount, humor often fades, with simply no time for fun anymore. Stressed and tired, parents feel overwhelmed with responsibilities. Often, they are simply too pooped to go out except for obligatory social functions. Further, with the passage of time, such men and women often completely forget how to relax and really enjoy lighthearted times together. Fun times spent with one another are not only energizing, but they are also a powerful tool to relieve stress. When such quality time becomes a marital priority, a home environment replete with warmth, fun times, and laughter begins to replace a house filled with negativity and work.

The bottom line is that you and your partner may need to literally relearn to "let go" again. This is necessary not only for your personal well-being, but also to preserve one of the most vital aspects of a marital friendship that will grow more fulfilling with the years. If every single day is filled to the top with work and more work, a question soon begins to cross each spouse's mind: "Is all this work really worth it? There's no fun anymore and living this way is definitely not what I wanted when I got married." These thoughts are a sure sign that stress is building and that more fun is needed in a marriage. Here are three suggestions to help you both "get away from it all" with one another again.

A. FIND AN ACTIVITY THAT YOU ENJOY DOING TO-GETHER. Young lovers spend much quality time together having fun, but spend little money doing so. They enjoy many activities with one another. Begin to experiment with new kinds of experiences you might enjoy or get back to something fun from your past. Joining other couples in pleasant diversions also helps.

B. MAKE SURE YOU HAVE REGULAR "ALONE TIME" AS A COUPLE. After children come, life changes in many ways. One of them is that finding time to be alone together becomes much more difficult. To counter this, train older children to respect your "couple's time" at home. In addition, get a sitter and go out alone together on a regular basis to have some fun.

C. DO NOT CONTAMINATE FUN TIMES WITH WORK. When you do spend time alone, it is very easy to contaminate it with bad habits related to work. When you're together, never take work along. Eliminate talk about work (or the kids) or what you must do tomorrow. Do not make notes or make/take telephone calls. Turn off your beeper; turn on the telephone answering machine.

VII. FRIENDS ACCEPT AND RESPECT CHANGE IN ONE ANOTHER

A good friendship that survives over long periods of time is never static. Rather, it is a fluid relationship that exists over the years as two people encounter different life experiences and change. Because of this, one foundation of such an ongoing friendship is a deep acceptance of one another based on trust, along with emotional support, as life circumstances evolve. In a good friendship, positive change is not discouraged nor is there an implication that both parties must stay the same for the relationship to continue. However, such deep acceptance also permits good friends to talk openly and give one another feedback and different perspectives without defensiveness or a feeling of rejection.

When they think about it for a moment, most men and women know that in a good marriage relationship, love and acceptance must never be conditional. However, too often, husbands and wives begin wanting their partners to "be what I want you to be" rather than who they really are. At that point, a marriage becomes a conditional relationship with an implied rejection and disappointment if one partner's expectations are not met by the other. The end result is that a spouse (or a child for that matter!) is not truly accepted and nurtured as a unique human being. The choices of the individual on the receiving end of such a conditional relationship amounts to a no-win situation. One choice is to be oneself and be rejected by a partner. The other choice is to give up being oneself to meet a spouse's expectations.

Whether expressed obviously or subtly in a marriage, such a nonaccepting attitude or set of expectations drives a wedge in the relationship that tends to deepen with the years. In fact, it is a primary reason why marriage partners begin to slowly grow apart. With your husband or wife, it is to your mutual benefit to change key behaviors in positive ways for oneself as well as for your marriage relationship. Why? Because, quite simply, it's the right thing to do. Here are three excellent ways to begin.

A. EXPRESS UNCONDITIONAL LOVE AND ACCEPTANCE. Good marital friendships are always built on the communication of deep mutual acceptance. Small acts of kindness and loving words reinforce this deep acceptance: "I love you just because you're you," or "You are the best husband/wife anyone could ever ask for." Such statements free both partners to love openly and change in personally positive ways.

B. INITIATE POSITIVE CHANGE IN YOURSELF. To reach your vision of the good life, it's a given that personal change will be necessary. Give up trying to change your partner or changing *for* your partner. Decide instead to make needed changes in yourself simply because such changes will make you a better friend and lover. Then you will both be evolving in the direction of the good life together.

C. BE WILLING TO COMPROMISE. When you encounter potentially divisive issues in your marriage, begin to resolve them by assuming that two married friends who truly respect each other are expressing two valid points of view. Then, reject selfish solutions to the problem and calmly look together for mutually satisfying ways to resolve the issue at hand.

Everyone Needs a Friend

The fact that everyone needs a friend stands in stark contrast to the unfortunate and painful reality that these days so many men and women, often married, don't have one good friend in the world. They may know lots of people and have lots of acquaintances, but for them a true friendship is elusive. In a world where impersonality is growing and families are often geographically separated, to have at least one good friend is even more emotionally necessary than in the past. It is certainly ironic that so many of these same men and women overlook the most important source of friendship of all—their spouses.

If you think about it for a moment, a special friendship is really what a marriage relationship is all about. At its root, the most important tie in a good marriage is not sex, romance, emotional highs, or pleasure. Certainly, all these things are part of the total relationship, but the core of marriage is a partnership built on emotional closeness, acceptance of one another, and fulfilling companionship. In other words, a best friends' relationship. To bring this point home, read once again the vows you made to one another when you married. They read like a description of a good friendship, don't they? Now ask yourself: "Have my partner and I neglected our friendship over the years?" If, on honest examination, the answer is "Yes," then both you and your husband or wife have your work cut out for you.

If you now recognize that you've lost that wonderful best friend part of your marriage, first make a verbal commitment to rebuilding this key part of your total relationship as husband and wife. Do understand that it will take time. Friendships are based on experiences shared with one another, not on promises. With your partner, begin to do all the things that reflect friendship. With time and consistency, the trust that is the core of any deep friendship will begin to grow. You will become closer and many of the divisive issues and sore points in your marriage will begin to fall into place of their own accord.

Furthermore, when you make a commitment to one another to renew your marital friendship, you will be bringing the good life that you've always wanted much closer. That's not all that will happen, however. There will be other important benefits as well.

1. YOU WON'T BE LONELY ANYMORE. It's a fact that without friendship, a marriage can be one of the most lonely places in the whole world. As you begin to renew this critical part of your marital partnership, that feeling of "We're really together again" will return. Then, the loneliness will begin to fade and you will become close friends working together for the good life.

2. YOU WILL HAVE AN EMOTIONAL ANCHOR. Good times are always easy to handle emotionally. It's during the bad times that you really need a friend. Knowing that your best friend and marriage partner will always be there for you becomes an extremely important source of personal security. Knowing that "We can get through anything together" becomes an emotional anchor for both partners.

3. YOUR PHYSICAL RELATIONSHIP WILL IMPROVE. There's a tremendous difference between "having sex" to satisfy physical needs now and then and really making love with your partner. As you renew your marital friendship, the deeper fulfillment of making love once again also usually returns. It reflects a broad new reality: "We're emotionally together once again."

4. JOY WILL RETURN TO YOUR LIFE. It's a wonderful feeling to know with absolute certainty that your partner deeply loves and cares about you. Such knowledge brings with it an inner peace. You can relax and enjoy your marriage. Along with personal fulfillment come feelings of joy that say: "I've got everything; this is the way it should be."

Perhaps you now realize that two workhorses living parallel lives under the same roof with a little sex thrown in is a far cry from a husband and wife who are best friends and lovers and who are sharing a fulfilling life together. Perhaps this striking contrast is best exemplified by the wit who wryly commented that "Marriage is the process whereby the account once held by the florist now belongs to the grocer." Tongue-in-cheek perhaps, but you know the difference. You've felt it. Now, as you become friends and lovers once again, you learn from past mistakes. You're not only closer, but also wiser about one of the most important sustaining qualities of all in a marriage— a lifelong friendship with your spouse.

Chapter 7

Getting Yourself Together: Overcoming Distorted Thinking

Most alert men and women are aware of a constant flow of thoughts running through their minds. However, because this flow is so constant and natural, most individuals do not take the time to carefully assess the quality of those thoughts. That's unfortunate because this stream of thought is that individual's personal representation of reality. And, in turn, these internal constructions of reality powerfully determine personal behavior, emotional states, and, certainly, self-esteem. In other words, over a lifetime of experience each person develops a set of filters that strongly influence the interpretation of other people's behaviors or responses. However, the big question is how well that man or woman's subjective reality corresponds to reality as assessed by more objective means.

Pushing this idea just a bit further, it can easily be seen that thought patterns can create either positive perceptions of reality or negative ones. In fact, it is the quality of those internal, and often unspoken, conceptualizations of reality that determine how well an individual deals with the inevitable problems and conflicts that are part of life. Further, these same ways of "seeing" reality also serve to create either personal contentment or the absence of it. In short, quality of life may not depend on objective reality as much as on how a husband or wife internally interprets all those big and small events that happen every day.

What is important for couples to understand is that positive self-esteem, personal confidence and security, and healthy coping skills, all heavily influenced by how the world is subjectively perceived, are necessary to function well as an individual. By extension, functioning well as an individual with an upbeat view of life is fundamental to being a caring and giving marriage partner. To reiterate, what you perceive and think is often exactly what you get because what you think is your reality.

To underscore the importance of the quality of thoughts, Dale

Carnegie once cautioned: "Remember, happiness doesn't depend upon who you are or what you have; it depends solely upon what you think." To the extent that this is true, then it is apparent that how each partner thinks about things will powerfully influence the ability of that couple to live the good life together. The contrast between an individual with positive perceptions of reality and one with negative ones is stark. Consider these two individuals.

Carl, a supervisor in a car dealership, is constantly overreacting. Every minor glitch is a major crisis, and he predicts all manner of catastrophic consequences if everything isn't just right. He goes home highly stressed each evening and responds the same way to every inconsequential problem with his wife, Sandy, and the children. Over the years, he has become extremely tense, cynical in his outlook, and personally unhappy. In fact, not only do Carl's kids avoid him, but because he is so negative and excitable, he has lost many friends. Even more seriously, he and Sandy have barely managed to maintain their marriage over the years.

Lucinda, superficially, is much like Carl — about the same age and married, with children. Life has never been easy for her. She works as an insurance adjuster and, over the years, has found this work personally fulfilling. Her friends constantly comment about how happy she seems to be and about her bright outlook on virtually everything. Life's little problems don't bother her; she takes them in stride. When she faces big issues, she confronts them directly. Although not affluent by any means, she and her husband, Jerome, live a full and rich life together.

Seeing this contrast, it is obvious that quality of life for these individuals, and for their spouses and children, has been clearly influenced by how each one perceives the little problems that occur each day — problems that cannot possibly be prevented, eliminated, or controlled. In fact, internal thought patterns can create at least five negative but interrelated effects on the individual and, by extension, on that man or woman's relationships.

1. PERSONAL STRESS LEVELS RISE. Negative perceptions of events create loss of any kind of objective perspective. As a result, fear and apprehension then give rise to emotional overreactions. Over time, these feelings are often transformed into chronically high tension levels within the individual. As years pass, such unnecessary stress can create serious health problems, not to mention impairing personal contentment.

2. DEPRESSIVE FEELINGS INCREASE. It goes without saying

that negatively-distorted thought patterns often reinforce a sense of loss of control. Further, it is well-known that a strong relationship exists between depression and an individual's perception of loss of control. While external events often cannot be controlled, the individual *always* retains the capacity to choose how to respond to problems and difficult situations.

3. SELF-ESTEEM IS DIMINISHED. Negative thought patterns and a perceived loss of control often contribute to low self-esteem as that person slips into a "victim" posture. The internal perceptions of the perennial victim are quite consistent: "I can't handle this problem" or "Something is going to happen that will overwhelm me." Self-esteem plummets as that person experiences apprehension and helplessness in the face of problems.

4. EFFECTIVE COPING RESPONSES ARE IMPAIRED. When there are habitual distortions of perceptions, negative emotions such as anger, depression, and tension are produced that consume tremendous amounts of energy. These powerful emotions often completely overpower an individual. The result is that the objectivity necessary to effectively assess and resolve even relatively minor life problems may be significantly compromised.

5. PROBLEMS IN RELATIONSHIPS ARE CREATED. When there is a problem (real or perceived!), many men and women oververbalize their negative perceptions and apprehensions. Or, negative perceptions may produce frequent emotional overreactions or trigger imprudent remarks that hurt others' feelings. When such negative responses are habitually directed toward a husband or wife, that person tends to withdraw or counterattack.

To summarize, depending on quality of thoughts, one individual can be personally content, enjoying life despite inevitable problems. In the very same circumstances, another man or woman can be reduced to a virtual "basket case" of insecurities that, over time, contributes heavily to poor relationships and to an extremely negative outlook on life. In other words, what you think is what you get. The bottom line is simple. To begin to live the good life — together — you may have to change the way you think about things — as an individual.

Varieties of Thought Disorders

Examining negative ways of thinking identifies a number of undesirable habits that are encountered again and again. And these self-defeating patterns of thinking are clearly learned. They may have been picked up from someone else, or they may have developed on their own. Some may have been learned recently, and others may have been creating problems for a lifetime. Whatever their origin, all are simply bad habits developed over the years, but because they have been learned, they can also be unlearned.

While some men and women have developed a variety of such "thought disorders," even the most well-adjusted men and women are prone to at least one or two of them. However, life can be made immensely easier by directly confronting these negative habits and by practicing alternative ways of responding. First, however, the dynamics of your particular distortion patterns must be understood. Here is an overview of a baker's dozen downers.

1. BASING REACTIONS ON ASSUMPTIONS ("WORRYING"). *Example:* Maria, an excellent student and well-trained in product design, asked one of her professors for a recommendation. She was nervous and thought she came across poorly in the interview. She returned home to her husband that evening inconsolably dejected because she just knew that her professor would give her a poor recommendation. Therefore, she would never get a job to help support the family.

When examined objectively, the problem here is clearcut. Maria simply did not know how her professor perceived her. Yet, she strung together three or four negative assumptions beginning with her perception of the interview and concluded that her career was over before it even began! Then, reacting to the assumed end result, she became depressed. Reacting to "catastrophic assumptions" as if they were true is, in fact, the central dynamic of most worry. The solution is simple and straightforward. First, refuse to react to anything except objectively demonstrable facts. Second, if there are questions that need answers, ask or seek out necessary information in lieu of making unfounded assumptions.

2. "BOXING" OTHER PEOPLE. *Example:* Alice, married to Jim for fifteen years, had a brief affair when she and Jim were having problems about five years after they tied the knot. Now, thirteen years later, no matter what she does, Jim refuses to trust her. Although she has been an exemplary wife and companion ever since, when Jim gets down, his continuing belief that she betrayed him and that he is an inadequate husband almost inevitably comes up.

Here Jim has put Alice into a psychological "box" and refuses to let her out. His mindset is that Alice has proven that no woman can really be trusted. This couple will never have an open and intimate relationship until Jim is able to see Alice for who she really is right now and appreciate all she has done over the years. Instead, he uses her brief affair to blame her and put himself down. This also helps him deny the fact that he heavily contributed to the marital problems they had at the time. His "box" for Alice is really a set of blinders he has created for himself, and the sad result is that neither he nor his relationship can grow until he takes those blinders off.

3. SECOND-GUESSING EVERY DECISION. *Example:* Whenever Melinda makes a decision, she immediately regrets it. No matter what she decides, it is never right, and she expresses sorrow and disappointment (sometimes tinged with anger) over her "poor choice." Then she berates herself unmercifully. Typically, she seeks reassurance from her husband Al, who cares deeply about her. No matter how positive and supportive he is, she isn't consoled.

Given a bit of forethought, most adults make responsible choices, including Melinda. The core of her problem, though, is that she wants a gain with no loss. However, the nature of choice is that there is always a loss whenever a decision is made. Men and women like Melinda focus only on the loss sustained, but never on what has been gained from that choice. This always results in personal regret and a tendency to put oneself down as basically incompetent, which in turn lowers self-esteem and makes future choices even more difficult. To overcome this problem, an individual must learn to accept the losses inherent in any choice and, without looking back, focus on the future and the possible gains from those decisions.

4. REACTING TO AN INTERNAL CYNICAL MONOLOGUE. *Example:* Kyle, perennially cynical, was perusing anniversary cards to find one for his wife. He found himself internally reacting to the card sentiments and thinking to himself: "Love? No one *really* loves anyone else. Caring? Yeah, but only if they want something. Togetherness? Only until one gets mad and dumps on the other." Kyle thinks this way about his relationships with virtually everyone.

Kyle has developed a cynical monologue that keeps him feeling bad about himself and everyone else in his life, even his wife whom he professes to love. A cynical monologue usually can't be seen; it streams through the mind while normal interactions are taking place. However, because it is negative and downbeat, such thoughts reinforce a distrustful mindset toward others, including loved ones, and also diminishes self-esteem ("I'll be hurt/betrayed/used again."). To break this self-punitive habit, first focus on what you are saying to yourself. Then, when you catch yourself, stop those thoughts cold and force yourself to substitute more optimistic ones. With time, your cynical monologue will disappear and relationships will blossom.

5. HABITUALLY FOCUSING ON THE "FAILURE GAP." *Example:* Everett has always had very high standards; in fact, he's a perfectionist. No matter what he attempts, he does his very best but it's never good enough. There's always something he could do better and he puts himself down because of it. Then, he imposes these same unrealistic standards on his wife and child who claim he is never supportive and finds fault with everything.

Everett's problem is the "failure gap." This is the gap, sometimes very small, between what has been accomplished and absolute perfection. Since no one is perfect, there is always room for improvement. This man or woman always focuses exclusively on what could be improved, hence the feeling that, "I'm not up to standard" on any given task. When receiving a ninety-eight on a test, such an individual berates himself or herself for the two points lost, completely forgetting about the ninety-eight percent done right. Almost always, these standards are imposed on others, making criticism and negativity the dominant theme in relationships. To break this habit, begin to focus on and personally acknowledge what you and others have done right.

6. CREATING NEGATIVE EXPECTATIONS. *Example:* Whenever Tonya puts on a beautiful new dress to go out, she tells her husband of ten years: "I know you won't like this on me, but I bought it anyway." When she gives a presentation as a financial planner, she tells everyone beforehand: "I'm not really good at giving talks, and I hope that I won't bore you!" No matter how many compliments she gets, they don't help Tonya trust herself.

Tonya habitually preempts everyone and puts herself down before anyone else has a chance to do so! This is an interesting, but very destructive, form of distorted thinking. By pointing out all her weaknesses to others, she "hooks" them into giving her reassurance and supportive comments, even compliments. Further, it sensitizes them to the very aspect of oneself about which there is insecurity. Ironically, others may now scrutinize that one particular area very closely! To break this bad habit, don't think it. Don't say it. Instead, do it. Let others judge for themselves. Then, after the fact, graciously accept their positive feedback and complimentary remarks.

7. NAME CALLING. *Example:* Overweight as a teen, Earl wasn't a good student, and was the class clown with a widespread reputation as a "goofball." Now, twenty years later, a slim and very successful businessman, whenever Earl encounters a personal problem, he puts himself down with the same old labels: "I've always been a screw-up" or "I can't do anything right" or "I'm just an overweight dummy that no one really likes."

It is amazing how many outwardly competent men and women are extremely insecure inside. They are sure that they are not likable or that no one could really love them. Often, these problems result from negative experiences during adolescence. During these critical years, a self-image is formed by peer (and sometimes parental) feedback that has nothing at all to do with later adult realities. Yet, the old self-image hangs on in the form of favorite put-down labels. These tend to emerge whenever there are problems. To overcome this bad habit, focus on defining your strengths and accepting yourself as a competent adult right now. Then, as you put your cop-out put-downs aside once and for all, deal directly with problems (and mistakes) on the basis of your present wisdom and skills.

8. BLOCKING POSITIVE FEEDBACK. *Example:* Rebekah, quite successful professionally, often receives compliments. Then, she proceeds to habitually reject and deny each and every one of them, even from Bob, her husband of fourteen years. "You really don't mean that" or "I really don't do that well; you're just saying that just to be nice" are her bywords. Rebekah is not being modest; she doesn't believe a word of any compliment given to her.

This common problem is typically born of a very poor self-concept. Starting from a basic premise ("I am incompetent/unattractive/naive/scatterbrained/lazy, etc."), this individual then sets out to reject any positive feedback that is inconsistent with this negative self-perception. Sometimes the rejection is overt and verbal; sometimes it is in the form of negating thoughts despite outward acceptance of compliments. The result is that an already low self-image remains poor. Conversely, in such men and women you can bet that any *negative* feedback received is immediately and painfully internalized! To overcome this bad habit, start by short-circuiting those rejecting thoughts or comments. Instead, with genuine sincerity, simply say: "Thank you so much for noticing. I really do appreciate it."

9. PERSONALIZING. *Example:* Scott, now married for twelve years, personalizes everything. When, Angie, his devoted wife and companion of two decades, fails to say hello in the morning, he thinks: "She doesn't love me any more." When she offers a helpful suggestion for a problem, his interpretation is immediate: "She really thinks I'm stupid." The result is that Scott feels rejected and put-down most of the time.

This mechanism of maintaining low self-esteem lies in the interpretation of events. The rule is simple: "Whatever happens, assign the most self-punitive interpretation to that event regardless of its relationship to reality!" This personal put-down — whether verbalized or not — is based on no objective evidence. In the above example, Angie didn't feel well that morning and failed to say hello. Then, she gave Scott a suggestion in a clearly helpful, kind, and supportive way. To break this very bad habit, two suggestions help. First, if there is a question about someone else's motives, check it out by asking that person directly. Second, at all times, assume you are okay until *objective* evidence (not your distortions) strongly suggests otherwise.

10. MAKING UNFAIR COMPARISONS. *Example:* Kathy's fantasy of married life is one of loving togetherness, white picket fences, companionship, and good times spent together every day. She looks at other couples at church and in the mall and perceives them as living out this wonderful life. Then she compares her marriage to them and reacts with disappointment and resentment toward Alex, her husband, who she blames for her lack of fulfillment.

What Kathy is reacting to is an illusion based partly on an unrealistic fantasy and partly on a superficial perspective on the lives others lead. She's personally unhappy and sees around her only blissfully happy couples, living together in complete marital harmony. She doesn't realize that these same couples are often grouchy, have fights, are stressed by all they have to get done each day, and often have different recreational interests. What she has set up is a rigged comparison: "I'm alone and everyone else has someone to love." "I'm ugly and every other man/woman is attractive." To relieve this kind of distortion, first decide what you want out of life. Then, set realistic goals for yourself based on solid information rather than illusions and fantasies. Finally, make concerted efforts to move toward your now more attainable personal goals.

11. BLAMING YOU FOR ME. *Example:* Arnie has always tended to avoid dealing with issues in his life. Instead, to himself and to his wife, Wendy, he constantly blames others for his passive responses: "I can't take a day off to be with you because my boss won't let me" or "I'm insecure because my parents ignored me while I was growing up." Arnie constantly feels victimized and resentful because of what he perceives as the "control" of others.

The theme of this destructive habit is: "I can't because. . . ." You fill in the blanks. A man or woman like Arnie has a plethora of excuses why life and its problems can't be handled in a direct, mature, and competent fashion. Instead, Arnie uses weak excuses for his consistent avoidance. This bad habit results from two distorted perceptions: First, constant blaming is a way of saying, "I'm not responsible because I'm an innocent victim of others" and second, always blaming other people or circumstances internally reinforces the idea that change is impossible. Both perceptions are rubbish. The trick here is to become more assertive and actively seek out what you want. Don't wait around for others to give you what is desired and then feel resentfully victimized when they fail to do so!

12. CREATING SELF-FULFILLING PROPHECIES. *Example:* Sharon truly believes that she and her husband can't talk about anything of importance. Whenever there's a difference of opinion, she immediately shifts away from the issue at hand and begins to hit Don "below the belt" in his vulnerable areas until he loses his temper. Then her belief is confirmed: "See, Don and I can't talk." Further, "He really doesn't care about my point of view."

The dynamics of a self-fulfilling prophecy are quite simple. Begin with a negative belief about oneself or others. Then, behave in ways that produce responses that confirm the belief. However, all self-fulfilling prophecies are setups. If key personal responses were modified, then the negative pre-existing belief would not be confirmed, and thus personal and interpersonal growth would result. Instead, when personal behavior sets up a situation to confirm a negative belief, low self-esteem and a negative view of others, even loved ones, is also reinforced. To overcome this problem, open your perception of others and then consciously respond in ways that do not (again!) produce confirmation of a negative belief.

13. SETTING YOURSELF UP FOR NEGATIVE EXPERIENCES. *Example:* Jim, an administrator of a medical clinic, doesn't understand why he is on the receiving end of so many negative comments by clinic staff members during weekly conferences and individual meetings. What Jim doesn't realize is that his staff has learned that to get action on a problem, they must be nasty to get his attention. If a problem is presented in kinder ways, Jim tends to ignore it.

A basic principle of communication is that all individuals, through their style or quality of responses, teach others how to respond in return. In this case, Jim, has directly taught his staff to respond to him in negative ways to get problems resolved. Other examples of this phenomenon are common: an individual procrastinates on decisions until others take the initiative to make a choice, an insecure man or woman reacts in an aloof or reserved fashion and is avoided by others. The end result of such situations is that self-esteem is damaged and personal effectiveness is eroded. When such relationship problems, often seen in marriages, are suspected, ask yourself a question: "How might I be teaching others to respond to me in this negative way?" Then experiment to change selected responses in order to change the ways others respond in return.

The Origins of Irrational Thinking

It must be evident by now that when even a few of these "dirty dozen" varieties of distorted thinking are present, it becomes much more difficult to have both a close and fulfilling marriage and positive relationships with your children. Further, it is well nigh impossible to really live "the good life" together unless these problems of perspective are substantially eliminated. However, to rid yourself of them means close self-examination, personal effort, and moving beyond what has happened in the past. That's no easy task, but it is eminently doable and well worth it. The benefits for you and for those you love last a lifetime.

A very legitimate question worth answering is often asked about these varieties of distorted thinking: "If these ways of relating are so self-defeating, then why are they so prevalent?" In fact, there are at least five reasons why they are so common and so persistent. As you read them, think about the origins of your distorted thinking habits.

1. MALADAPTIVE LEARNING FROM PARENTAL MODELING. Without doubt, many negative responses of adults are picked up during childhood directly from what parents were seen doing, including patterns of distorted thinking. Children watch and listen to their parents for at least eighteen years before leaving home. Many of these responses, observed for years, are internalized and become part of personal response patterns later in life, particularly when the stresses and strains of married life and parenthood grow.

2. PERSONALLY DIFFICULT EXPERIENCES. In many instances, patterns of distorted thinking develop on their own during childhood or adult life, particularly during emotionally difficult times. And, they often develop without the conscious awareness of the individual involved. Then, with the years, these inadvertently-developed habits persist to continue exerting their negative influence, even though the emotionally "tough times" are over and the good life is within reach.

3. EMOTIONAL NEEDS. Many types of distorted thinking offer emotional rewards. These payoffs are called secondary gains. For example, as the result of negative or distorted ways of thinking, particularly when verbalized, an individual might receive attention from others, sympathetic responses, or emotional support. Or, the payoff might be protection from emotional vulnerability or the avoidance of disappointment. Without exception, personal growth cannot take place when there is conscious or subconscious motivation to seek such payoffs.

4. PROJECTED RESPONSIBILITY. It is strange but true that many people believe feeling bad is easier than confronting and solving life problems. By using various patterns of distorted thinking, responsibility for negative feelings is projected outward toward a perceived oppressor (either an individual or even to life itself!) and, *ipso facto,* one then becomes a victim. Because a "victim" isn't responsible for a problem, the problem and negative feelings continue.

5. ERRONEOUS ASSUMPTIONS. Often operating just below the level of conscious awareness, these kinds of tenuous emotional connections are easily seen in the case of worry. For example, it is surprising how often worry is often equated with love ("I wouldn't worry if I didn't love you!") and the more worry, the greater the love. Or, worry is seen as a protection from catastrophe: "If I worry, it won't happen." Later: "See, I worried and it didn't happen!"

Leaving Your "Head-Trips" Behind

It is sad to see how many otherwise well-adjusted, talented, and accomplished men and women are limited by distorted thinking. These destructive habits were recognized years ago by Mark Twain, that indominitable wit with wisdom: "Life does not consist mainly — or even largely — of facts and happenings. It consists mainly of the storm of thoughts that is forever blowing through one's head." How true, but the trick is not to stop the ongoing storm of thoughts. That's impossible. Rather, it's to change the nature of those thoughts from negative and destructive to positive and life enhancing. When that happens, then you've made a giant step toward living the good life — together — based on your own positive self-esteem and the personal confidence to deal effectively with problems.

As you commit yourself to eliminating these negative ways of thinking from your life, three facts about distorted thinking must be clearly understood. First, these bad thinking habits are much more likely to emerge when you are fatigued, highly stressed, or faced with a significant problem. Because these kinds of situations weaken your ability to cope, various kinds of distorted thinking are likely to emerge under these conditions. Ironically, they tend to surface when there's a problem, and that's exactly when effective coping responses are most needed! Conversely, when things are going reasonably well, they may not be apparent at all.

Second, be aware that for many men and women, the areas (or kinds of problems) which precipitate these distorted thoughts is often quite diagnostic. In other words, many individuals do not experience such thought disorders with all problems. Rather, these distortion habits tend to emerge when a problem impacts on an area of personal vulnerability or emotional sensitivity. By noticing exactly where and when distortion patterns emerge, unresolved conflicts can be pinpointed and personal awareness is consequently enhanced. These are your emotional "soft spots" where coping skills clearly need to be strengthened.

Third, all of the various forms of distorted thinking have one attribute in common: When they are used, they put the individual in the role of victim — of circumstance, of others, of life itself. For too many men and women, a victim posture with all the negative feelings it produces reflects not only a habitual way of thinking, but also a way of living. Keep in mind that everyone makes choices and that doing so does not automatically result in becoming a victim. The first important choice you must make is to break out of these self-defeating and emotionally destructive ways of thinking.

Now comes the big question: How do you get rid of these self-defeating ways of thinking, these distortions of reality that interfere with living life to the fullest? Be assured that it can be done, but it will require self-awareness, patience, practice, and the help of your spouse or a good friend. Make these changes for yourself, but do it for your marriage as well. Remember that it takes an emotionally-together man or woman to build and sustain a fulfilling marriage relationship. Here are nine helpful steps to eliminate these "thought disorders" once and for all.

1. VERBALIZE YOUR THOUGHTS WHEN THERE IS A PROBLEM. To build awareness of distorted thinking, when there is a problem, think out loud. As you do so, don't censor anything and listen to yourself. You may be very surprised at how persistently negative and self-defeating your thoughts actually are. Keep in mind that these thoughts internally reinforce negative perceptions of you and of reality. *Note:* Sometimes it helps to tape record your negative or self-defeating thoughts about a particular problem. Don't censor yourself at all. Then listen to how you sound; it's the same way others hear you.

2. DO NOT PROJECT NEGATIVE THOUGHTS TO YOUR SPOUSE OR LOVED ONES. It's easy to unfairly attribute negative thoughts to loved ones or close friends: "He doesn't love me" or "They don't care" or "Everyone's out to take advantage of me." To eliminate distorted thinking, you must first take full responsibility for your thoughts. Then, open yourself to give loved ones a chance to love and care about you.

3. WORK ON ONE HABIT AT A TIME. Most individuals are prone to several different negative thought patterns. To tackle them all at once is usually self-defeating. There is simply too much to deal with at once. Instead, clearly identify one distortion habit and work on that one alone until it is eliminated. Then move on to the next one, and so on, until all such negative habits have been overcome.

4. PRACTICE NEW THINKING ON INCONSEQUENTIAL PROBLEMS. In other words, start small and slowly work up to bigger problems or issues. It also helps to redefine how you see events when you are feeling good. At such times, negative feelings about yourself are less likely to interfere. With consistent practice on insignificant problems, new ways of thinking and coping will become ingrained and therefore easier to use when bigger or more difficult problems are encountered.

5. ACT AS IF YOU WERE COMPLETELY COMPETENT AND IN CONTROL. Acting "as if" even if you don't necessarily feel it or believe it will be necessary in the beginning. Force yourself to do this in lieu of negative thinking to give new ways of relating to a problem a chance. Once positive results are experienced, you will feel better. And problems won't seem so overwhelming because you are coping more effectively.

6. USE THOUGHT-STOPPING AS A TECHNIQUE. When you find yourself slipping into distorted thinking, internally shout loudly to yourself: "Stop." Or, accompany this by clapping your hands to associate stopping with a strong and clear external cue. Another effective thought-stopping technique is to wear a rubber band loosely around one wrist. When negative thoughts occur, snap yourself with the rubber band to negatively reinforce inappropriate thought patterns.

7. PRACTICE POSITIVE SELF-STATEMENTS/AFFIR-MATIONS. Even when you feel good, it's helpful to make self-reinforcing positive statements. Repeat them frequently out loud. Doing so in front of a mirror helps. No matter where you are, keep self-affirming thoughts going: "I have many strengths and others appreciate these in me" and "I am a good person and loved by others." As these perceptions are reinforced, negative thoughts are less likely to overwhelm you.

8. PUT POSITIVE SUGGESTIONS BY OTHERS INTO PRACTICE. It is often helpful to solicit and then carefully listen to feedback from your spouse or a good friend you trust. When you do so, make it a point not to become defensive because receiving uncomfortable feedback often triggers negative distorted thinking. By remaining calm and receptive, you may find yourself gaining insight and good ideas about how to cope more effectively.

9. SEPARATE YOURSELF FROM NEGATIVELY-THINKING PEERS. Far too often, negative perceptions are inadvertently (or directly) reinforced by friends, especially when discussing personal or marital problems. First of all, take time to think out a problem for yourself. Then, if you need to "check it out," find *one* upbeat friend who is helpful to use as a sounding board. Let the naysayers in your life bring someone else down, not you!

Cutting right to the core, you've lived too long with negative thoughts and distorted thinking. By overcoming these habits, you are not only doing something for yourself, but you are also freeing yourself from the past. When you begin to think more positively, unwanted baggage from the past, perhaps going all the way back to your childhood, is left behind. The result is that you throw away major roots of personal discontent that have been barriers to personal growth and a close, fulfilling marriage.

By now, it must be obvious that it's very difficult, if not impossible, to live the good life when you feel insecure, unloved, distrustful of others, and threatened by events around you. But, you also realize that most of this is nothing more than a "head-trip." You can't change the world — or your past — but you *can* change yourself. That old sage Mark Twain, once quipped: "My life has been filled with terrible misfortunes . . . most of which never happened." I disagree. Many of your misfortunes have happened . . . between your ears.

And, when you eliminate those misfortunes, good fortune will be yours and the good life will be closer.

Chapter 8

Reducing Marital Materialism: Making Your Needs Your Wants

There is little question that this country is among the most wealthy on earth. All over the world, our nation is perceived as the land of plenty. And, it's true. Compared to the material wealth of average citizens in most other countries, men and women in the United States live with a virtual cornucopia of available goods and services. Here, for most, the question is not whether you have a car. The fact is that the vast majority of adults assume that car ownership is an entirely normal state of affairs. The real question may be how many cars and what models. Men and women, and especially couples where both have careers, are so used to this life of abundance that it is taken for granted.

It is interesting that when many couples visit other industrialized nations, they often experience a materialistic "culture shock." How can they live without all the comfort and convenience of X, Y, and Z?" is the often unspoken question. On closer examination, the answer is surprising: "Very well, thank you!" The fact is that in this country, "wants" and "needs" have become confused. An ethic has developed in which acquiring possessions has become an end in itself. Unfortunately, this highly-developed and reinforced materialistic orientation has great potential to create problems. Consider these individuals and couples.

• Jacob keeps the family finances in constant chaos by unilaterally purchasing status items he thinks he needs without informing his spouse. His latest acquisition is an extremely expensive watch. Because of this purchase, there will be little extra money, and the family's budget will be tight for months.

• Jeremy and Betsy are constantly fighting about money. Together, they have spent so much that they have no savings, and credit limits have been breached on all their credit cards. They've promised themselves to cut back on spending numerous times. It hasn't happened yet, nor is it likely to in the near future.

• Maxine buys and buys, but it's selective. She desperately wants to "keep up" with the other women in her office. Whatever item they purchase, it's a sure bet that Maxine will have a similar (or better) one shortly. Her office mates see the pattern and even joke about it. This need has kept Maxine broke for years.

• Mike, a fisherman, goes on occasional fishing trips with an old friend, Fred. Before each trip, he goes to the tackle shop and makes it a point to buy all the latest fishing gear that he thinks will insure success. In fact, Fred consistently catches more fish with a beat-up old rod and reel that he's had for years!

• Cydney, a good midlevel manager, had to accept a lesser position after a company reorganization. When finances forced her to move from her home in an upscale neighborhood, a severe emotional crisis was precipitated. Although she still made enough money on which to live, she entertained thoughts of suicide.

Given the above symptomatic problems, all associated with the accumulation of possessions, a legitimate question is: "Just exactly what is wrong with having nice things?" At one level, the answer is, "Nothing at all." Any man, woman, or couple who has worked hard to reach a comfortable standard of living has absolutely nothing to apologize for. There is a catch, however. Possessions must be kept in reasonable perspective and not assigned psychological meanings that create problems. Unfortunately, not one of the above individuals or couples is emotionally secure and comfortable with personal successes. The characteristic problems they are experiencing are the result.

In short, a materialistic orientation becomes a serious problem when men and women begin to use possessions to define themselves as successful. When this happens, by definition, a materialistic dependency has developed.

MATERIALISTIC DEPENDENCY: *A state of ongoing emotional vulnerability that exists when self-esteem and personal adequacy are excessively linked to ownership of status-oriented items.*

In other words, the man or woman who has become materialistically dependent has crossed a line from enjoying possessions to emotionally *needing them* to support an underdeveloped internal sense of personal adequacy. Of course, the vulnerability is that when self-worth is defined externally, what is needed to define self-esteem can be lost or taken away. Then, that man or woman is left with few internal resources to feel good about oneself. To make matters worse, a materialistic dependency then drives an "acquisition compulsion" which often produces additional problems.

ACQUISITION COMPULSION: *A persistent emotional need to purchase or upgrade material possessions to support self-esteem and validate personal adequacy.*

It certainly doesn't take much imagination to see how materialistic dependency and an associated acquisition compulsion can create many personal and marital problems that significantly interfere with living the good life. It goes without saying that this orientation to life is emotionally shallow and, ultimately, unfulfilling. In fact, left unchecked, the end result is often overwork, excessive debt, and tremendous wasted energy used to create and maintain a "successful" public image. Without confronting and resolving these issues that often cause great conflict in their marriage, a couple simply can't get better together.

The Social Context of Materialism

Much of the materialistic orientation seen these days has its roots in the superficial values rampant in this culture and the institutions that communicate it. And, these questionable values receive constant daily reinforcement. Over a lifetime, men and women, even children, are encouraged in subtle and not-so-subtle ways to become increasingly materialistic and to define themselves through their possessions. Without a healthy value system that is clear and well understood, the consistent reinforcement of such superficial values becomes extremely difficult to resist.

It is truly unfortunate that this destructive and materialistic patina of social values is so very pervasive and powerful. It is additionally unfortunate that all that it represents flies in the face of what is deeply fulfilling, enduring, and emotionally healthy. Needless to say, its effect on the ability of couples to "live the good life" together can be devastating. Understanding the origins of materialistic dependency is important as a base to resist its corrosive influence. At least ten interrelated reasons help explain why this possession-oriented way of life has become the status quo for so many.

1. THE RISE OF DUAL-INCOME FAMILIES. Two-career

marriages have significantly raised the income of many families. When both husband and wife are working, they usually have less available time for one another, but more money to spend. One significant consequence is a strong tendency to begin providing "things" to a spouse and children in lieu of time and shared experiences. Giving material goods helps assuage guilt stemming from the significantly diminished amount of quality time spent together, with its resulting emotional neglect of loved ones.

2. THE NEED FOR INSTANT GRATIFICATION. The value system of contemporary culture is heavily oriented toward a very fast pace that gives rise to an ingrained "I want it all right now" attitude. These days, in contrast to years past, it has become easier to bypass waiting and sacrifice to obtain significant possessions. The unfortunate result is a strong "buy now, pay later" ethic. Frequently, the ease of accumulating possessions gives rise to decreased appreciation of what is already owned.

3. THE RISE OF EASY CREDIT. Instant gratification of needs would certainly not be possible without easy credit available to virtually everyone. Once a credit record has been established, a variety of credit cards are easily obtained. Offers of thousands of dollars in credit lines are regularly received in the mail. With the use of spending on credit constantly encouraged and with credit itself readily available, it becomes very easy to begin abusing it through unwise spending and consequent excessive debt.

4. MATERIALISTIC MODELING BY PARENTS. It is often true that in materialistically-oriented families, acquiring more possessions may have a higher priority than family time or relationships. Children naturally learn and internalize this value system. In such families, love and caring can easily become associated with how much is given to children. Some parents compete with other families in terms of what they are able to materially provide for their children.

5. THE AVAILABILITY OF MATERIAL GOODS. In a consumer-oriented society, competition has insured that there are many varieties available for virtually every kind of product. Further, new products are constantly being marketed as new materials and technology evolve. As a result, "new, better, and more" prestigious models regularly show up in the marketplace. Keeping up with "top of the line" products becomes ever more expensive for the consumer whose income may not be increasing as rapidly as the need for new possessions.

6. INSTANTANEOUS COMMUNICATIONS NETWORKS. From

coast to coast, reports of new products, technological innovations, fads, and fashions are transmitted nationally via a very sophisticated and multi-faceted communications network. In fact, mass marketing of products via this communications network has insured saturation coverage of consumers about their availability. In every hamlet, town, city, and rural area, men, women, and children are exposed to literally hundreds of such product-based "media" messages every day.

7. PERSUASIVE ADVERTISING. These days, advertising uses extremely sophisticated and subtle persuasion techniques. Using extensive market research, products are "packaged" through advertising to appeal to the needs and vulnerabilities of specific consumer groups. A favorite ploy is to link a specific product, especially top-of-the-line status items, to the self-esteem of the consumer. Advertising nowadays promotes such linkages even to children as young as four or five years of age.

8. THE EFFECT OF PEER INFLUENCES. Adult men, women, and couples tend to develop peer reference groups just as they did when they were adolescents. For example, attorneys compare their "success" to other attorneys. When an adult peer group promotes through its value system a materialistic orientation and status-based acquisition, it becomes a very powerful motivating influence. Implicitly, others link their own success and their perceived acceptance by that peer group to the adoption of similar, materialistic values.

9. THE BREAKDOWN OF SOCIAL INSTITUTIONS. Couples trying to overcome a materialistically-oriented lifestyle must ask themselves this revealing question: "What social institutions in this society promote and reinforce healthy life values?" These days, the answer may be reduced to *some* parents and the church. As a strong, psychologically persuasive, and materialistically-oriented value system has become more dominant, the influence of other social institutions in reinforcing deeper and more enduring life values has become correspondingly weaker.

10. DISTORTION OF THE AMERICAN DREAM. In the past, the American Dream was characterized by adequate employment, a fulfilling marriage, healthy children, and time to relax and enjoy life. Now, the "good life" has slowly become defined by the acquisition of a plethora of expensive possessions. Top-of-the-line cars and clothes, expensive vacations, the latest electronic equipment, the largest affordable home, and adult toys have become the goals of the American Dream.

Ego-Needs and Materialistic Motivation

As social exposure and reinforcements become heavily oriented in the direction of rather shallow materialistic values, beginning in childhood and never ceasing, it is not difficult to see the roots of materialistic motivation. This, then, becomes a powerful driving force with its focus on acquiring even more possessions. As the superficial values of this consumer-based, buying-oriented commercial culture overshadow the teaching of deeper and more fulfilling ways of living, then the stage is set for high levels of stress to develop along with marital conflict and great personal unhappiness.

At the root of many of these problems is a man or woman who has unwittingly allowed self-esteem, career success, or personal adequacy to be defined through the number and quality of material possessions. However, once this motivational system has become established, there is no end to it. Bigger, better, and more not only become driving forces, but purchasing something "bigger, better, or more of it" generates but a fleeting positive impact. Then, because it never lasts, the cycle of "bigger, better, more" must be repeated.

In short, such materialistic self-definition is similar to an addictive force, akin to trying to fill a bucket with a hole in the bottom. No matter what you put into it, it's never enough, it never lasts, and you must keep filling it. Typically, such an inappropriate personal validation system, stemming from materialistic dependency, only drives debt and results in increasingly high levels of personal stress. Such an orientation to living has four interrelated forms.

1. MATERIALISTIC SELF-VALIDATION. *Defining Theme:* "I know I'm successful every time I look around and see the kinds of things I possess."

This man or woman revels in personal possessions because they allay basic insecurity. A glance at the label on a blouse or jacket, viewing a new car with all the latest gadgets, seeing the big house in the prestigious neighborhood are all used to reassure such individuals that they are indeed adequate and okay. The real question is: "Okay at what?" Making money and acquiring possessions certainly doesn't insure happiness, guarantee a fulfilling marriage, or create life satisfaction. In fact, once the basics have been acquired, living the good life doesn't require great materialistic success at all.

2. MATERIALISTIC COMPETITION. *Defining Theme:* "I've got more than you do; therefore I'm more successful."

This very competitive individual measures personal self-worth through constant materialistic comparisons to the possessions of friends, colleagues, and even strangers. Square footage of a home, number of cars, salary, even the numbers of adult toys all become materialistic bases for comparison. As a result of this kind of materialistic competitiveness, living life becomes an ever more expensive game of trying to stay ahead of others. On the other hand, because of the "game," such a man or woman can never really relax and enjoy current possessions.

3. MATERIALISTIC GIVING TO CHILDREN. *Defining Theme:* "I know I've made it; just look at what I'm able to give to my children."

Over time, this form of materialism has very destructive effects on the kids. Sometimes children are indulged because parents feel they can demonstrate their success to the world this way. Unfortunately, such indulged children come to selfishly expect to be given everything without giving much back. Further, they also often fail to learn work values that help them become economically self-sufficient later in life. As adults, such children may continue to rely on parents for support. When parents fall into this materialistic trap, everyone loses—the kids perhaps for a lifetime.

4. MATERIALISTIC IMAGE-ENHANCEMENT. *Defining Theme:* "Just take a look at what I have. Aren't you impressed?"

Here, personal validation is derived from the impact of status-oriented possessions on others. Everyone—friends, colleagues, relatives, even strangers—are all fair game for this person's constant need to impress. The "ooh's" and "ah's" generated by possessions are music to his or her ears. For such an individual, to be the object of such adulation is equated with being liked, accepted, and respected by others. Too often, such men and women are blind to the fact that this isn't so. When the truth finally dawns, it can be devastating.

Vulnerabilities of the Acquisition Compulsion

Once a materialistic orientation to self-validation is established, it tends to continue until that individual or couple directly confronts the pattern and changes it. Unfortunately, this motivation may develop very early in life unless there is exposure to emotionally deeper and psychologically healthier value systems. As a result, some of the most fulfilling life experiences may be entirely missed as men, women, and couples strive only to acquire more possessions to reassure themselves of their own self-worth and "success."

With the years, especially after marriage, personal vulnerabilities that result from an acquisition compulsion slowly grow, often without the awareness of the individuals involved. Sooner or later, this shallow and materialistic-oriented way of living creates serious personal and marital problems. There are at least ten of them.

1. FINANCIAL PROBLEMS. With age, the financial cost of defining personal adequacy through possessions steadily rises. Left unresolved, the costs of this type of self-validation sooner or later begin to outstrip income. Credit limits are reached and debt load grows. There are few or no financial reserves. In a less-than-robust economy, overextended couples can become extremely vulnerable to any kind of financial setback.

2. ESCALATING MATERIALISTIC NEEDS. When self-esteem depends heavily on one's possessions, there is no end point. If purchasing is not continued, personal insecurity begins to grow, and eventually depression may set in. Further, the financial ante usually escalates as new possessions typically must be bigger and better than those already possessed to be personally validating. The acquisition compulsion never allows time to develop financial security.

3. MARITAL STRESS AND CONFLICT. When spending outstrips income, marital stress and conflict usually increase. There are more frequent arguments about "who is spending what on whom and for what reasons." Accusations and fights about finances can become part of daily life. The end result is that such financial pressures can drive a couple apart emotionally. Intimacy wanes as criticism, put-downs, and denials continue unabated.

4. "IMAGE ENERGY" RISES. For materialistically-oriented couples, maintaining a public image of success is extremely important. However, with time, the cost of this kind of public image, based on possessions and conspicuous consumption, increases. Correspondingly, fear of not being able to maintain the image steadily grows, thus creating more fear and personal insecurity, along with draining emotional energy. When the fall comes, it is usually a hard one.

5. WORK BECOMES UNFULFILLING. At its best, a life's work is an important part of one's total identity. It is a growing, interesting, and expressive part of oneself. When an acquisition compulsion develops, debt increases and then work is soon driven by a need to make money to satisfy creditors rather than remaining an important source of personal fulfillment. Distress builds further when second jobs become necessary to maintain possessions and service excessive debt.

6. CAREER DEVELOPMENT MISTAKES. The need to acquire more possessions frequently causes men and women to look only at financial gain (more to spend!) when considering career moves. Frequently, not seriously considering other factors leads to emotionally expensive career mistakes. For example, accepting a position for which one is emotionally unsuited and untrained "just for the money" often turns out worse than no promotion at all.

7. ABSENCE OF "FAILURE RESOURCES." When self-esteem is heavily dependent on possessions, a significant emotional vulnerability is created. The reason? Income or possessions can be lost any number of ways. Without internal bases for self-esteem, loss of income (and consequently, possessions) becomes emotionally devastating and leads to severe emotional crises, depression, and, not infrequently, suicidal feelings.

8. ENVY AND COMPETITIVENESS. Along with the need to acquire ever more possessions, a "keep up with the Joneses" mentality develops. This mindset leads to an envy of others who have more and to a competitive attitude toward them. This results in difficulty accepting others as true peers. Instead, other couples are seen in a vertical hierarchy as having "more than" or "less than" we do. In short, such envy produces a subtle, but significant strain on friendships.

9. MATERIALISTIC PARENTING. It is common for parents who are materialistically oriented to parent their children in ways that transmit these same values. Children are often indulged and become very materialistic from a very young age ("Only the best will do"). With the years, parental indulgence causes the kids to want more and more without work or sacrifice. Because of this "entitlement mentality," these indulged children do not develop emotional maturity, personal accountability, or achievement motivation.

10. LOSS OF PERSONAL CONTROL. One consequence of a possession-orientation is a lifestyle that eventually spins out of control. The financial costs, the concomitant heavy workload, the ever-present creditors, and the expectations of unappreciative children all converge to create a perception of loss of control. Resulting problems may include depression, daily tension, personal insecurity, intense marital discord, and a desire to run away. Too often, the end result is separation or divorce.

Materialism and Marital Crises

With all of the above liabilities of a materialistically-driven lifestyle adversely affecting a couple's life, it is typical to find a husband or wife (or both) beginning to experience growing marital discontent and personal unhappiness. These feelings slowly become stronger and more dominant as months and years pass. These distressing feelings become stronger until they are virtually always present in that man or woman's awareness. However, because that husband or wife is outwardly responding in responsible ways, casual observers often believe that everything is just fine.

At deeper emotional levels, however, that individual or couple is slowly moving into the uncomfortable grip of a personally painful marital crisis. When this occurs, their entire marital relationship and their future, not to mention living the good life together, is often jeopardized. While marital midlife crises have many roots, an excessively materialistic orientation to life with its many consequences is frequently found to be a powerful trigger. Conversely, directly confronting and moving beyond the superficial value system that materialism entails is often the single most meaningful step a couple can take to bring more togetherness and fulfillment back into their lives together.

At this point, before explaining how marital midlife crises develop, it would be helpful to outline in general terms what such a crisis actually is. From a psychological perspective, the definition is quite straightforward:

MARITAL MIDLIFE CRISIS: *A developmental point of transition, marked by deep unhappiness in a husband, a wife, or both, where previous lifestyle values and priorities have become unfulfilling and new ways of relating must be found to recreate personal contentment and life satisfaction.*

Now, the question is how a materialistic orientation to life creates such a crisis point in an individual's life. While there may be many perspectives from which to view this very common, but quite uncomfortable state of affairs, examining it from the vantage point of personal development is best. A young couple, newly married, experiences three phases as they work hard to become established and economically successful. Unfortunately, as part of this process, this same couple may drift, years down the road, into a crisis point in their marriage and in their personal lives.

To understand this development, it is necessary to see how

Standard of Living and Quality of Life relate to one another in each of the three stages. Remember that Standard of Living is measured by economic and materialistic criteria for success while Quality of Life is primarily reflected in an emotionally satisfying way of living. Figure 3 illustrates these phases in graphic form.

PHASE ONE: SIMPLICITY. This is the first phase of a married couple's life together and might be termed the period of *Striving.* The typical workday schedule affords adequate time for recreation, good times, and friends. Because of these realities, Quality of Life is very high, but Standard of Living may be quite low because the couple is just starting out and has not created an economic base as yet. However, as these first heady years pass, life begins to become more complex with home ownership, more responsibilities at work, marriage and children, and community responsibilities. Toward the end of Phase One, the Standard of Living for a hard-working couple is steadily rising while Quality of Life is slowly declining. However, at this point the decline is not serious and is therefore hardly noticeable.

PHASE TWO: CRISIS. This second phase (also termed the time of *Deciding*) actively begins when a couple's Quality of Life has deteriorated to create the Ironic Cross (see Figure 2, page 73). While Standard of Living may continue to grow because of hard work, overwhelming demands in every part of life preclude time to relax and enjoy life. As this trend continues, personal distress slowly increases and marital problems grow. Husband and wife do not communicate well. They are irritable, stressed, and so chronically tired that there is little motivation to spend quality time with one another. Emotional closeness and their physical relationship suffer. Eventually, the emotional pain of this work-dominated and materialistically-oriented way of living becomes so constant and so great that new lifestyle choices must be made.

PHASE THREE: INTEGRATION. Phase 3 is when a couple begins *Arriving.* It occurs when a husband and wife begin to actively put decisions to improve their Quality of Life together into practice. While they continue to work hard, regular time is taken to enjoy life and one another. They decide to reduce their debts and buy for functional value rather than for status or image needs. As they simplify life, time for one another is taken at all costs. As a result, stress levels are reduced and they begin to have fun together again. Gradually, they grow closer emotionally and their physical relationship then often improves. Standard of Living continues to rise, but more slowly. It is never again allowed to overwhelm the Quality of Life that

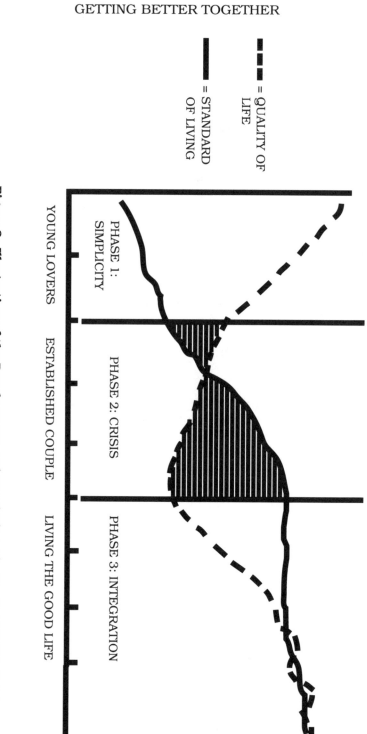

Figure 3: Illustration of the Development and Resolution of a Marital Midlife Crisis.

a couple has recovered together.

Steps to "Dematerialize" Yourselves

Every problem has a solution. And, anyone who has experienced the consequences of strong marital materialism knows that it can be a huge problem. As you already know, it can seriously affect an individual, a marital relationship, and certainly the ability to live "the good life" together. At worst, it can completely destroy a marriage. Here are some tried and true suggestions that will help with this problem. It will take time to implement them, but, in the long haul, adopting them will pay emotional dividends that last for a lifetime.

1. DEVELOP A SHARED, NONMATERIALISTIC VISION FOR YOUR MARRIAGE. To do this, begin a series of discussions with your spouse. Ask yourselves questions and then answer them. For example: "Why are we living like this?" "What do we really want out of our life together?" "How are we going to get there?" "What is really fulfilling in this short life we live?" Such questions, contemplated together, often lead to defining and then taking the necessary steps to "get better together" and really begin enjoying life.

2. ADOPT A FUNCTIONAL ORIENTATION TO PURCHASES. This purchasing strategy requires that status value be reduced or eliminated from purchases. First, ask yourselves, "Is this purchase really necessary?" If it is, then seek an item of good quality (without attaching much importance to status value) that will adequately meet your needs. Comparison shopping, purchasing good used items, and buying for the long-term breaks the expensive "designer orientation" to living. Over time, this strategy for making purchases begins to relieve financial pressure.

3. GIVE TIME TO LOVED ONES, NOT EXPENSIVE GIFTS. In many distressed marriages and dysfunctional families, couples have all kinds of "things." What they do not have for one another, nor for the children, is time to enjoy being together, to talk, and to share interesting experiences. Instead of giving materially, start taking regular time to chat with your spouse, play or talk with the kids, and create the kinds of experiences that make memories. Remember, good memories last a lifetime. "Things" don't.

4. FOCUS ON OTHERS' PERSONAL QUALITIES. At social gatherings, couples meet and conversation quickly turns to status-oriented questions: "Where do you live?" "Who do you know?" "Where did you go to school?" "What is your profession?" This "name, social rank, and income" orientation to conversation should be completely dropped. Instead, focus on getting to know and enjoy *people*. In addition, make it a point to studiously avoid talking about yourself in similar, status-oriented ways.

5. FIND FRIENDS WHO APPRECIATE YOU AS A PERSON. To really live the good life, it is extremely important to find friends who know and appreciate you as a person. It is certainly preferable to form at least some friendships outside your profession. This eliminates the tendency to "shop talk." At best, such friends have no interest in what you do, where you live, or what your income level might be. They just enjoy you. Experiences shared with this kind of friend validate you as a person and also expose you to healthier, nonmaterialistic life values.

6. CREATE A PLAN TO REDUCE YOUR DEBT LOAD. Overcoming a materialistically-oriented lifestyle requires not only reduced spending, but also a plan to bring your debt load down to manageable levels. It may take several years, but it's well worth it. Begin by creating a budget. Initiate a savings plan. Pay off credit cards. Do not spend over $50 on a nonbudgeted item without agreement of your spouse. There are many possible strategies, but they all lead to reduction of financial vulnerability and enhanced ability to enjoy life together.

7. LEARN TO ENJOY LIFE'S SIMPLE PLEASURES. Instead of going broke with expensive and glitzy vacations, begin to spend regular time with your spouse enjoying life's simple pleasures close to home. The many possibilities are limited only by your imagination: hiking in a nearby state park, putting together a special picnic lunch for two, making crafts together to give as gifts, or just puttering around in your shop. Experiences like these slow you down enough to discover new meanings and deeper fulfillments.

8. LOOK FOR YOUR MATERIALISTIC ROOTS. Almost by definition, a materialistic orientation to living stems from deep personal insecurity. And, frequently, these insecurities have developed from experiences growing up. For example, a possession-dominated lifestyle may stem from a poverty-stricken childhood and fear of future poverty or from parents who were only interested in their public image. Taking time for introspection helps you understand the past origins of personal insecurity so you can start resolving them.

9. KEEP AND APPRECIATE WHAT YOU HAVE. Move beyond the fashion-oriented, "throwaway" mentality that is so prevalent these days. Purchase good-quality items when you buy (*e.g.*, a fishing rod, car, or home) and then keep them. Such items become like old friends; they last and last with good care. Specific items can become heirlooms with great sentimental value that can be passed on to children along with happy memories of good times spent together. Valuing what you already have helps to break the "newer and more and bigger" mentality of a materialistic orientation.

10. DEVELOP YOUR SPIRITUAL LIFE. It is easy in this society to completely avoid exposure to deeper and, ultimately, more fulfilling values. For too many, values are defined primarily by television, advertising, and peers. Through involvement in a church of your choice, a forum for self-examination and learning to live in more deeply fulfilling ways is created. Church membership also brings with it a peer group that subscribes to healthier and more positive life values.

Arriving in Time

To have an acquisition orientation to life is quite characteristic of young adults. And, while certainly not desirable, it is understandable. After years of post-secondary schooling with sacrifice of time and income, along with living with the constant stresses of academia, graduation day finally comes. With diploma in hand, most young men and women then start out in life with very little in the way of possessions. As soon as employment begins, money starts coming in and credit is available. These new financial realities often trigger a tendency to begin purchasing all they could not afford during the college years.

While this early "buying binge" is very natural for those just starting out on their own, the question of importance is when the heavy orientation toward acquiring possessions will end. Sadly, for some, a shallow and materialistic orientation to life goes on indefinitely. Such men and women never really mature to enjoy some of the more fulfilling experiences in life. Others come to their senses only after experiencing a personal downfall or a financial tragedy, often of their own making.

For an ever-larger number of couples who are emotionally aware, there comes a time in life when the realization hits that just having more "things" is not really fulfilling and is not what life is all about. Although it can happen almost anytime during adulthood, this awareness occurs most frequently in couples who have reached their thirties, forties, or even fifties. These couples, who are successful and have achieved the basics of an adequate income, a home and family, and a car or two, find that life has slowly become less fulfilling. They start striving to find more life satisfaction and personal contentment through sharing time and experiences with loved ones.

The old saying that "The best things in life are free" is absolutely true. In fact, healthy men and women know that the good life is not the most expensive or materialistically extravagant at all. Unfortunately, far too many couples never find that out. There's another sound saying: "The road to contentment lies not in increasing wealth, but in reducing needs." The point? It is easy to let the good life be subverted by the pursuit of materialistic wants, but wants are not really needs. Until this confusion is resolved, many couples cannot emotionally arrive in time to enjoy the good life together.

Chapter 9

Beyond Financial Chaos: How to Eliminate Money Problems

It should certainly come as no surprise that financial pressure is a very common problem in families these days. That pressure can be found in couples at every single level of the economic spectrum. And, no matter how the economy is doing, such problems have always been present to one extent or another. In fact, money problems have consistently been found to be among the top three sources of conflict in marriages. Beyond outright conflict, financial pressures have been linked to a decrease in intimacy between a husband and wife, a decline in their physical relationship, and the inability to relax and enjoy one another.

It is interesting that money problems are often completely independent of income. Someone has commented, quite accurately, that "Quality of life depends not on how much you make, but on how much you have left over." In other words, the good life depends more on how money is managed rather than on how much money is being made. Conversely, consistently spending more than is made can create serious marital and family problems and, at worst, financial ruin. That's exactly the state of affairs found in many educated and otherwise savvy couples. For them, no matter how much money is coming in, it's never enough to purchase everything they want and cover their bills and debts, too.

Left unaddressed, the ongoing stress produced by money problems can easily become a serious threat to emotional well-being and personal health, thus endangering living the good life. The vulnerability created by these reckless and ill-considered spending patterns is especially deep at times when the economy is less than robust. Beyond a basically materialistic orientation, such patterns have at their root psychological issues that have not been addressed and resolved in such men and women. Until that happens, the symptomatic spending patterns tend to continue unabated with all the resultant negative consequences.

From early in life, most people with a solid work ethic are preparing to go out into the world and make a good living. Parents and teachers emphasize this goal and, indeed, it is a worthy one. Once out in the real world, however, this aspiration is inadvertently, but significantly, changed. Making a "good living" subtly evolves into a focus on making more and more money. Slowly, it becomes the central focus for many couples and becomes a problem when erroneous assumptions about money fuel a driving force to mindlessly make more and more of it. Three false ideas in particular are often found.

1. HAVING MONEY AND PERSONAL HAPPINESS GO TOGETHER. Nothing could be further from the truth. If money brings happiness, then why are there so many unhappy, but relatively affluent, men and women and couples to be found these days? Strictly speaking, money is nothing more than a medium of exchange. And, by virtue of being so, there is absolutely nothing inherent in money that brings personal contentment and emotional fulfillment. In fact, for many couples, more money brings personal distress and great unhappiness.

2. MORE MONEY MEANS PEOPLE WILL LIKE YOU MORE. The mistaken rationale here is that other people will accept and love you because you have money. Not true at all. No one can buy a relationship. Although others may be attracted to what you possess, fulfilling friendships do not depend on your wealth. Nor does having more money define you deep inside as a more adequate person. No matter what your economic status, it's always who you are as a man or woman that counts the most.

3. MONEY TENDS TO SIMPLIFY YOUR LIFE. "If I had lots of money, all my worries would be over." Since this relationship appears logical, many individuals dream of becoming wealthy, but it simply isn't true. The fact is that the more money you have, the more complicated life tends to become. Increased wealth brings with it worry, stress, personal insecurity, and many difficult decisions that must be faced. Do you remember when life was truly simple? It was when you were young and poor and had only a few possessions!

Looking beyond these common misperceptions about wealth, it might be easy to assume that if income was kept in perspective, many problems in marriages and in families would be solved. To some extent, at least, this assumption is true. Beyond making enough for the basics, blindly seeking to make more and more money simply does not contribute much to attaining the good life. On the other hand, making money is only half the problem. More problems these days stem from *how money is spent*, not from an inability to make enough for a reasonably decent living. To bring this key point home, consider these two families, the Ables and the Lesscans. Superficially, they are much alike, but under the surface they are actually quite different.

The Ables, Manny and Claudia, both have strong careers and their joint income is over six figures. They live in an upscale home in one of the prestigious developments in town. They dress expensively and whatever the kids want, they get. The Ables' problem is not apparent until their finances are closely examined. They purchase on credit. On more than one occasion, they have not been able to pay their credit card bills on time, leading to constant fights about money and how to make more of it so all their bills can be paid. On some occasions, neither Manny nor Claudia have had enough cash on hand to pay the kids their weekly allowance! Financially, they live from hand to mouth every week and it has always been so.

Now let's take a look at the Lesscans, Troy and Erin. Living in the same small city, they both have careers, but their joint income is modest compared to the Ables. While living in a moderately priced neighborhood, their finances are in order. They coordinate their spending according to a well-thought-out and tested budget, which includes a savings account for emergencies and small trust funds for the kids' college. The outstanding balances on their few credit cards are always paid on time. And, the Lesscans have enough left over each year for a reasonably nice vacation. They are living the good life every day, and they don't want for much of anything.

The stark contrast between the lifestyles of Ables and the Lesscans illustrates a very important lesson when it comes to living comfortably. That is, as you already know, Quality of Life and Standard of Living are definitely not the same. Once you have the basics, sound money management becomes the key to living an emotionally comfortable and fulfilling lifestyle. And, to bring counterproductive spending habits under control definitely not only reduces stress, but also enhances a sense of personal security and improves strained marital relationships.

Conversely, far too many couples these days are seriously overextended financially. These unfortunate couples and families, many of whom make entirely ample amounts of money, have never come to terms with the basic tenets of money management. Nor have they ever paused to take a good hard look at the reasons why they wind up living beyond their means. Further, many of these couples have never teamed up to develop the sound spending habits that will enable them to move, together, in the direction of the good life. They haven't discovered — yet — that personal contentment lies not in the accumulation of wealth as much as in the reduction of needs. Instead, for them, the daily theme of their lives is best exemplified by the tongue-in-cheek bumper sticker that is now frequently seen: "I owe. I owe. So, it's off to work I go!"

Financial Danger Signs

It is not difficult to spot a financially overextended couple suffering all the worry and distress that such unwarranted spending entails. The signs are almost classic. Further, most couples who wind up in this position do not set out to live this way. They have simply not taken the time to think about the motivation that drives their spending. All too often, that motivation has to do with issues that have little or nothing to do with money *per se:* personal unhappiness, need for control, sexual stereotyping, even revenge against a partner. In many instances, persistent problems in financial management reflect unresolved issues that are also preventing a marriage from becoming more fulfilling. And, because this is so, the good life becomes more difficult to attain.

Here are fifteen of the most common financial "red flags" that signal serious money management problems in a marriage. Carefully consider each one of them. The more of them you see in how you and your spouse handle your money, the more important it is to take appropriate steps to put your financial house in order. Remember, many of these bad financial habits reflect unresolved personal or couple's issues that must be addressed. Keep in mind that whatever your level of income, if you do not moderate these negative personal or marital habits, they can easily keep you both chronically pressured financially, personally stressed, and essentially broke!

_____ 1. You or your spouse have made major purchases in the past that you have not agreed on in advance.

_____ 2. There seems to be a clear "double standard" on how money is spent or allocated in your marriage.

_____ 3. Too often, not enough cash is on hand to pay for little things like the kids' school lunches or gas for the car.

_____ 4. Despite good intentions, you have virtually no reserves put away for emergencies or for a rainy day.

_____ 5. In your marriage, there is a pattern of making purchases and then informing your spouse about them after the fact.

_____ 6. On your credit cards or credit lines, you have reached limits on one or more of them and can't seem to get that balance down.

_____ 7. You and your spouse cannot talk about money and budgeting anymore without getting into a big argument or a fight.

_____ 8. Many months you must shift money from one account or credit line to another just to get the bills paid.

_____ 9. You have a tendency to spend on impulse even when you know you have no money to cover the cost of your purchases.

_____ 10. In the past, there have been instances of lying or deceit between you and your partner when it comes to money matters.

_____ 11. With your finances, there is too much separation into "his money" and "her money" with little emphasis on "our money."

_____ 12. You don't know exactly how much money your spouse makes and have only vague ideas where that money goes.

_____ 13. There is no household budget or you make budgets which are quickly violated by one or both of you.

_____ 14. Despite a reasonable income, there have been instances when you or your spouse have borrowed money from parents or friends to help "bail you out" of a financial difficulty.

_____ 15. You find it difficult or impossible to say "no" to purchases for your children even if they really don't need that item.

Bad Money Habits for Couples

It would be easy to assume that bringing sound financial management to a family where it isn't present is simply a mechanical process. That is, you take how much money you make and begin to allocate it according to a budget plan created with sound principles of financial management in mind. In some few instances, this is all there is to it. However, for most couples who have trouble establishing a true financial partnership in their marriages, creating fiscal control is not quite so straightforward.

Besides sex, there is perhaps no other area where unresolved psychological issues contaminate the process as much as in developing healthy spending habits in a marriage. Before this "mechanical process" of modifying spending priorities can begin, such underlying issues must be confronted and resolved. Some of these issues are personal and must be worked out within the individual. Others are basically interpersonal and involve both husband and wife. Whatever the case, solving these psychological issues creates the foundation on which sound financial management strategies can be developed.

Here are a number of such issues that are very commonly encountered in marriages with suggestions for resolution. Do understand that each one of them can involve either sex.

1. THE "GOOD TIME CHARLIE" HABIT. *Vignette:* At dinner, Ned always picks up the tab. Or, he buys drinks for all his buddies if they are out together. Never offering to reciprocate, Ned's friends know that an evening out won't cost them at all! In reality, Ned just can't afford to treat his friends. It's already hard enough to get the bills paid. His generous spending is driving him and his wife, Ruth, apart.

At one level, it might be easy to assume that Ned's problem is that he wants to present an affluent image to his friends. To a minor extent, this is true. However, the real issue lies in Ned's chronically low self-esteem. Since his adolescence, he has been picking up the tabs and treating his "friends" because he desperately wants them to like him. And, they do! They just love the way Ned picks up those tabs. They'll go out with him anytime. Ned uses his financial generosity to avoid finding out if his buddies really like him just for himself. Now married, Ned and Ruth have had many arguments about this bad habit that keeps them financially strapped. Although it's gotten a bit better when they are out with other couples, when he's alone with his friends, Ned's pattern continues unabated.

RESOLUTION: The solution is for Ned to stop habitually treating everyone and see what happens. If friends continue to spend time with him when he doesn't pay, Ned can assume that they accept him personally. If they don't, they were financially using him and were never friends in the first place. In this case, he must look for new friends who can appreciate him for who he is as a person.

2. USING MONEY TO CONTROL OTHERS. *Vignette:* Marc makes an excellent living, and Judy is happy being a homemaker. Virtually since day one, Marc has used "his" money to control his wife and his two children. If they do what he wants, they get what they want. Should they stand up for themselves or defy him, he withholds from them financially as a way to inflict punishment.

Marc has a very distorted way of dealing with loved ones. What he does, in effect, is strive to keep everyone close to him very dependent financially. That way, he can be in total control of their actions. On the surface, this may seem to be a power trip reflecting a need to dominate others. While there is some truth to this assertion, the deeper issue lies in Marc's insecurity. Deep down he does not really believe that he can be loved for himself. Instead, he "captures" others through use of money. His children resent his control, and one day they will reject him and his money to establish their own emotional independence. Judy, his wife, puts up with Marc's style, but she harbors a deep resentment of him and has often thought about leaving.

RESOLUTION: Marc needs to relax and allow others to care about him for who he is instead of using money to coerce and control. By promoting the autonomy of family members, he will increase their respect for him and nurture the deep kind of caring that he craves. But, to gain this acceptance and respect, he must give up his financially-controlling ways.

3. THE SHOPAHOLIC PROBLEM. *Vignette:* Kyla has always had a low tolerance for frustration. When she becomes emotionally upset or distraught, she heads for the nearest mall and begins to spend. Temporarily, shopping does help her feel better. Often, though, her purchases are unneeded, and habitually draining family finances this way only creates more stress and conflict at home.

Kyla has fallen prey to the classic "shopaholic syndrome," which is psychologically similar to overeating as a response to anxiety or tension. After she has given in to the buying urge, her frustration and anxiety are replaced by a transient sense of well-being. As a coping mechanism, shopping certainly has its drawbacks beyond the financial costs. First, shopping under such circumstances has an addictive quality and the "high" wears off quickly. Second, such shopping frequently leads to regret because the consequence is additional debt. This in turn creates more conflict with a marriage partner over the spending, resulting in even more frustration and stress, triggering the need to shop even more!

RESOLUTION: With lots of support from her husband and friends, Kyla changed how she copes with frustration. First, she regularly exercises to prevent tension and frustration from building up. Second, she takes walks with a friend or her husband to just chat whenever she feels overwhelmed. With these changes, the urge to shop has lessened, and she feels more in control.

4. LINKING WORTH TO OTHERS' EARNINGS. *Vignette:* Deep down, it is apparent that Harold does not respect Kay or her opinions, decisions, or needs. He listened to her when she had a career outside the home and was bringing in a salary. But since the kids came along, and she became a full-time homemaker with no income, in many ways, including financial ones, Harold treats her as less than an equal.

Harold doesn't respect Kay because deep down he links her worth directly to her value in the marketplace. If she makes a good salary, she is worthy. If she does not, she doesn't deserve much respect from him. Ironically, she gave up a solid career (with some reservations) because they *both agreed* that being at home with the kids during the early years was what they both wanted. Despite himself, Harold finds it difficult to recognize Kay's contributions to all that makes their life good. Although she loves being at home with the kids, Kay feels acutely that she has been diminished in Harold's eyes and has to fight constantly to participate in marital decision-making, particular financial decisions.

RESOLUTION: It is obvious that Harold must reestablish a true partnership with Kay based on mutually-defined goals and family priorities. More than ever, Kay needs to be included in decision making and to be reassured that her contributions are both valued and valuable. She needs to insist on this in direct and firm, but tactful ways. For his part, Harold needs to help out more around the house.

5. GIFTS TO SUBSTITUTE FOR INTIMACY. *Vignette:* Sam, now married to Lila, sees his primary role as a husband as being a provider. Financially, Lila gets what she wants, including expensive gifts. When he hurts her feelings, Sam soon gives her a gift to atone. Lila is lonely because Sam never tells her he loves her and isn't there for her emotionally when she needs him.

Sam and Lila actually have a dual set of problems. His gift giving is not only expensive, but he often purchases things that Lila doesn't really want or need. This habit has created financial problems over the years and placed unneeded pressure on their marriage. Although Lila knows the intent of Sam's gifts, she acutely feels the lack of intimacy between them. She has tried to explain to him that what she really needs is for him to share intimate moments, to just talk now and then, to be a shoulder to lean on when she feels overwhelmed or upset. He just doesn't seem to listen. In fact, sometimes she believes that Sam uses his often-lavish gifts to her as a license to do whatever he pleases.

RESOLUTION: In his marriage, Sam is clearly copping out. Instead of blaming his discomfort with intimacy on his upbringing, both his marriage and his financial condition would improve if he focused on learning to convey kind words, to give big bear hugs, and to often say "I love you" to Kay. Kay really doesn't want gifts. What she desires most is for shared intimacies to become part of their daily life.

6. PURCHASING TO PUNISH. *Vignette:* Rhonda's husband, Deshon, often ignores her as he spends most of his time in pursuit of *his* hobbies and interests. Frequently, this leads to big fights between them which Rhonda always feels she loses. Indirectly, she gets back at Jim by going out and making an expensive purchase for herself. This response only infuriates Jim even more.

In her marriage, Rhonda is clearly using her credit card to punish Deshon for neglecting her. She knows that though he will be angry when he becomes aware of her purchases, he can do little about it. It has become, for her, a way to fight back when she feels neglected and overwhelmed by her husband. The problem is that, over the years, he has drawn even further away from her because of this habit. And, the more he avoids her, the greater her anger and the need to punish him for neglecting her. Then, out comes the credit card. A vicious circle is in motion in this marriage. This problem has gone on so long that sometimes both Deshon and Rhonda wonder whether their marriage can be saved.

RESOLUTION: An excellent solution for Rhonda is to take a course where she can learn to be assertive in a direct and positive manner. Then, she can begin to deal more directly with the problems in her marriage without feeling intimidated by Deshon. When she does so, she will feel more in control and will increase the chances that the problems in her marriage will improve.

7. MONEY AND DOUBLE STANDARDS. *Vignette:* Though Ben has always been somewhat selfish, Laura didn't see this trait in him during courtship; however, it became quite evident soon after they married. While systematically squelching any purchase Laura needed for herself, the kids, or the house, Ben would unilaterally spend extravagantly on himself for clothes, adult "toys," and other frivolous items.

Basically, Ben has never grown up. During his growing years, he was never taught to give to anyone; he became a taker instead and always got his way with his parents. Now, in his marriage, his self-centered attitudes are creating problems. His standards for himself and his standards for Laura vary greatly. Further, his personal indulgences, most often made unilaterally and without discussion with Laura, have created financial problems for the family, not to mention the lack of a close and fulfilling marital relationship. Although she has a career of her own, Laura spends most of the money she makes for basics and for paying off debts accumulated by Ben.

RESOLUTION: Ben just isn't going to grow up until Laura puts her foot down. He needs to accept family responsibilities rather than treating Laura like his mother. She must stop rationalizing his selfishness and begin to confront the issues in a reasoned, firm, and tactful way. Then, she must follow through even in the face of Ben's temper tantrums designed to intimidate her . . . again!

8. SELF-INDULGENCE AND IMMATURITY. *Vignette:* Andrea grew up in an affluent family who consistently indulged her. When she fell in love and married Tim, she expected things to continue as they had. She bought and bought, thinking that Tim would pay the bills just as her parents had always done. Instead, the result was constant marital conflict and severe financial problems.

Andrea and Tim represent a frequently-encountered financial problem in marriages these days. Many children, now adults, grew up in families where they never learned financial accountability, as well as other life responsibilities. When these indulged youngsters must later cope with the real world, their irresponsible and uncaring ways create many personal hardships for them and sometimes cause unbearable strains in a marriage. In essence, such adults have never learned to deny themselves anything and often see themselves as deserving whatever they want. When parents aren't there to bail them out financially or rescue them from problems, these impulsive, pleasure-oriented, and emotionally-immature adults simply can't cope.

RESOLUTION: Overcoming this kind of immaturity takes time and commitment. First, the individual (or couple) must want to grow up emotionally. Then, removing sources of temptation such as credit cards and dedicating oneself to abiding by a strict budget help. Great support is needed during this learning process as traditional sources of "rescue" (parents, spouse) are eliminated.

9. COSTLY COMPETITION. *Vignette:* Carla's sister had always been successful growing up and deep down Carla always felt second best. When she married Duane, a subtle competition began. Whatever her sister bought, Carla "one-upped" her with a bigger or better purchase. Duane loved Carla, but as time passed, their steadily-worsening financial condition had to be stopped.

Carla's sense of inadequacy is slowly driving Duane and Carla into dire straits financially. Interestingly, others in Carla's family are more aware of the competitiveness with her sister than she is. It has been going on for years, but as time passed and as her sister become more successful, the cost of competing has steadily increased with no end in sight. Duane knows what has been going on, but he has given in because he wants Carla to feel good about herself. The problem is that whenever Carla makes a purchase to prove herself her sister's equal (or superior), it doesn't last and the cycle is repeated.

RESOLUTION: Carla must understand that, indirectly, her sister is actually controlling what she purchases! Second, she must put aside childhood rivalries and define herself as okay from within, not solely in reference to her sister. Only then will she feel comfortable purchasing what she and Duane really need, rather than buying things just to compete with her sister.

10. FINANCIAL SELFISHNESS AND SECRETIVENESS. *Vignette:* Week to week, Jewel hardly has enough money to pay for food. She has to beg Rick, her husband, for money although he makes an excellent salary. Jewel has no idea how much her husband makes nor where the money goes. When she asks about finances or even to see their tax returns, he always manages to avoid the issue by getting mad or refusing to discuss it.

The basic problem here results from a number of factors. First, sexual stereotyping on Rick's part: "Women can't handle money and shouldn't have to bother with finances and taxes." Second, the need for control: "I don't want anyone telling me what to do or even to make suggestions about money." Finally, there is pure selfishness: "What's mine is mine and I don't want to share it with anyone, not even my family!" What a prescription for sabotaging open communication and the development of a financial partnership in marriage. Such marriages are often unions in name only, with one partner rigidly enforcing not only financial, but other forms of separateness as well. Sharing information about money, much less the money itself, is simply not possible.

RESOLUTION: Rick, never personally secure enough to share, must learn this in adult life. To do so, he must begin to trust Jewel with information and with financial decisions. Otherwise, he and his wife will grow further apart. For her part, Jewel must cease accepting putoffs. Instead, she must insist on being part of family financial planning.

Creating a Financial Partnership

Removing the emotional barriers to a true financial partnership in marriage is no easy task. You now know that the spending patterns that create problems in a marriage have often been there for many years, frequently having their origins in childhood and family experiences. Further, many of these emotional problems, most obviously manifested in how money is handled within the marriage, often have other unrecognized facets that negatively impact on the total marital relationship. For example, a financially-indulgent man or woman may not have the self-discipline to follow through on projects around the house. Or, an individual who is financially selfish and seclusive often cannot share feelings with a spouse.

The point is that resolution of many of these issues can be tackled on several fronts at once, including nonfinancial ones. In addition, the act of creating and following through together on a financial "master plan" for family money management can become a major vehicle for a couple to confront and resolve these emotionally-based issues. When this occurs, the result is a win-win situation in which not only do sounder money management practices develop, but also a closer and more open marital relationship evolves. To create a financial "master plan," consider the following suggestions.

1. DECIDE TO COOPERATIVELY BRING YOUR SPENDING UNDER CONTROL. Without this critical first step, nothing may change. And, bringing your finances and debt load under control does take time. In some instances, two or three years is not unrealistic. It necessitates not only continual self-examination, but also specific changes in spending patterns that bring finances under control and the good life within reach.

2. SET ASIDE A SPECIFIC TIME EACH WEEK TO TALK ABOUT FAMILY FINANCES. This step is often difficult because spending patterns are at the root of much conflict. However, it is necessary to begin; try talking about finances over dinner at a restaurant or in the den. Go over all the bills together and decide what extras will be required in the week ahead. Make it a point to be open and tactful, so defensiveness doesn't shut down communication.

3. CREATE A HOUSEHOLD BUDGET. To accomplish this absolutely crucial step, tabulate where every dollar of income was spent for a period of two months. Then, create categories of expenses and examine where the money went. From this information, put down on paper a reasonable household budget to cover all necessary expenses. While cutting down on unneeded expenses, don't forget to budget some money for the inevitable extras that crop up.

4. DECIDE WHO WILL TAKE PRIMARY RESPONSIBILITY FOR MAKING SURE THE BILLS ARE PAID. Usually, either a husband or wife will assume this sometimes onerous task. While this decision is often fraught with conflict, an agreement must be reached. In the beginning, paying the bills together may be required. Regardless of who writes the checks for the bills, it is critical to keep the checkbook and the expenditures open to both parties.

5. CREATE A PLAN FOR BRINGING UNWANTED DEBTS UNDER CONTROL. Often omitted, this step means making a commitment to systematically use extra money, bonuses, or a small second job to reduce debt load. However, this will only work if there is a simultaneous decision to prevent any additional debt from accumulating. This takes "couples discipline" and is often a test of the basic commitment to family financial restructuring.

6. INCLUDE IN THE BUDGET AN "ALLOWANCE" FOR EACH SPOUSE. This is discretionary money to be spent as wished. If a budget is so tight that literally nothing is left over to spend on personal items, then the budget may break down. In the beginning, such free money may be a small amount until a couple's debt load is under control. Later, it can be increased. In some marriages, spouses jointly "save" this personal allowance for a desired item.

7. REDUCE THE NUMBER OF CREDIT CARDS YOU CARRY. The "instant gratification" of credit card purchases is an extremely bad habit. Unless a separate one is needed for business expenses, one regular credit card and one gasoline credit card should be sufficient. Put away or cut up the remainder; then work systematically to pay off those credit card balances with high interest rates. Together, move toward cash purchases.

8. AGREE NOT TO SPEND MORE THAN A GIVEN AMOUNT WITHOUT YOUR PARTNER'S CONSENT. This strategy makes both partners accountable to one another for spending beyond budgeted items and prevents much financial conflict. It also resolves the problem of one partner unilaterally "raiding" a savings account or using a credit card. Further, this agreement also tends to reduce impulse buying and purchases of frivolous or status-oriented items.

9. DECIDE TO IMPLEMENT SPECIFIC MONEY-SAVING STRATEGIES. Many savings strategies that add up to significant amounts at the end of the month can be brought into a marriage. For example, use the telephone to comparison shop for prescriptions or purchase generic brands of food or toiletries that you both agree on. After defining a number of such strategies and agreeing on them, put them into practice. *Note:* Excellent books that outline many such money-saving tips are on the market.

10. WHEN MAKING PURCHASES, FOCUS ON THE "SOLID CENTER." Begin to shift your purchasing away from prestige items to those products representing good quality with lasting power. In other words, buy primarily for functional value rather than for status. Consumer guides can be extremely helpful here. Not only do such purchases last longer, but when items have become solidly established, the "bugs" have been worked out and they need fewer repairs.

11. BEGIN TO CREATE AN "UNTOUCHABLE FUND" FOR EMERGENCIES. Not having an emergency fund catches many families completely off guard when unexpected events occur that require money to be immediately available. To prepare for unanticipated problems, start to systematically build such a fund with modest amounts at first. Agree to never use this "nest egg" money except in dire emergencies and then, only after discussion and mutual consent.

12. USE SOME OF THE MONEY YOU SAVE TO TREAT YOURSELVES. As you both begin to cooperatively bring your finances under control, it is helpful to reward yourselves from time to time. For instance, take a little money now and then to have some fun or buy that inexpensive item that isn't really needed. These small financial "breakouts" are fun and make the necessary self-discipline of financial belt-tightening more tolerable.

13. DON'T STOP PREMATURELY. Men and women struggling hard to control spending are initially successful. However, as soon as they create some modicum of financial relief, then it's back to old spending habits again. The inevitable result is another financial crunch down the road. It's a habit akin to "yo-yo" dieting. The real solution is to change your spending habits permanently. Don't stop until you've done just that.

Getting Better Financially

As the financial pressure on them increases, it should be dawning on many couples that their money problems have occurred because, over the years, they have mistakenly traded quality of life for an increased standard of living. As couples strive for more and better possessions, quality of life is typically diminished. Despite entirely ample incomes, these hard-working and striving couples have lost their way to the good life without realizing it. They feel the stress and tension not only from incessant financial pressure, but from the lack of time they have to spend together.

The solution for couples facing this dilemma does not lie in making more money. That's the mistake. Rather, the good life lies in changing their life priorities and managing the money they do make in better ways. As already seen, many of these problems in money management have their roots in childhood experiences; they stem from the failure of parents to teach their children healthy life values, as well as specific money management skills. In adulthood, "catching up" on such skills can be quite difficult, but doing so is well worth it, given the personal and marital benefits that result.

The bottom line is simple. An old adage states that we are good at teaching men and women how to make a good living, but we fail at teaching them how to live a good life! For such marriage partners, the lesson that must be learned is as simple as it is difficult. Perhaps it is best put in a very astute comment made by an unknown, but very wise, individual: "Contentment lies not in the accumulation of wealth as much as in the lessening of wants." That's what the good life is really all about.

Chapter 10

Couples in Conversation: Small Talk Pays Big Dividends

"Small talk." "Passing the time of day." "Chattin' a bit." "Shooting the bull." It's known by many names. Kids do it all the time. Adolescents are experts. It's an integral part of daily life in college. In young marrieds and those who are courting, it's a way of being together and affirming the bond between them. Casual conversation. It's fun and it's an enjoyable way to pass the time. It's so simple you don't even think about it. Everyone knows how to do it. And, everyone does it naturally. Don't they?

Not exactly. Not these days. In those who have been married for a while, casual conversation slowly and inexorably begins to disappear. It's usually a matter of time until there just isn't enough of it. With the hectic and intense lifestyles that most families live these days, it seems that casual conversation is becoming a lost art. It goes the way of the dinosaurs. With so much to do, sadly, there's no time for "just talking." This stimulating and important way of relating slowly slips to the bottom of the priority list. And, when it does, the relationship loses. Consider the reactions of these couples to one another.

When *Ez and Annie*, always busy, find a few moments to be alone without the kids, they both focus immediately on schedules and what must be done and what didn't get done. When they're not talking about work or schedules or problems that must be solved, they quickly lapse into an uncomfortable silence.

Holly and Al hardly ever go out alone anymore. When they do, they almost always wind up in an argument. It's usually about some minor point, and they both come home unhappy with one another. Now, when they go out, it's primarily with other couples whose presence keeps the conversation civil and fun.

Fernando and Connie have been living together, but gradually growing apart for a number of years. Fernando has become an inveterate couch potato who watches television constantly in all his free time. In the evening, Connie works around the house. They're both "too busy" to really talk with one another anymore.

It's a fact that spending time casually conversing with one another is an absolute must for any healthy marriage. Conversely, in those many relationships that have grown distant and unfulfilling, it is almost axiomatic that easy and comfortable conversations have disappeared. Ironically, these same husbands and wives who don't seem to have much to say to one another anymore can and often do talk regularly with friends, relatives, and colleagues. These animated "extra-marital" conversations stand in stark contrast to the strained and stilted interactions that are characteristic of marriage partners living pressure-packed lifestyles.

Furthermore, the absence of regular and interesting conversations is a sure diagnostic sign that a husband and wife have grown apart. Under the same roof, they have started to live separate lives with very little in the way of adventure and stimulating diversions in their lives. As routines slowly dominate them, husbands and wives find there is little to talk about beyond problems they encountered and the mundane realities of everyday life. Then, with the passage of time, chronic irritability, withdrawal from one another, and bad communication habits all come to the fore to further erode the possibility of fun and easygoing conversations.

The bottom line is that casual conversation is more important than it may first appear for the well-being of a marriage. From a relationship perspective, regular and interesting conversations with your husband or wife meets a number of important needs.

1. IT EXPRESSES PERSONAL INTEREST. It's sad that so many couples don't really listen to one another anymore and thereby express disinterest. Giving your full attention to a spouse and responding directly through casual conversing is an important relationship message. It strengthens a marriage because it says, "I'm interested in you and what you have to say."

2. IT IS A FORM OF INTIMACY. Think back to the "good old days" of your relationship when courtship was in bloom and romance was in the air. Regularly communicating about your hopes and your dreams of a life to be shared made it real. Conversing in this way not only builds closeness, but small talk also helps to mutually define a couple's direction toward the good life.

3. IT AFFIRMS THE RELATIONSHIP BOND. It's easy these days to inadvertently take a marriage relationship completely for granted. There are always a million and one other things to do besides talk to one another. Even short talks serve to affirm the marital partnership. When regular conversations are present, it says clearly: "We have responsibilities, but we're important, too!"

4. IT IS A WAY OF RELAXING TOGETHER. Good conversations are emotionally fulfilling because they are relaxing. No goals need to be accomplished. All that is expected is the pleasure of the experience. Just enjoying the process of conversing tends to release tension. The worries and concerns of the day seem far away (if only for a little while) when you're casually "shooting the bull."

5. IT IS STIMULATING AND CREATIVE. A good conversation is almost by definition interesting. Further, in many men and women, creative thoughts are stimulated by the exchange of ideas. New ways of seeing things are learned. Or, a conversation can take the form of playful banter with lighthearted humor and laughter. Such conversations create a desire for more of the same.

6. IT IS EMOTIONALLY HEALTHY. Regular conversations help maintain positive attitudes and mental health. When there is a problem, having someone there to listen and respond is immensely helpful. A listener helps you sort out feelings and more accurately assess options. Talking about a personal concern also relieves emotional pressure and prevents distortion or magnification of feelings.

7. IT COUNTERS PERSONAL RESERVE. Some men and women are so reserved and shy they have trouble talking to virtually everyone. For such individuals, learning to converse with a spouse easily and comfortably about nonthreatening topics is excellent practice. Over time and with repetition, it builds social comfort that often extends to other important relationships outside marriage.

It is ironic that while regular conversing is essential for any good relationship, it is in a marriage, the most important bond of all, where casual communication is most likely to deteriorate or disappear entirely. With friends and colleagues, there is a social expectation that an effort be made to keep communication reasonably open and tactful. On the home front, however, such expectations for communication cease to be important. With fatigue, responsibilities, pressure, and stress, casual conversations go by the wayside. They are replaced by withdrawing into oneself, constant bickering, or diving in to get more work done.

Unwritten Rules for Conversing

It is a sad commentary on personal and social values to find that so many once good marriage relationships wither to become uninteresting and personally unfulfilling. Restoring the art of casual conversation is an important and often unrecognized way to bring back many of the good qualities that were once part of a marital relationship. Keep in mind that conversing is a two-way street, and it will take you both to bring it back. Three requisites are necessary, however. First, you must desire to improve your marital relationship. Learning to converse is a nonthreatening way to begin doing just that. Then, you've got to make regular time to have comfortable conversations. Finally, you must both be patient with one another while you're relearning this critical marital skill.

Certain qualities must be present in any casual conversation. These are the rules for communicating in an easy and stimulating way. When these unspoken but nevertheless powerful conversational norms are violated, one or both partners may become frustrated and the conversation then deteriorates.

RULE #1: THERE MUST BE AN EASY RECIPROCITY IN THE CONVERSATION. In other words, the best conversations are characterized by an easy balance of both listening and responding to what has been heard. It's like tossing a ball back and forth, but one party never holds the ball for too long. When one individual dominates the interaction, the reciprocal nature of casual conversation is destroyed and the interaction becomes less attractive.

RULE #2: GOOD CONVERSATIONS ARE VERY FLUID. In other words, a good conversation usually has no set structure or goals. It can focus on one topic for a while and then shift to something quite different. In fact, an interesting talk may wind up far afield from where it began. Either partner can initiate easy shifts from time to time. This fluidity is what makes a good conversation fun for both partners.

RULE #3: AVOID FOCUSING ON SENSITIVE SUBJECTS. Good conversations are stimulating when they are kept comfortable for everyone. But every husband and wife have unresolved conflicts, emotional vulnerabilities, and personal sensitivities. When these issues are made part of every discussion, conversing is inhibited. Further, never talking about anything but problems or emotionally volatile topics gets old.

RULE #4: FREE EXPRESSION AND ACCEPTANCE OF A PARTNER'S VIEWPOINTS ARE PROMOTED. There is a difference between listening with acceptance to another point of view and defending one's own perspective by rejecting everything else. It's very helpful to remain open and understanding. Accepting your partner's views doesn't necessarily mean agreement, but you must always respond with tact and consideration. If the conversation starts becoming contentious, subtly guide it into a more neutral area.

Some Conversational Bad Habits

In marriage relationships where the personal unhappiness and withdrawal of a spouse has become obvious, personal self-esteem usually plummets. Within, a question is asked: "Am I so uninteresting that not even my spouse is willing to listen to me?" The answer is usually, "Probably not." However, perhaps you have a problem in conversational style that is putting a spouse (or your children) off so that they avoid even casual conversations with you. If this is the case, the problem is exacerbated because the avoidance or rejection of conversation is so blatant. At least friends and colleagues usually make at least some attempt to be diplomatic!

Here are fifteen of the most negative habits commonly found in poor conversationalists. Keep in mind that these communication problems may be tolerated more by friends because friends don't live with the man or woman using them. However, these same habits become an outright turnoff if heard every day at home. A suggestion for correcting each of these conversational problems is included. As a point of interest, take a moment as you read through the description of each one of these habits to determine which of the four unwritten rules of comfortable conversation is being violated.

HABIT #1: FRAGMENTING. *Recognition:* One partner consistently responds in ways that have nothing to do with the theme of the conversation or what has just been said. When a spouse responds with an irrelevant remark, the other is left asking: "Where did that come from?" The problem is that the response is to a personal agenda or to a free-association rather than to what a partner has said.

REMEDY: To break this communication problem, listen carefully. Then, briefly paraphrase what your partner has said and add your own comments. Although using this technique may be awkward initially, it is an effective way to help maintain the topical flow of the conversation. If you slip up, be sure to stop and explain to your partner where your "out of the blue" response came from.

HABIT #2: INTERRUPTING. *Recognition:* This man or woman never lets a partner finish because that individual has something much more important to say. This problem may arise from excitement about what has been said or from a need to dominate or take over the conversation. In either case, this habit is discourteous to a spouse who may give up feeling that "I can't get a word in edgewise."

REMEDY: This frustrating habit can be broken by following two simple rules. First, never, ever break into what your partner is saying, especially in the middle of a sentence. Allow your spouse to completely finish a thought first. Wait for a pause. Second, always allow your partner to complete three or four sentences (on average) before responding with your ideas.

HABIT #3: CHALLENGING. *Recognition:* This person loves to stir up controversy. It's done by habitually taking an opposing or adversarial view on anything a spouse says. The hidden message comes out loud and clear: "You're wrong, so defend what you've just said." Not only does comfortable conversation become virtually impossible, but such an adversarial stance often provokes conflict and stubborn defensiveness.

REMEDY: The easiest way to resolve this problem is to learn to accept other perspectives as valid. There does not have to be a right and a wrong in the conversation. You both may have good ideas. Instead of challenging your partner's perspective, try responding by adding to it your thoughts and insights. It will be more interesting, and the conversation will probably continue.

HABIT #4: VERBATIM REPORTS. *Recognition:* Also known as the "He said . . . She said" problem. When conversing, this man or woman persistently recounts precisely and without end or omission a dialogue with someone else. While extremely trying to the patience of a spouse, the core problem is that the reporter frequently never quite gets around to making a clear point so a partner can respond.

REMEDY: Make a commitment to yourself to avoid recounting verbatim conversations at all costs. Instead, think for a moment about the point that you want to make. Then state it clearly and concisely. If a partner wants more information (and only if asked!), relate no more than a sentence or two of a past conversation. Then stop to allow your husband or wife to respond.

HABIT #5: ONE-TRACK MIND. *Recognition:* These speakers are personally obsessed with one (usually controversial) idea or topic. They can't get it out of their minds or out of their conversations. No matter where a talk starts, it will be brought back to this topic again and again. Always focusing on this single topic gets so monotonous that even short conversations are avoided.

REMEDY: First, figure out what your "tiresome topic" is. Then, commit yourself in a specific conversation never to bring it up under any circumstances. Your spouse can also help you by gently reminding you that you are getting into "it" again so you can change the subject. With practice, avoiding that topic will become easier and your conversations more stimulating to you both.

HABIT #6: MONOPOLIZING. *Recognition:* These loud and often boisterous individuals manage to take control of every conversation. They don't respond to others; rather they constantly force others to respond to them. These talks aren't dialogues; rather they are monologues with only a sporadic comment by a spouse allowed now and then. This "run on" style of discussing anything turns everyone off.

REMEDY: Bringing back some "give and take" (really "respond and listen") in your conversations is the byword here. To do this is easy by following one simple rule: the Monopolizer should state no more than can be said in one breath. Then, stop and allow your partner equal time to respond.

HABIT #7: EXPERT COUNSEL. *Recognition:* These "advisors" love to tell a spouse (and everyone else!) exactly what to do and how to do it. Whether asked to or not, these men and women will perennially give advice on anything and everything. They mistakenly hear requests for expert counsel in every conversation. In reality, their spouses may just want to chat and enjoy a casual conversation.

REMEDY: The solution here is simple and has two parts. First, do not offer any advice to your spouse unless you are clearly and directly asked for it. If suggestions are requested, help your partner define alternatives rather than impose your solutions. Second, practice paying close attention to your partner. Your husband or wife may just want you to listen with empathy and understanding, not solve a problem.

HABIT #8: NAYSAYING. *Recognition:* The users of this conversational killer unfailingly find the negative side of every topic and state it. Dyed-in-the-wool pessimists and cynics, these men and women seem constitutionally incapable of seeing the positive side of anything. No matter how upbeat it begins, this obsessive Naysayer quickly puts everything said into a negative framework.

REMEDY: "If you can't say something positive, don't say anything at all" is the beginning solution for this problem. Once you've mastered the art of stifling yourself, then force yourself to start making positive and upbeat comments. It will stimulate a much more interesting conversation. Don't forget that negative thought processes also reinforce negative feelings and keep you feeling low.

HABIT #9: CHRONIC COMPLAINING. *Recognition:* Consistently talking about how awful their problems are, what others have done to them, and how victimized they feel are the hallmarks of the Complainer. "Let me tell you my tale of woe" becomes the central theme of every conversation. This martyristic, attention-seeking style of relating can severely damage communication in any relationship, not to mention a marriage.

REMEDY: The best solution is to deal with problems, not incessantly complain about them. Begin immediately to treat yourself as a competent adult and begin handling most problems on your own. Tell others how well you handled these problems, not why you couldn't. If you want suggestions, concisely state the problem and ask your spouse for some ideas. Then drop the subject and go on to more pleasant topics of conversation.

HABIT #10: ZAPPING. *Recognition:* Those who zap regularly are individuals who make insensitive and tactless remarks to a spouse, sometimes publicly, often in the guise of being "funny." With indirect expressions of hostility in the air, who can converse and enjoy it while waiting for the next thinly veiled insult? The Zapper is often too insecure to permit comfortable closeness, so trust diminishes and conversation dies.

REMEDY: Sometimes this man or woman is unaware of the full impact of what is said. Bring this to awareness through helpful and nondefensive feedback, including tips on better ways to phrase one's concerns. Or, if this problem is an indirect way of expressing anger, bring concerns into the open and discuss them rather than letting putdowns ruin every conversation.

HABIT #11: INTERROGATION. *Recognition:* The Interrogators relate only by asking a multitude of very direct and pointed questions. In business, obtaining information as quickly as possible is often necessary because time is at a premium. But, that's not what casual conversations are all about. Too many direct questions are unduly intrusive, tiresome, and often provoke defensive responses.

REMEDY: First, understand that the purpose of a conversation is just to enjoy relating to one another. To reduce questioning when you converse, try paraphrasing what your spouse has just said. Or, turn a potential question into a statement. Often, just nodding or saying something like "That's interesting" or "Tell me more" helps immensely. Then, how you come across will soften.

HABIT #12: "ME-DEEP" IN CONVERSATION. *Recognition:*

This insecure man or woman simply doesn't stop talking about personal accomplishments and successes. Within, each has a strong need to impress a spouse (and everyone else!) with what great things they have done. The real intent is to solicit reassuring praise or pats on the back. Others' accomplishments are often diminished to support this egotist's own fragile sense of self-esteem.

REMEDY: To break this habit requires that you start becoming more comfortable with yourself. Take a risk and trust that others will like and accept you just for yourself. Then, interest yourself in your spouse. Listen carefully to what is being said and encourage your partner to continue. Eliminate the egocentrism from your speech by significantly reducing use of the pronoun "I" when you talk.

HABIT #13: POLYPHASING. *Recognition:* Polyphasic activity is defined as attending to two (or more) things at once. This "juggling" habit not only contributes to high levels of stress, but also can severely inhibit conversation. In a word, it's just plain difficult to talk easily and spontaneously when you are really focusing on something else. The usual result is a nonattentive and disjointed attempt at conversation that's not fun or fulfilling for anyone.

REMEDY: Any good conversation requires that you care enough to give your spouse your full and complete attention with good eye contact and active listening. In essence, the habitual polyphaser must learn to converse without "doubling up" with something else. While initially frustrating, talking without distractions helps slow you down and, at the same time, promotes your ability to relax.

HABIT #14: TEACHING. *Recognition:* This style, sometimes also referred to as the "Plato Problem," is created when one partner habitually adopts a teacher-student stance in relating to a spouse or others. Once a topic about which this individual is even superficially knowledgeable is brought up, others learn everything they didn't need to know about it because a nonstop monologue about the subject will inevitably ensue. *Note:* A variation of this uncomfortable teaching mode is a "selling style." Here, an individual persistently tries to "sell" others on personal ideas, products, or the "proper" ways to do things. The goal becomes persuasion, not conversation.

REMEDY: The bottom line is that a conversation is not a teaching forum. Therefore, becoming an *ad hoc* professor imparting knowledge to the ignorant isn't appropriate. In fact, such a style subtly puts others down and often bores them. Instead, tune in to topics that others are interested in. "Go with the flow" of the conversation to become an interesting participant instead of a teacher.

HABIT #15: MARTYRISM. *Recognition:* No matter what the nature of the issue, or in what area of life, this individual will quickly assume a victim's stance. There will be comments about how others are unappreciative, selfish, and uncaring. This person is being perennially "dumped on" and will tell you all about it. Why? Usually, because there is a need for attention and getting a spouse to express sympathy is one way to do it.

REMEDY: The solution here is quite easy. Just state directly what you want. If you want your spouse to just listen, say that. If you want a hug, just ask your spouse for one. Instead of being a victim, strive to present yourself as a competent man or woman with normal needs. Remember, by being a victim, you victimize yourself because sooner or later it will trigger avoidance.

Conversational Exercises

As couples strive to renew their ability to converse easily and openly with one another, it is sometimes helpful in the beginning to use structured exercises. By relating to one another using guidelines that focus on specific skills or problem areas, couples are able to "hear" a conversation in a very different way than when it is free-floating and unstructured. Structure also helps to keep a conversation focused and less likely to deteriorate into uncomfortable silences or even an argument. At first, short conversations of about ten to twenty minutes seem to be better than long ones that stretch into an hour or more.

In addition, when using conversational games to develop their communication skills, it is helpful for both husband and wife to keep their talks easy and light. Remember to laugh and have some fun with the exercises. That's what conversations should be. Here are some exercises to get started. Or, make up your own as long as they are basically positive. Remember that developing positive communication skills is like anything else; with practice, better ways of relating will develop and become easier. And, as you practice together, you'll also be getting better together!

1. BOUNCING THE (CONVERSATIONAL) BALL. This is an excellent exercise for those men and women who tend to run on . . . and on in their conversations. A husband and wife monitor one another with a hand signal, in accordance with one simple rule: Neither one can say more than three sentences before pausing to allow the other one to respond. This technique helps to recreate an easygoing and comfortable "bouncing ball" reciprocity in conversations.

2. KILL THE QUESTIONS. This is a fun exercise to use during idle time together, for example, while riding in a car. Each partner monitors the other one for use of questions. There is only one rule: The first one to use three questions loses and must pay a penalty to the partner. Perhaps a big smoochy kiss or a bear hug would be appropriate. Hints: turn questions into statements, use empathic leads, or make a statement about how your experiences relate to the topic of discussion.

3. EXTEMPORANEOUSLY SPEAKING. Here, a husband or wife begins to talk about a subject that is more or less picked at random. It should not be anything either one of you know a lot about. Open the dictionary to pick a subject. Or, take turns choosing something to talk about. Keep it interesting and avoid your relationship, your problems, or your feelings. For best results, don't go more than ten or fifteen minutes before changing the subject to something else.

4. TACTFULLY TALKING. This exercise helps couples become more aware of saying things in nonhurtful ways. First, in a very objective or neutral way, describe a specific response by someone else (not yourselves or relatives) that has bothered you. Then, describe the same behavior using negative adjectives or an adjective that is guaranteed to create hurt feelings. Then, as a contrast, describe the behavior under discussion in a way that is positive, very tactful, and that keeps communication open. *Note:* A tip is that tactful responses usually require more words than hurtful responses, which often take the form of labels or put-downs.

5. OPTIMISTICALLY YOURS. First, flip a coin to decide which one of you will be an optimist and which one a pessimist. Then, take a situation that either one of you has encountered that day. The pessimist describes that situation in an exaggerated negative way that will be a "downer." Next, your partner describes the same situation in an upbeat and optimistic way that maximizes the positive. When you're finished, change optimist and pessimist roles.

6. ADJECTIVES, ADJECTIVES. Which positive statement has more impact: "You have a nice sense of humor" or "You have a *sparkling* sense of humor." The rather dramatic difference lies in the choice of one single word, an adjective. As an exercise, take positive personality attributes of friends or of yourselves. Then, describe those characteristics using the most descriptive and flattering adjectives possible. This is wonderful practice and it's fun.

Increasing Conversational Compatibility

It is a truism that the general status of a marital relationship can easily be assessed by examining the quality of the communication between a husband and wife. In far too many marriages, couples consistently and quickly drift into conflict, constant criticism, and a sense of estrangement whenever they attempt to talk about anything. Granted, they have many problems and frustrations in day-to-day living, the resolution of which requires understanding and acceptance of one another. On the other hand, how can a couple expect to deal effectively as a team with sensitive issues when they can't casually converse with one another about neutral topics anymore?

To reiterate, regular time spent "just talking" is more important than it seems on the surface in maintaining a healthy marriage. And, bringing back comfortable, casual conversations is an excellent place to start rejuvenating a marriage that has become distant, stressful, and unfulfilling. Conversations build a base of mutually positive experiences that generate sensitivity and awareness. This is a major first step in restoring the closeness between you that has slowly dissipated over the years. It also becomes a base of together-ness that enhances a couple's ability to compatibly resolve the problems that will inevitably confront them.

To bring regular casual conversations back into your relationship, here are some guidelines that have proven helpful to many couples. Remember, relearning how to talk easily together takes time and persistence. Keep at it and give one another room to make mistakes and goof up now and then. With some practice, conversing together will once again become natural and easy.

1. MAKE TIME FOR CONVERSATIONS A HIGH PRIORITY. Despite all that needs to be done each day, taking time to talk to your spouse is an absolute must. Regular time is much more important than big blocks of time. For most couples, thirty minutes or so three or four times each week is an excellent conversational baseline to shoot for.

2. GET OUT OF THE HOUSE WHEN YOU TALK. In the beginning, talking together inside the house is extremely difficult. There are just too many distractions there—the kids, TV, telephones, chores—to really talk easily together. You don't have to go far for your conversations—sitting on the back porch or deck or taking a walk together will do fine.

3. STRICTLY AVOID ALL EMOTIONALLY SENSITIVE OR CONTROVERSIAL SUBJECTS. At first, until you establish comfort and trust with one another, conversations should be easy and stimulating, not hard emotional work. Set aside other times to talk about "heavy" subjects or problems. Remember, to continue, conversations must be a positive experience for you both.

4. TREAT YOUR SPOUSE AS YOU WOULD A GOOD FRIEND. Most people treat friends with kindness and caring. This is not necessarily true of their spouses. In any good marriage, a husband or wife must be a good friend, if not your best friend. Conversationally respond with tact, sensitivity, and awareness so your marital friendship will once again blossom.

5. WORK ON YOUR OWN BAD COMMUNICATION HABITS. To become a better conversationalist, it will be necessary for you to take full responsibility for the bad habits you've slipped into over the years. Solicit feedback about your verbal style from a good friend who will tell you the truth. Sometimes taping a conversation and listening to it helps. Then, work diligently to improve your conversational quality.

6. DO SOMETHING TOGETHER TO TALK ABOUT. Too many couples have nothing to say to one another because they've drifted away from doing fun things together. To stimulate conversation, create an experience to talk about with one another. Take in an interesting movie. Attend a seminar. Play a game of tennis or golf. As you converse, don't forget to laugh and have fun.

One other often-missed point is pertinent here. Many couples complain that they can't talk about their personal or marital problems because of negative communication habits. And it's true. Many of these habits not only put a spouse off or make a husband or wife feel bad, but they may also widen a growing emotional distance between you. Conversely, by learning to comfortably converse with one another in lighthearted ways, a level of trust begins to grow again. As this conversational comfort grows and as bad habits are eliminated, a couple may then find that the stage is set to talk about the big issues, or controversial ones, more easily and without dissension.

At another level, deep down perhaps you've been thinking: "Where did the good life go? We used to have fun together and talk all the time about all kinds of things. Now daily life seems to be a drag, and we never even talk anymore." You're certainly not alone with such feelings. George Bernard Shaw hit the nail on the head when he talked of men and women who had "lost the art of conversation, but not, unfortunately, the power of speech." Think about it. In your marriage, you may not have lost the power of speech. But, the real question is whether stimulating conversations still exist. If the answer is no, it's probably well past time to start talking about it!

Chapter 11

Marital Madness: The Emotional Misuses of Anger at Home

Anger—an unpleasant emotion to be sure. Kids get mad. Adolescents are rebellious and confrontational. And busy adults blow their stacks regularly. The experience of anger—certainly part of the human condition—seems to abound these days. It is obvious that too much of it can ruin relationships, including the marital bond between a husband and wife. And, it does. Every day. No other emotion can produce more personal hurt and destroy intimacy the way unbridled anger can. Even so, it is also true that anger is part of every *healthy* marital relationship.

The question is not whether anger is present, but rather how it is expressed. Some men and women, unfortunately, habitually suppress anger or deny its existence. At the other extreme, many other men and women express far too much anger each day. For this sizable group, defining the real emotional sources of their angry outbursts is helpful. Such introspection is conducive not only to personal well-being, but to improved communication and more loving marital relationships. Witness these scenarios that occur daily in households across the country.

• Brooke, tired from a hectic day at the office and then from a committee meeting at a volunteer agency, finally arrives home. Within minutes, she's taking her daughter to task for some minor infraction that she would let pass if she weren't feeling stretched to the limit. Later, she feels guilty for blowing up.

• After they've had an especially good time together and after he has been feeling particularly close to his fiancee Marge, Dale gets mad. It's obvious to her that he has picked a fight and then withdrawn into himself. It can be days before he's his old self again.

• Late in the day, after being told by a client that his work on a big project just wasn't quite what was wanted, Morrie unmercifully berates his wife. Why? Because the dinner she had thoughtfully prepared just wasn't "right." He's done this so often that she doesn't even care anymore.

• Esther is typically very accommodating and usually yields to others' wishes. But sometimes at home, she unexpectedly becomes intensely angry and habitually tells off any family member who makes even a simple request of her. Sometimes she is surprised at how intense her anger is and doesn't know where it came from.

It is very easy, indeed entirely erroneous, to assume that angry feelings always involve the target of the anger with a legitimate issue to be dealt with. While it is true that anger maturely expressed can help resolve relationship issues, in none of the angry interactions above is this the case. In each situation, the source of anger lies primarily within the individual. That is, the anger being expressed has nothing to do with the other person or that individual's responses. And these men and women exhibit little maturity when expressing this kind of irrational anger.

An immediate perception is that this outpouring of anger is unfair to others . . . and it is. The fact is that because the emotional misuse of anger comes easily, it can become a very bad habit with extremely destructive effects on a marital relationship. The bottom line is that everyone loses when this kind of unfair anger begins to contaminate a relationship. The spouse who "lets go" is in less control and often feels guilty following displays of unwarranted anger. Those on the receiving end learn to become defensive. Over time, a spouse who constantly expresses inappropriate anger may be ostracized. Or, such an outburst may provoke a counterattack by the family member being used as a scapegoat.

The unfortunate end result of misused anger is a strained marital relationship that becomes distant and emotionally unfulfilling. And, all the hurt and pain it causes for both husband and wife are entirely unnecessary. The primary object of eliminating emotional misuses of anger is to help the individual to both resolve personal issues and develop healthier and more mature coping responses. As this occurs, the level of general tension and acrimony in a marriage relationship lessens. Then, both husband and wife feel better and can begin to relax and love one another again.

Certainly, eliminating inappropriate uses of anger cannot be construed to mean that there will not be conflict even in the very best of marital relationships. Differences will always crop up now and then. However, as unfair expressions of anger pass by the wayside, legitimate issues can be addressed in more emotionally mature and positive ways. Then, a husband and wife feel safer and more trusting of one another. With growing trust, a couple has taken another step toward creating "the good life" for themselves.

Understanding Inappropriate Anger

To really understand what the emotional misuse of anger is all about, it is necessary to go beyond the surface of what might appear to be a fairly typical conflict between husband and wife. However, appearances are deceptive. The real problem often lies at a deeper level than the obvious issues that seem to be provoking a confrontation. As a way to begin building a solid psychological foundation for understanding the emotional misuses of anger, here are seven key points to remember.

1. ANGER ITSELF IS NOT AN INAPPROPRIATE EMOTION. At a very fundamental level, the experience of anger is not bad. It is just one of a range of different human emotions, some of which are pleasant and some very uncomfortable. However, while anger itself may be a healthy emotion, the manner in which it is expressed to a husband and wife (or anyone else for that matter!) can range from helpful to extremely destructive. It is truly unfortunate that so many men and women have never been taught to cope with the anger they experience in positive and interpersonally healthy ways. The individual, as well as the marriage relationship, suffers as a result.

2. ANGER SERVES MANY PSYCHOLOGICAL PURPOSES. It is easy but naive to think of anger only in terms of personal conflict. On close examination, that assumption simply doesn't hold water. The fact is that anger can be used to meet a variety of emotional needs. In a surprising number of instances, it is found that expressions of anger are completely independent of the person toward whom it is being discharged. When angry interactions are psychologically scrutinized, it is seen that the individual using them does so to meet selfish personal needs which may not be immediately obvious.

3. EMOTIONAL MISUSES OF ANGER REFLECT UNRESOLVED PERSONAL ISSUES. These inappropriate patterns of using anger may have their origins far in the past. Often these misuses of anger begin during a person's developmental years as a child still living at home. As such, these patterns represent unresolved conflicts that have never been addressed by that individual. Typically, these conflicts persisted and created a vulnerable adult. Now adversely affecting a spouse and children, the individual can't grow until those underlying conflicts are defined and resolved.

4. AN INDIVIDUAL MAY NOT BE FULLY AWARE OF HOW EMOTIONAL NEEDS ARE MET BY ANGER. The expression of anger is typically rationalized by the perceived behavior of someone else, for example, a spouse or children. However, this external justification often masks the hidden purpose of anger. To understand the psychological purpose of anger, the individual must begin to examine himself or herself internally. Until the true purposes of angry outbursts are defined, loved ones may bear the brunt of frequent and emotionally unfair expressions of this often destructive emotion.

5. EXPRESSING INAPPROPRIATE ANGER TOWARD LOVED ONES IS SAFE AND EASY. This unfortunate reality creates many distressed marriages. A spouse and children are most vulnerable to being treated with unwarranted anger because of two factors. First, the consequences are not as great as they are at the office when reprimands or even termination may be the consequence of an inappropriate angry outburst. Second, the closeness of a marital relationship brings with it personal vulnerability. As a result, routine interactions with a spouse can sometimes trigger the underlying and unresolved issues that motivate such anger.

6. "DISINHIBITING FACTORS" MAY EXACERBATE THE PROBLEM. It is generally true that when an individual is feeling emotionally together, undesirable responses are usually not as evident and may disappear entirely. The same is true of the emotional misuses of anger. However, any number of factors loosen personal control and encourage undesirable responses. Primary among them are high levels of chronic stress, excessive fatigue, and use of alcohol or drugs (even small amounts). Some level of relief can be gained by eliminating these disinhibiting factors. However, such efforts do not resolve the causal problem which lies under the surface.

7. PRIMARY RESPONSIBILITY LIES WITH THE PERSON UNFAIRLY DISCHARGING ANGER. In other words, a spouse who is the object of emotional misuse of anger has very limited ability to eliminate the outburst. Even if the recipient of the anger makes changes suggested (or demanded) by the person misusing anger, it may, in fact, help very little and that's a telling diagnostic sign. Why? Because the issue lies within the individual emotionally misusing anger for personal psychological purposes. It is incumbent upon that husband or wife to do some soul searching to discover and resolve the underlying issue that is creating the need to use anger in such unfair and maritally-destructive ways.

Inappropriate Uses of Anger

To gain more insight into your possible misuses of anger, the next step is to identify several recent occasions during which you became angry toward your spouse for questionable reasons. When anger is being misused in a marriage, most of the time a pattern is involved that can be detected with just a little thought. Ask yourself the following kinds of questions to discover and define your pattern. Then ask your spouse to answer the same questions about your anger to give you additional information.

In what setting does your anger most frequently emerge?

What was going on immediately before your outburst?

Who else was involved?

Was the anger expressed disproportionately intense?

Were there any other specific feelings present other than anger?

Does your anger seem to arise at any particular time of day?

Any consistencies you can find will help you narrow your search for an unresolved issue which is generating anger. Once the pattern of your anger has been clarified as much as possible, you are ready to define the specific emotional use it serves. Here are a number of possibilities to consider, along with suggestions for resolving each one. Some of these misuses of anger are more common than others. A few are quite blatant and obvious. Others, more subtle. However, all are emotionally destructive to close and loving marital relationships.

1. ANGER USED TO ESCAPE PERSONAL RESPONSIBILITY. *Example:* When Josh went to run an errand, he found the car out of gas. Frustrated, he immediately and angrily put down his wife, Kara, for "letting things go" around the house. The fact is that *he* had run most of the gas out of the car the day before!

This pattern represents the blaming syndrome. It occurs in men and women who are so personally insecure that they are unable to admit any kind of fault. Responsibility for every problem is always shifted on other people or the circumstances involved. Blaming others for problems is a very common reaction in children. However, in an adult, such blaming is a signal of personal immaturity. At a deeper level, habitually blaming others for any problems or frustrations puts that individual in the position of always being a "victim." This, then, reinforces a negative perception of other people (or the world in general) as either oppressors or incompetents.

RESOLUTION: A first task for the blaming husband or wife is to realize that fallibility is only human. Everyone makes mistakes and goofs up now and then. When this happens, it doesn't mean that you are a bad person or a failure. Begin to openly admit your mistakes. It is a sign of emotional maturity and personal strength. If you blame your spouse without thinking about it, then sincerely and directly apologize. When you do, respect for you will grow, thus setting the stage for closeness to return.

2. ANGER GENERATED BY A SENSE OF FAILURE. *Example:* With so much to get done each day, Shawndra has a tight daily schedule. When unforeseen problems delay her, her impatience quickly turns into anger. Inside, she experiences a deep feeling of failure if she doesn't get everything done she sets out to do each day. Though controlling her frustration with clients and coworkers, she lets her husband have it if the least little thing gets in her way at home.

As life grows busier and more complicated, there is a tendency to speed up to get everything done. One result is hurry-sickness. A husband or wife begins to work faster, talk faster, drive faster . . . and becomes steadily more impatient with anyone or anything that gets in the way. In these individuals, personal self-esteem is too highly linked to total control and to "productivity." For some, the object each day is to get more and more done in a given amount of time. When unforeseen problems prevent completing what has been personally scheduled, the resulting guilt, anxiety, and sense of personal failure generate anger that is often let loose at home.

RESOLUTION: An important first step is to recognize that in a healthy individual, self-esteem cannot be defined by how much is accomplished each day. Give yourself a break. Schedule more reasonably what you absolutely must get done, taking into account the inevitable glitches that will get in your way. Many men and women must also lower the level of their daily goals because they're so high it's impossible to accomplish them. When problems or delays do occur, remind yourself that anger not only isn't necessary, but that it doesn't help. Getting angry is just easier.

3. ANGER DISPLACED FROM ONE SITUATION TO ANOTHER. *Example:* Alex is a calm and usually unruffled attorney for a large firm. When he is occasionally blocked during the negotiation of an important contract, however, he often becomes angry. During the actual negotiation, he smiles and holds it all in because that's what is expected. Later, though, his wife Liz or one of the kids, gets blasted for anything minor that displeases him, even though it was at work he became frustrated.

This bad habit is also known as the "kick-the-cat" problem. A husband or wife becomes angry in a situation in which it would be difficult or extremely inappropriate to express anger directly. Because of possible negative consequences, anger is then suppressed until a safe target becomes available. Unfortunately, the easiest targets of all are found at home. A spouse, children, the dog or cat, sometimes even the door gets it. These innocents receive the brunt of pent-up anger generated elsewhere because they're handy, they're vulnerable, and it's safe to let go.

RESOLUTION: As a first step, calm down. Then, make an attempt to tactfully deal with the real source of your anger. If this proves impossible, ask your spouse (or find an empathic friend) and talk out the situation to defuse angry feelings. You need someone to listen, but not necessarily to give advice. If desired, and as a bonus, your spouse can also help you see your blind spots or, as a couple, you can work toward defining alternative ways of responding to specific situations that will avoid future conflict.

4. ANGER USED AS A MOTIVATIONAL TECHNIQUE. *Example:* Nick grew up in a strict military family. His father consistently used hard spankings, serious threats and ultimatums, and physical intimidation to make him behave. Now, without thinking out what he is doing, Nick habitually intimidates his wife and children the same way. Although he would deny it, in his view it's the only way to get anyone to do anything.

Sometimes called KITSE (Kick In The South End) motivation, this use of anger is favored principally by men and women who believe that the only real motivation is fear. Typically, fear is produced through outbursts of anger (too often in public) accompanied by threats and sometimes physical abuse. An unfortunate by-product of this style is that an adversarial relationship is established with a spouse or children. And, while they may comply with your demands, a relationship based on intimidation breeds resentment. "Respect" generated by fear is not really respect at all, and family relationships always suffer in the long run.

RESOLUTION: There is no substitute for positive incentives and rewards to make others want to do well. But, first you must train yourself to see the positive and consistently comment on it. With praise, encouragement, support, and loving comments, an entire family draws closer and positive motivation grows. Soliciting and respecting others' ideas about how to deal with specific situations and problems also helps. When this happens, a true partnership develops and a cooperative atmosphere at home is created.

5. ANGER EXPRESSED TO REDUCE INTERNAL TENSION.
Example: As coordinator of a volunteer agency, Joanna encounters a myriad of minor frustrations each day that create tension. And, that tension slowly builds during the course of the day. Contained at work, when she goes home, the tension she feels is transformed into intense irritability. Sean, her husband, and the kids usually get the brunt of it.

This is by far the most common emotional misuse of anger. Though origins lie in the tension and frustration arising out of the pressures of a hectic workday, these feelings are usually well-suppressed in the workplace. The individual's sense of appropriateness or of a professional way of relating helps control any unpleasant emotion. Once out of the workplace, however, general tension is quickly transformed into anger and expressed at any opportune target. Again, a spouse or children are very easy targets indeed. After an angry outburst, calm usually returns as tension is reduced. But, the cost to a marital relationship and to the family as a whole is high.

RESOLUTION: The best way to overcome this common problem is to build a transition routine that follows the day's work. Typically requiring about one-half hour, this activity enables a husband or wife to discharge tension built up during the day before it is transformed into anger and expressed at home. The best transition routines are those practiced every day and that involve some physical activity—a short workout, a walk, a bicycle ride with a spouse or the kids.

6. ANGER USED TO CREATE EMOTIONAL DISTANCE.
Example: Growing up, Dan had a very manipulative mother who, sooner or later, would use anything he revealed about his feelings against him. Now married, whenever he and Abby, his wife, experience some real emotional closeness, he inevitably picks a fight right afterwards. Then, he usually stomps out to spend time with his friends.

Although reasonably common, this misuse of anger as a way to reduce the emotional threat of closeness and intimacy is sometimes difficult to spot. Its origin lies in the vulnerability that an insecure man or woman feels in the face of too much closeness to a loved one for too long. To reduce the personal threat and discomfort of too much emotional vulnerability, something is done to reduce intimacy and create psychological distance. Picking a fight is common. So is being very close to a spouse only during a trip out of town. Sometimes it takes the form of always socializing with friends, thereby never being intimately alone with a spouse except for very short periods of time. All these maneuvers are, at their root, defenses against emotional intimacy that are extremely threatening to one vulnerable spouse.

RESOLUTION: Resolving this problem entails developing trust in a spouse. That requires efforts by both partners. The spouse with a fear of closeness must take the risk of revealing inner feelings and thoughts to a husband or wife. Then, that vulnerable individual must make it a point not to withdraw for any reason. The other partner, on the other hand, must never, ever use what has been revealed in ways that hurt or punish during arguments. To do so only makes distrust worse in a spouse who is already distrustful!

7. ANGER RESULTING FROM GIVING TOO MUCH TO OTHERS. *Example:* Cal consistently volunteers when asked to help out citizens' groups and friends. His after-hours commitments are tremendous. As a result, time he used to spend relaxing with his family or fishing, his hobby, has become virtually nonexistent. It's used for community involvements. Simultaneously, he has become quite grouchy and irritable whenever he is at home, which is not much anymore.

No doubt about it. There are many giving people around. They consistently respond to the needs of community, friends, and family. A problem occurs, however, when such men and women fail to give to themselves. With the passage of time, a deep personal resentment grows that often results in angry outbursts directed toward the easiest targets, a spouse or children. Even loved ones are eventually perceived as "takers," and outbursts occur even when a minor request is made. The anger expressed is really a message: "I'm giving and giving to everyone. I'm just not appreciated, and I don't understand why no one is giving anything back to me."

RESOLUTION: A principle of healthy emotional functioning states: "If you want to give to others and feel good about it over the long run, you must consistently give a little bit to yourself along the way." To resolve this problem, the overgiving man or woman must, at all costs, begin to give to himself or herself. A little bit of time, consistently taken, to do something just for you, just for the pleasure of it, is necessary. This may mean saying "no" to new commitments. Or, gradually phasing out of one or two responsibilities. Make sure that the time you gain is used just for you. When you do so, your internal anger dissipates and you will again become a loving (not resentful) spouse.

8. ANGER USED TO GET YOUR WAY. *Example:* It was early in childhood when Doris learned to get her way with her parents by having a tempter tantrum. Now, years later and married, she still does it. Whenever her husband balks, Doris makes his life miserable until she gets what *she* wants—right or wrong. With the resultant distance between them, they can't and don't talk about anything anymore.

As with Doris, this immature ploy is often a holdover from childhood. Unfortunately, many children learn to emotionally coerce parents into giving in by having temper tantrums. In adulthood the same technique is often used in a marriage relationship. Vicious personal attacks on a spouse often occur. Or, there may be a sullen withdrawal with constant indirect jabs at a spouse's self-esteem. The immature message is clear: "I hate you because you won't give me my way." The man or woman who responds this way has never learned to solve problems or differences through open discussion and compromise. Instead, anger is used to browbeat a partner into submission. The usual result is a decline in closeness and a deterioration in the ability to really talk out problems and solve them in ways satisfactory to both.

RESOLUTION: Understanding and respecting others' needs in a marriage, along with finding creative compromises when problems are encountered, requires action by both partners. First, the spouse who is prone to temper tantrums must stifle that impulse and instead seek an open dialogue with a partner. The other spouse must make it a point never to give in to a temper tantrum, while at the same time remaining open and flexible when a dialogue about a problem does begin.

9. ASSERTIVENESS JUSTIFIED BY RIGHTEOUS ANGER. *Example:* Dewayne is assertive only when he becomes intensely angry, usually after feeling slighted many times. At home, with Carol, his spouse, his habit is never to talk about issues or uncomfortable feelings as they develop. Then, after saving up his resentments for weeks or even months, he jumps all over her and becomes irrationally angry. It's usually over some minor incident that, objectively speaking, doesn't really matter.

Far too many basically passive people can be assertive only when they are angry. In fact, they are often not assertive at all! Instead, they are aggressive and attack others. These men and women do not communicate about problems until they feel pushed to the absolute brink. Then self-righteous anger which is called up becomes the impetus to aggressively push back. Because this anger has been saved up and stored from past perceived slights or put-downs, when it comes out it is often disproportionately intense. The scenario usually ends with negative feelings all around, and, of course, the marital relationship suffers.

RESOLUTION: To resolve this misuse of anger in marriage, two fundamental changes are necessary. First, make a commitment to consistently talk with your spouse about even small problems at the time they occur instead of letting them pass and becoming resentful. Then, respond to such problem situations in a calm, direct, and very tactful fashion that is not driven by anger. These changes help you define yourself and your needs in healthier ways within the marital relationship.

Growing Beyond Unfair Anger

The intense and frenetic pace of today's lifestyles certainly creates more than enough frustration and anger to go around. But life is too short, and family relationships too precious, to see them compromised (or even destroyed) by inappropriate and unpleasant displays of anger. And, as already stated, the relationships most prone to the misuse of anger are the marriage or with the children. This is truly unfortunate because family members are victimized by a problem that has nothing to do with them. The only sure remedy is to grow within to completely eliminate inappropriate expressions of anger.

When such emotional growth has occurred and more marital maturity has developed with the elimination of unfair anger, there is usually corresponding improvement in the quality of a marital relationship that may have waned with the years. Both personal and marital benefits of such positive changes slowly and surely become apparent.

1. YOUR HEALTH IS ENHANCED. Evidence has been accumulating for some years that of all forms of stress, walking around constantly angry is the most destructive. It not only erodes healthy emotional functioning, but, over the long run, too much anger may also impair physical health as well. By eliminating the misuses of anger within you, you begin to feel better emotionally *and* physically.

2. SECONDARY NEGATIVE FEELINGS ARE REDUCED. Husbands and wives who misuse anger in a marital relationship often experience damage to their own self-esteem. After becoming unfairly angry, they feel personally down and often quite guilty about it. Further, energy must be exerted to repair the damage done to family relationships. By eliminating misuses of anger, secondary negative feelings are also eliminated and the nice person you really are emerges again.

3. YOUR SELF-ESTEEM RISES. The consistent misuse of anger in a marriage is often a diagnostic signal of low self-esteem. But, misuse of anger also directly lowers self-esteem! By resolving these issues personally and striving toward a more loving marital relationship, self-esteem begins to rise. It frees a husband and wife to again love and be loved in ways that have been lost over the years.

4. PERSONAL MATURITY IS ENHANCED. In short, to define and resolve the underlying issue that generates unfair use of anger means that a personal vulnerability has been removed. As a result, that husband or wife begins to mature emotionally and becomes more secure as a man or woman. The individual then displays less negative sensitivity to others, stronger coping responses, and a sense of completeness not present previously.

Finally, two additional points about the misuse of anger at home are worth making. First, it must be said again that many of the emotional abuses of anger seen in adults are learned in the family during childhood. And, if not modified, these unhealthy expressions of emotion are likely to be picked up by your children and cause problems for them. Striving to create emotionally healthy marital and family relationships for *your* children to model will help them to be healthy and live the good life with their own loved ones later on.

Second, don't forget that the experience of anger consumes tremendous amounts of emotional energy. And, it's all negative energy that does nothing but create more problems in family relationships. Becoming unnecessarily angry just isn't worth it. When you become less prone to inappropriate anger, you not only feel calmer within, but you free energy to reestablish emotional closeness and have good times with your spouse. Then, you'll both have taken another step toward getting better together and living the good life for yourselves.

The message is clear. Making the effort to mature beyond easy, but interpersonally destructive uses of anger has tremendous benefits not only for you, but for your entire family. A new and more easygoing you will emerge; your spouse and children will like and respond to the new you in positive ways. Little things won't bother you as much. Family members won't be apprehensive in your presence. You'll also become more comfortable with yourself as your self-esteem rises. No doubt about it. Eliminating the misuses of anger in your life is a most worthwhile personal goal.

On the other hand, should you choose to let inappropriate emotional sources of anger remain, you must accept the consequences of remaining at the mercy of your mouth. Cutting right to this point, someone wryly commented: "Speak when you're angry, and you will make the best speech you'll ever regret!" Let such marital orators beware. The consequences to the health of your marriage may be very serious. Whatever your age, you may have already made more than enough such platform speeches to an apprehensive family audience to last a lifetime.

Chapter 12

Conflict and Communication: Resolving Marital Differences Amicably

It's certainly true that relationships of any kind are based on communication. And, it goes without saying that communication in a marriage involves many different levels of relating. In a good relationship, husband and wife might banter and joke around when first meeting after work. A bit later, they sit down for a few minutes to talk about the day and the comings and goings of folks at the office or in the neighborhood. Still later, a problem situation looms that must be sorted out and resolved. Regularly, they have romantic moments and share the most intimate thoughts and feelings. No question about it. Without good communication, there just can't be a good marriage relationship.

Conversely, many once-good marriage relationships grow very distant and unfulfilling when communication between a husband and wife begins to break down. Unfortunately, many relationships end for the same reason. In fact, when couples complain about the quality of their relationship, the lament is classic and very telling: "We just can't communicate anymore." What this statement really means is that negative ways of relating have overwhelmed all that is positive between them. When pressed, the concerns become more specific:

"We seem to bicker an awful lot more these days than we ever did in the past."

"Whenever we have a big argument, it takes us both longer to get over it and back to normal again."

"We argue all the time over little things that don't really mean anything."

"Every time I say anything at all, my spouse either attacks me or withdraws and won't talk."

"When we fight, it gets very hurtful and nothing ever seems to get resolved."

"These days, I take things the wrong way and get defensive in spite of myself."

"Every little disagreement we have seems to escalate into a big fight."

"Whenever there's a problem and we try to talk about it, there always has to be a winner and a loser, and I'm tired of it."

These complaints reflect marital relationships where the ability to relate easily and openly has declined. As this process occurs, a husband and wife grow further apart and, to protect themselves, begin to maintain an emotional distance from one another. To make matters worse, the credibility of anything one spouse says to the other often drops to zero. Helpful suggestions and good advice are rejected out of hand. Any kind of feedback, however well-intended, evokes a defensive response or an outright counterattack from an offended partner.

When this point is reached, both partners feel vulnerable and, as a result, are very wary of one another. Having been hurt in the past, each questions the other's motives and is likely to take anything the other says the wrong way. As this defensive posture grows stronger and more pervasive, good times spent together correspondingly diminish in lieu of constant bickering or taking jabs at one another. Ironically, this husband and wife were at one time very close and could talk about almost anything with one another for hours at a time! Now their communication, unless it is kept very bland, is chock full of potential conflict and misunderstanding.

As frequently as such marital communication problems occur, they don't have to happen at all. In fact, even touchy subjects and areas of deep personal disagreement can be handled without damage to a relationship. Not convinced? Take a look at these situations:

• Two attorneys battle it out with everything they have in the courtroom, yet remain good friends afterward.

• College students on a debating team do their level best to beat their opponents and then go out with them for a pizza.

• Negotiating a new contract, labor and management representatives drive hard bargains, but eventually come to an agreement and then continue to work together amicably.

Granted, in these settings the individuals are relating within the framework of clearly defined adversarial roles. However, the real difference is that in each of the above situations, procedural guidelines keep communication about the issues respectful, courteous, and to the point. Because of adherence to these protocols, the personal relationships among the parties involved do not suffer much, if at all.

Certainly, these very same guidelines can also work beautifully in marriage relationships which are challenged by problems. At the same time, more often than not this simply does not happen and the entire relationship eventually begins to suffer. There are several reasons why basic courtesy and respect for a partner break down when a husband and wife encounter a problem.

1. FEELINGS. Living life each day and meeting personal responsibilities in every part of life generates many kinds of feelings. At first, early in a relationship, positive and fulfilling feelings outweigh the negative. However, as life becomes busier and more intense and as leisure time needed for emotional recovery declines, frustration, fatigue, stress, resentment, and outright anger grow and become dominant.

2. FAMILIARITY. Living with a marriage partner for years permits a husband and wife to get to know one another intimately. Along with an awareness of a partner's strengths comes knowledge of vulnerabilities, soft spots, weaknesses, and gaps in ability to cope. Unfortunately, these awarenesses, along with real and per-ceived personal slights, often become weapons to be used when there is conflict.

3. FREEDOM. At home, husbands and wives are freer to let out negative feelings toward one another, feelings that are often generated in other parts of life. And, these feelings are expressed to one another in ways that would never occur in public. Respect and courtesy, in addition to maintaining focus on the real issues, dissolve in lieu of loud, hurtful, and punitive remarks. Does famil-iarity breed contempt? Yes, too often in a marriage.

As time passes and as frustrations in every part of life grow, this volatile mix of negative feelings, familiarity with a spouse's vulnerabilities, and freedom to openly express oneself at home steadily increases conflict and creates more emotional distance in a marriage relationship. In fact, as this occurs, the entire relationship begins to spiral downward. Self-esteem of both partners begins to plummet as emotional battering (or constant picking at one an-other) continues and often worsens. Intimacy declines as defensive ways of relating and distrust of a partner become the norm.

Slowly but surely, if this type of communication breakdown is not stopped, a marital crisis grows. If caught early enough, such crises can be entirely prevented with focused efforts by both partners.

If relating has already started to become excessively harsh and punitive, growing marital distance can be rolled back. However, under these circumstances it may take some time. In either case, some personal understandings must form the foundation for change. Here are some ideas to think about as a way for both of you to get started.

Two Principles of Conflict Resolution

It is a mistake to assume that the difference between a poor marriage and a good relationship between spouses lies in the presence or absence of conflict. The fact is that conflict occurs in all marriages, good and bad. The real difference is that in a good marriage, differences and problems get resolved in emotionally healthy ways that are satisfactory to both partners. Further, finding such solutions does not damage the relationship. In a poor marital relationship, conflict is present, but problems don't get resolved. Husband and wife relate in ways that erode their closeness and damage the trust they have in one another.

At first glance, understanding the dynamics of conflict and conflict resolution seems to involve very complex issues. However, when examined from a psychological perspective, certain fundamental principles and strategies not only work, but also form the basis for positive ways to address and resolve differences amicably. To bring conflict in a marriage under personal control and thereby enhance positive relating when problems do arise, two principles of conflict resolution form the foundation.

PRINCIPLE #1: REDUCING UNHEALTHY RELATING REQUIRES ENHANCING PERSONAL PERSPECTIVE AND THE ABILITY TO COPE, SO THAT INSIGNIFICANT EVENTS DO NOT ESCALATE INTO UNNECESSARY CONFLICT. The bottom line is that many conflicts in marital (and other) relationships are entirely unnecessary. They do not result from real or legitimate differences that must be resolved between two individuals. Negative feelings, differing perceptions, or personal frustrations that have nothing to do with a spouse cause conflict. Adopting humane time management strategies, respecting physical limitations, accepting minor glitches that can't be changed, and eliminating emotional misuses of anger all help to prevent unnecessary marital arguments or fights.

PRINCIPLE #2: HEALTHY CONFLICT RESOLUTION NECESSITATES ADDRESSING DIFFERENCES IN WAYS THAT

KEEP COMMUNICATION OPEN AND NONDEFENSIVE, SO THAT ISSUES CAN BE DISCUSSED AND RESOLVED IN A SATISFACTORY MANNER. When legitimate differences or problems are encountered in a marital relationship, the primary goal is to keep communication from deteriorating into either defensive withdrawal or counterattack. Partners require trust in each other not to hurt or attack in unfair ways, along with adhering to healthy ways of addressing problems. However, this trust by a partner must be earned. Once it is lost through hurtful or punitive responses in the heat of conflict, it takes time and commitment to change and recreate enough trust to keep communication open in the face of a problem.

Controlling Aggressive Responses

At worst, interaction between marriage partners comes to be dominated by aggressive responses by one or the other or both. Aggressive responses consist of attacking or other offensive (literally and figuratively) ways of relating. When this happens, the probability of a positive outcome dramatically drops. Why? Because aggressive communication provokes defensive (*i. e.*, protective) responses by a partner. Then, as you already know, the real issue tends to become lost as the two parties involved either shift into an attack mode or withdraw physically or psychologically from one another.

To prevent aggressive responses from taking over, husbands and wives must make it a point to prevent any one of the three basic needs from becoming primary motivators during conflict resolution. These responses are very easily aroused and correspondingly difficult to control once brought into play. However, with conscious awareness and commitment to positive relating when problems arise, it can be done. Most of the time, only one of these needs is primary in any given individual, although all three may be brought into play if "discussion" of a particular issue deteriorates enough.

1. DOMINANCE NEEDS. Here, the fundamental motivation is to control the other person or the situation. Psychologically, this is a way to reduce the perceived threat of being controlled and subjugated by others, particularly by a spouse. As the motivation to control and avoid being controlled takes over, the end result is that reasoned and open discussion of the core issue either becomes extremely difficult or disappears entirely.

2. COMPETITIVE NEEDS. When competitive motivation is present, the intent is simply to win at any cost. While competition itself is not bad, this need becomes very destructive when compromise solutions to problems are required. Discussion quickly degenerates into a "your way" or "my way" contest of wills. Typically, the end result is a selfish solution with one spouse the resentful loser, or at best, a stalemate with no resolution.

3.   REVENGE NEEDS.   The basic drive here is to punish a husband or wife. Not only do emotionally hurtful responses take discussion away from the issues, but they create a widening wedge of distrust between two people. Further, punishment damages a partner's self-esteem and arouses very strong emotions. This, then, creates the perfect climate for a very volatile situation to develop.

YOUR FIRST DECISION in effective conflict resolution is to prevent any of these three needs from producing aggressive responses toward your spouse. Sometimes such maladaptive responses are so ingrained they are almost automatic. It often helps if both spouses monitor one another with caring reminders when aggressive responses are taking over. If done tactfully, personal awareness grows because these kinds of responses feel uncomfortably different than healthy ones. Eventually, self-monitoring becomes possible and the problem of aggressive responses can be virtually eliminated.

Reducing Angry Interactions

Now, with the understanding that aggressive responses triggered during conflict resolution are decidedly unhelpful, the question then becomes what to do with any anger that you do feel. After all, anger is not only a normal emotion, but one that is extremely difficult, if not impossible, to eliminate entirely. However, a number of additional decisions can be made to help defuse angry feelings. Before those decisions can be defined, you must understand first of all that more often than not, the experience of anger is not a true feeling.

Anyone who experiences anger would immediately argue that anger is indeed real! And, at the experience level, that fact certainly cannot be denied. However, what is meant by the idea that anger is not a real feeling is that often it is instead a meta-feeling. To understand how angry meta-feelings can trigger unnecessary conflict, this term must be defined.

META-FEELING: *A feeling that is derived from and has as its root another emotion.*

In other words, a base feeling is aroused within an individual which is then transformed into anger, the meta-feeling, and is overtly experienced as such. The transformation of base feelings into anger can occur very quickly, sometimes instantaneously. And, in some men and women, such changes have become so habitual that they are no longer consciously aware of the base feelings unless there is a concerted attempt to define them.

When deeper feelings that have transformed into anger are examined, seven common base emotions are found. No matter how well-adjusted a man or woman may be, in all probability at least one or two of these feelings are habitually transformed into anger in any given individual.

1. FEAR. *Example*: A parent whose child runs out in front of a car experiences instantaneous fear which then quickly turns into anger. The common transformation of fear into anger typically occurs very rapidly. The base fear may involve any number of issues either personal or interpersonal, but the underlying feeling that spurs the transformation into anger is always some form of emotional or physical threat.

2. LOSS. *Example*: A man or women whose job is terminated when the company reorganizes experiences a deep burning anger. Virtually any kind of significant loss can quickly generate anger within an individual. When a loss is a major one, anger—even irrational blaming anger—is a normal stage of the grieving process. As healthy grieving progresses, the loss is reconciled and the anger then begins to dissipate and eventually disappear.

3. PERSONAL HURT. *Example*: A husband calls his wife "stupid" for making a specific decision, and she becomes extremely angry. Basically, any interaction that damages the self-esteem of an individual is likely to generate anger. And, the more insecure that man or woman is to begin with, the easier and more likely it is that anger will be generated. When personal hurt is thought to be deliberately inflicted, the anger is usually more intense.

4. EMOTIONAL SENSITIVITY. *Example*: A husband who has been teased all his life about being "fat" overreacts with anger whenever anyone brings up his weight. Here, past hurt is so intense that benign, even helpfully intended remarks are likely to be misinterpreted. Such comments bring up old feelings of rejection or hurt that are then transformed into anger. Almost everyone has at least one such sore spot.

5. INTERNAL TENSION. *Example*: An individual who has encountered many minor frustrations during the day becomes furious with other drivers on the way home. Internal tension or anxiety often generates irritability or anger. Part of the reason is that this individual's ability to cope effectively is diminished by a high level of internal tension. Then, with tension transformed into anger, it is discharged when an insignificant event triggers it.

6. FEELINGS OF FAILURE. *Example*: Husbands or wives become angry when they are criticized—once again—about something they did or didn't do. Often, feelings of failure, or of not adequately meeting expectations, can arouse intense anger in susceptible individuals. The failure may lie in not meeting one's own expectations or those of others. This emotional transformation is exacerbated when the individual has historically been on the receiving end of constant criticism.

7. PHYSICAL DISCOMFORT. *Example*: An individual who has a bad cold becomes angry in a situation that would ordinarily be taken in stride. Significant loss of sleep, a physical ailment, or hormonal fluctuations may all generate anger. The ability of the individual to cope effectively with daily frustrations is weakened. This situation can often be prevented by taking care of oneself and respecting physical limitations.

YOUR SECOND DECISION comes after you've decided not to allow any anger you do feel to turn into aggressive responses. The focus of this second decision is to deal effectively with any anger that is being experienced in ways that are helpful to you and to the successful resolution of a problem situation. At this point, two options are available.

OPTION A: TO DESCRIBE YOUR ANGER TO THE OTHER PERSON. The individual steps back from the emotion of anger and indicates that it is present to another person. Further, it is described in a fashion that is not likely to arouse a defensive reaction. This is a far better choice than to act it out by letting the direct expression of anger trigger aggressive responses. A neutral statement that calmly describes one's anger seems to be best: "I have angry feelings right now."

OPTION B: TO DESCRIBE THE UNDERLYING FEELING THAT IS CREATING THE ANGER. This is the best option because it often effectively short-circuits any kind of angry response. At times, it is difficult to determine the underlying feeling, but with practice it becomes much easier. It is interesting that after such deeper feelings have been personally acknowledged, problems can usually be discussed calmly and resolved more easily. Again, a simple statement is best: "That really hurt my feelings."

Note: It is often very helpful for a husband or wife to respond to underlying or base feelings instead of the meta-feelings (anger) being displayed by a partner. Such responses often help not only to understand what the true feelings are, but also to defuse the anger being generated by those feelings. When such empathic statements are on target, an angry husband or wife feels understood, and the stage is set to really talk about and resolve the issue at hand. Simple direct responses that show you understand and care will usually be accepted: "That must have really hurt your feelings."

Deciding Not to Become Angry

YOUR THIRD DECISION is perhaps less obvious than the first two. It involves a decision not to become angry at all. Of course, this is not going to be possible one hundred percent of the time. Sometimes anger will be aroused no matter how well you cope. On the other hand, many small incidents occur each day when an individual can consciously decide not to become upset or angry because of them. In fact, most of the time these small events represent the routine glitches and unforeseen problems that cannot possibly be prevented and that are a normal part of daily life.

Look at it this way. You already know that a typical husband or wife who is established in a career, who owns a home, and who has a family to care for is going to encounter no less than ten to fifteen minor problems and inconsequential but frustrating events every day. Because these minor glitches cannot be eliminated, controlled, prevented, or even anticipated, it is an exercise in futility to waste energy becoming angry about them. You also know that examples of minor daily problems are legion because you've experienced them.

- An important telephone call comes in just as you are about to catch your ride to work.
- Your teen finally comes clean and tells you about poor grades that will be brought home this grading period.
- At the office, two key employees working with you on an important project with a close deadline call in sick.
- While you check on arrangements for a business trip, the hotel can't find the reservation you made weeks before.
- You've been playing "telephone tag" with another person for three days now.
- While making dinner, one of the kids has a problem and the vegetables burn.

• On your way to work, you discover that one tire is low and probably going flat.

• You give your last three dollars to your son or daughter for a school item and find you now have no lunch money.

• Trying to fix a broken lamp, you must track down a neighbor who borrowed a tool and didn't return it.

• On a trip to the store, you completely forget to buy an item that your spouse specifically requested.

The litany of life's small problems goes on an on. However, by learning to accept them calmly as a normal part of life, you can significantly reduce angry feelings, eliminate aggressive responses, and effectively prevent subsequent relationship problems. Begin to learn this very important skill by keeping an important adage right in the forefront of your mind: *"Life is mind over matter. If you don't mind, it doesn't matter."* Then, as you decide to become more accepting and to "go with the flow" when small problems crop up, here are some techniques that will help you do so more easily.

1. STAY OUT OF A "VICTIM" ROLE. You create anger when you slip into a negative mindset: "They are doing this deliberately just to create problems for me." This is the victim mentality, which in most cases is simply not true. Most problems occur inadvertently due to human error, fallibility, or some necessity that just happens to affect you. As you begin to understand that these minor events are not personal, you can remain calm more easily.

2. DECIDE THAT YOU CANNOT CONTROL EVERYTHING. Some men and women believe that if they only tried hard enough, they could free themselves of these kinds of small problems. Lots of luck! No individual is in control of everything. When small problems occur, stop and make a conscious decision: "This is not a big deal and I refuse to become upset about it." As time passes, making such decisions will become easier and almost automatic.

3. PUNISH YOURSELF FOR BECOMING ANGRY. Self-imposed punishments help when you become irrationally angry at some minor and inconsequential event. Make yourself go around the block and "do it right" the second time when you get upset at another driver. At home, set up a "goof box" in which you put a dollar for every expletive that slips out. Or, give yourself a reward if you don't let anything upset you for twenty-four hours.

4. USE IMAGERY TO PRACTICE MAINTAINING PERSPEC-TIVE. Behavior rehearsal using imagery is very effective in reinforcing calm acceptance of life's little irritations. On a regular basis, find a quiet place to relax, close your eyes, and visualize yourself in a very pleasant setting. Then, see yourself encountering a small problem or glitch, but visualize yourself handling it very calmly without any anger or irritation whatsoever.

5. MAKE IT A POINT TO BE COURTEOUS. Always giving others the benefit of the doubt and remaining ever courteous helps to avoid "foot in mouth disease" when small problems are encountered. Not only do you remain calm and in control (in lieu of allowing a minor event to create unwarranted outrage), but you come across to others as an individual with dignity, personal respect, and class. Because courtesy is contagious, you will get back the same.

Tactfully Talking About Touchy Topics

Even in the very best of marriage relationships, touchy subjects must be discussed from time to time. The issues might involve critical feedback, inadvertent hurts, decisions that must be made, different ways of doing things, or simple misunderstandings. Someone has accurately defined tact as "the art of making a point without making any enemy." How true! And tact is an art that is essential in any close and fulfilling marriage. Unfortunately, in busy lives, as frustration builds, insensitive responses, hurtful remarks, and discourteous responses flourish.

When a sensitive issue must be addressed, there are definitely some do's and don'ts as far as what to say and how to say it are concerned. Do keep in mind that as communication in a marriage deteriorates, a husband and wife become extremely sensitive to any slight, criticism, or perceived put-down from a partner. You can begin to rebuild your trust in one another by giving your spouse the benefit of the doubt in what is being said instead of overreacting. Now, here are fourteen specific suggestions to get you both started.

1. LISTEN CAREFULLY TO YOUR PARTNER. Give your partner your undivided attention. Good eye contact and expressed concern convey the right message. When your partner is describing the problem, make it a point not to interrupt, withdraw, or become defensive and try to justify yourself. All this does is shift the interaction away from the problem that must be resolved. Then, your spouse will probably extend this same kind of courtesy to you when you respond.

2. AVOID MAKING ACCUSATIONS. When life becomes busy, most people have a tendency to ask many direct questions to get information quickly. Very direct questions combined with the pronoun "you" come across as an accusation (whether intended or not) that often produces a defensive reaction from a spouse. For a better response, reduce the number of questions and eliminate the accusative pronoun "you" (as in "Why did you . . .?"). Instead, change questions into neutral statements: "The lights were left on."

3. ELIMINATE SELFISH SOLUTIONS. This guideline is especially helpful when a decision needs to be made or a compromise must be reached. Each partner defines the most selfish solution to the problem. After those two self-serving solutions are automatically eliminated, subsequent discussion can then focus on in-between options. When a couple does this, the win-lose struggle that contaminates so much marital problem-solving is also eliminated. Finding mutually satisfactory solutions then becomes much easier.

4. DO NOT USE PROVOCATIVE LANGUAGE. In short, neutral descriptive statements of a problem work best. Name calling, put-downs, judgmental remarks, swearwords, personal attacks, and martyristic speeches are emotionally provocative. "You were stupid and inconsiderate to make that #@!%*& mess; you just don't care about me," just isn't helpful. Instead, try: "There's a mess here." Period. Remember that mature men and women attack problems, not people.

Note: Your posture and gestures can also be extremely provocative. If you find yourself pointing your finger at a spouse or shaking your fist, stop immediately. If you find it hard to control your gestures, sit down while discussing a problem and keep your hands permanently folded in your lap.

5. DO NOT RAISE YOUR VOICE. When angry, many men and women have a natural tendency to turn up the volume of what they are saying. Then a spouse does the same. The end result is a shouting match in which both partners are trying to overwhelm the other. As this occurs, hurtful or insensitive remarks emerge to make the situation worse. By making it a point to speak in a normal tone of voice, you not only control yourself, but also reduce the tendency of your partner to become loud.

6. VALIDATE YOUR PARTNER'S POINT OF VIEW. When there is a difference of opinion or perspective, both husband and wife want their viewpoints heard. More often than not, both perspectives have validity. When your partner has stated a point of view, validate it: "I see what you are saying" or "I can understand how you feel that way." When a husband or wife listens and acknowledges that a spouse's feelings and perceptions are valid, it helps that partner to relax and discuss possible solutions.

7. FOCUS ON FINDING SOLUTIONS, NOT "REASONS WHY." Frequently, finding mutually satisfactory, reasonable solutions to problems is lost as the focus of problem solving. Instead, "why," something happened dominates discussion. The fact is that whatever happened *did* happen. Instead, emphasize how to prevent similar problems in the future. There are virtually no problems for which reasonable solutions can't be found if caring husbands and wives set their minds to it.

8. CHOOSE AN OPTIMAL TIME TO TALK. Many men and women have developed a bad habit: If they see it or think it, they say it. This may not only produce indiscreet comments socially, but it becomes very destructive when you're trying to solve a problem. The following times are far from optimum for discussing problems: when your spouse is hurrying out the door, at 2:30 a.m. when your husband or wife is asleep, or in front of friends. Waiting a bit until you find a time when you both can talk comfortably also helps you calm down and gain more objectivity.

9. FOCUS YOUR DISCUSSION ON A PROBLEM. When a problem arises, discussion often strays far from the issues. Four major irrelevancies which tend to occur must all be eliminated: shifting to past problems, bringing up other present problems, responding to emotions instead of the issue at hand, and trying to figure out the "why's" instead of working on solutions. When any discussion is limited to calmly attempting to resolve one circumscribed issue right now, then the probability of a successful outcome goes up.

10. ADD STATEMENTS OF LOVE AND AFFECTION. Giving negative feedback to a partner or addressing a touchy issue between you is much easier for a partner to accept if it is combined with sincere statements of positive regard. "I do love you" is certainly not too strong nor is "I care deeply about you." Sometimes it helps to preface discussing the issue with: "Please don't take this the wrong way; I'm really trying to be helpful." Such statements reduce the probability of defensive reactions. Some couples even find it helpful to hold hands while discussing sensitive issues.

11. USE INDIRECT APPROACHES. Sometimes, a direct face-to-face discussion of a problem isn't necessary or even helpful. These days, even finding the time to talk about a small problem may be a big problem! With minor issues, indirect approaches sometimes work better. For example, leave your partner a note tactfully describing the problem and a possible solution. Or, leave a message on his or her computer at work (E-mail). Don't forget to combine your message with a statement of love and affection.

12. DON'T LET YOURSELF BE PROVOKED. In other words, don't allow anything your spouse says to drag you down to the same immature level of functioning. Maintaining your dignity when discussing touchy subjects results in several payoffs. First, not allowing yourself to "lose it" does a lot to keep the interaction calm and respectful. Second, if your spouse becomes abusive, your maturity will serve as a mirror for your partner to see himself or herself. This positive effect is lost if you lose control.

13. AGREE TO DISENGAGE. If at any time during discussion of a problem your self-control (or that of your partner) is weakening, agree to take a break and come back to the problem later. This allows you both to calm down, regain personal control, and develop some objectivity about the problem. A simple statement is enough: "Honey, we're both getting too emotional. Let's stop now before we both say things we'll regret and talk about this again later today."

14. REINFORCE THE PARTNERSHIP APPROACH. A marriage is a partnership where two people live together *and* solve life's problems as a team. When you're talking about problems, it helps to take some personal responsibility for solving the problem while emphasizing the "we" approach to "our" problem. "We can figure out this problem by working together. Let's really try" is the kind of response that helps produce a cooperative effort and reduce an adversarial "you versus me" approach to solving problems.

Adding Class to Conflict

One of the most telling changes that might have occurred as your life became more hectic is that deep down inside, you've become an angry person. And, more likely than not, so has your spouse. You may both be filled with far too much stress, frustration, and resentment. Most of the time, you manage to hold it in at work, but then it comes spilling out in very destructive and aggressive ways at home. You may have even noticed that your husband or wife and children have become wary of you because of your outbursts. The hurt and damage to self-esteem you've inflicted on them may be starting to show.

You may not even be fully aware just how angry you are inside

. . . until it begins to explode over little things that really don't matter (and that wouldn't even bother you if you felt better). This unfortunate but common state of affairs makes a kind and tactful discussion about virtually anything extremely difficult. In short, you're unhappy, but worse yet, you've lost a lot of class. Class is easy to define.

CLASS: *The ability to relate with unshakable personal dignity and respect toward other people, manifested by consistently courteous responses, no matter how personally distressing the situation.*

As you've lost your ability to relate with kindness and courtesy, not only have you lost some class, but you've made a spectacle of yourself on far too many occasions. In the process of overreacting, you've repeatedly hurt the feelings of loved ones. Then you feel bad because of your unnecessary outbursts, and your own self-esteem is damaged because of what you've done. You don't like yourself and what you've become anymore. Further, your spouse may love you, but may not like you very much these days. And, vice versa.

All of these problems can be reversed, but how you deal with anger is a personal decision that you must make for yourself. You can choose not to become angry. And, you can choose to express anger in healthy and nondestructive ways once it is felt. By making these healthy choices, in a broad sense you are making a decision to recover personal control of your life from within. And, you are deciding that it's time to reestablish comfort with your husband or wife and move closer to living the good life together. It's a wonderful feeling to begin breaking out of old habits and easy but destructive ways of responding. You'll become a class act once again and everyone around you will soon recognize it.

With your commitment to reestablish control of your emotions in general and your anger in particular, a number of preventive measures can be of immense help. Here are six of the most important. Adopting those that apply to you will help you personally, as well as your marital relationship.

1. DO SOMETHING FOR YOURSELF REGULARLY. If you give to everyone else, but not to yourself, you will eventually become deeply resentful. And, your resentment will take on an angry, martyristic flavor: "I work so hard and no one cares about me." To reduce this kind of anger, it is necessary to take a little bit of time to enjoy yourself on a daily basis, if possible.

2. REFRAIN FROM SAYING THREE OR FOUR CRITICAL THINGS A DAY. As pressure on you increases, you don't feel good and your perceptions reflect your feelings. You see negative things around you and you comment on them constantly. These critical comments create even more distance in your marriage. For more closeness, zip it. Don't make those three or four choice comments a day; just let them go by.

3. GIVE REGULAR POSITIVE FEEDBACK TO OTHERS. Keep in mind this simple principle of human nature: Those who receive consistent positive feedback are then much more likely to listen to and accept needed criticism when it is tactfully given. If all others hear from you is criticism and negative comments, your husband or wife, even your children, will quickly tune you out.

4. RESPECT YOUR PHYSICAL LIMITATIONS. As you age, your body simply cannot handle abuse as it did years ago. Chronic loss of sleep, bad eating habits, and lack of exercise all contribute to diminished ability to cope. And, weakened coping capacity leads to angry overreactions to even minor events. By taking care of yourself, your ability to handle routine problems is enhanced.

5. TOUCH BASE DAILY WITH YOUR SPOUSE. One of the best ways to prevent glitches and miscommunication is to take a few minutes every day to touch base with your spouse. At this time, you can discuss schedules, who will be doing what when, and the times you will be together. Without this regular but very critical time, misunderstandings mount and irritability begins to build.

6. DO NOT DRINK AND DISCUSS PROBLEMS. Many couples consistently have horrendous arguments only when they've had a few drinks. They say and do things that would be absolutely unthinkable when cold sober. Make it a point never to try to discuss problems when drinking. For even better results, make it a point to drop drinking altogether as a way to relax!

As you both strengthen your commitment to getting better together, deciding to handle conflict in better ways is giving a wonderful gift to yourselves as a married couple. At the same time, you will be giving an even greater gift to your children. The kids will grow up seeing an emotionally close relationship between two adults who can resolve their differences amicably. Then, as adults, they will know how to do it because they've observed it for years. Sadly, many children grow to adulthood who, while bright and well-educated, have no earthly idea how to build a healthy marriage relationship because they've never seen one!

And, as you get better together and the emotional distance between you disappears, you'll become good friends, even best friends, once again. The lonely feelings, born of distrust and distance, that have been part of your life for years will soon disappear because you'll be putting a high priority on taking care of yourselves and one another. The fear that you're not going to make it personally and as a couple will also fade away. Who knows, as destructive angry interactions disappear, you might even find that you'll fall head over heels in love with one another again. And, you'll never tire of getting along better—together. Remember the immortal words of Mae West: "Too much of a good thing is wonderful!"

Chapter 13

The LAST Factors:
Four Essential Ingredients
for a Fulfilling Marriage

Having a partner to share life's joys and sorrows is at once a source of strength and a wellspring of personal fulfillment. For most, it's so much better than facing the vicissitudes of life alone that it's a major reason why marriage is here to stay. Furthermore, as children grow toward adulthood, most of them envision themselves as adults marrying and raising children and eventually nurturing their grandchildren. As it has been for generations, marriage is the cornerstone of family life and remains an essential part of the "good life" for most men and women. That's the good news.

The bad news is something that you've already begun to realize. It's that maintaining a strong and healthy marriage relationship over a lifetime is much more difficult now than at any time in the past. The obvious pitfalls are well-known. There has been much recent publicity about resultant spouse and child abuse as pressures build and anger is expressed at home. Certainly, there is increased use of alcohol and drugs among far too many successful and educated men and women. Talk shows and articles have documented the staggering numbers of men and women who have been unfaithful to their spouses. These are the big social issues that make the headlines.

While these problems are an undeniable reality in today's society, to believe that these are the major causes of failed or unfulfilling marital relationships would be erroneous. The fact is that most marriages that eventually end don't do so because of a few very blatantly destructive events. Rather, most are destroyed by a thousand and one small problems and hurts that occur over years. Sometimes, these small problems or differences eventually culminate in bigger and more publicly recognized problems. And, just as often, they don't.

In stress management, someone wryly said: "There are two rules for living these days. Rule #1: Don't sweat the small stuff. Rule #2: It's all the small stuff." The same is true for marriages that fall apart.

The root cause is that myriad of small decisions, unwarranted remarks, insensitive responses, unresolved differences, and consequent emotional neglect. The cumulative effects produce an end result that is as unfortunate as it is destructive to the marriage: A man and woman, once in love and very close, begin to grow apart while living together. Eventually, if the hurt and neglect continue, they go their separate ways.

The most unfortunate part of most failed relationships is that they simply don't have to happen. Too many men and women just forget to say those three important words to one another anymore. And, for some who do, the words simply do not ring true. In essence, and perhaps at the risk of simplifying matters too much, the trick of keeping a marriage healthy and strong is to bring "I love you" into believable terms for your marriage partner every single day. In short, love must be communicated through actions, not words!

Furthermore, in those marriage relationships that remain close and fulfilling, certain kinds of responses are almost always present. Or, conversely, in those relationships that are falling apart, it is interesting to note what kinds of interpersonal behaviors are consistently absent. These critical elements are by no means infinite in number. In fact, their numbers are actually quite few, but they represent core elements in any good relationship. For marriage partners who are growing apart, each of these kinds of responses must be reintroduced into their relationship and practiced enough to become a natural part of how they relate each day.

At this juncture, here's a riddle for you to think about: "What do an ear, a mouth, a shoulder, and a hand all have in common?" Your immediate answer might be: "Well, they're all parts of the human body." Certainly, you would be right, but think about these four things in terms of what a good relationship is all about. In fact, in relationship terms, the correct answer reflects four core elements in any good marriage. They are all critical modalities for giving of oneself to a husband or wife: Listening (ear), Apologizing (mouth), Support (shoulder), and Touching (hand). Put them together and the first letter of each one becomes an easily remembered acronym: LAST.

To bring these LAST factors back into your marriage, or to build them if they've never been present, requires a positive attitude and some know-how. Begin by understanding these five essential parts of any marital change process.

1. PERSPECTIVE on what is important in a marriage. Many men and women these days come from homes where parents simply did not model healthy relationship skills for their children. The net result is that the kids, now adults, have to gain a clear perspective on what a close relationship is all about without the benefit of watching their parents or from personal experience.

2. FORGIVENESS for what has happened in the past. That is, the neglect, the hurts, and the insensitive responses that have created a giant wedge keeping marriage partners defensive and apart must be put aside. It is critical that both partners make a joint decision to improve their relationship. On that day, they can begin to focus their efforts on making positive changes.

3. INITIATIVE is essential to change. Begin to make needed changes yourself. Don't wait for your husband or wife to start and then follow along. The changes required are beneficial for individuals as well as for their relationship together. Understand that these critical relationship skills are as important in friendships and in parenting as in a marriage.

4. RECEPTIVITY to new responses that your partner is making. Be aware that new responses may make your spouse feel awkward or that they may be emotionally difficult. Because of this, make it a point not to diminish or reject new responses in any way. Instead, encouragement and positive reinforcement will insure that those responses will be repeated and refined.

5. REGRESSIONS are certainly part of any change process. New responses are very vulnerable simply because they are not yet ingrained and habitual. Hence, slip-ups do occur especially when the individuals involved are under stress or pressure or very fatigued. Be understanding when goofs occur and then get back on the track of positive change instead of giving up.

With this framework as a foundation and a basic commitment to positive change, you're ready to begin. Here is an overview of each of the LAST factors that are necessary for any healthy and strong marriage relationship. Specific suggestions are provided for each one in the form of several do's and don'ts. Read over all four relationship skills to gain an understanding of what needs to be done. Then, pick a place to begin making positive changes for yourself and for your marriage. You'll be surprised at how well these changes work to make your marriage close again.

I. Listening: Expressing Your Interest

It is remarkable how often and how heavily the act of not

listening to a spouse contributes to the decline of a marriage relationship. When no one listens anymore, it becomes very frustrating to discuss anything meaningful. In fact, the translation of the common marital malady that "We can't talk anymore" is really: "We don't listen to one another anymore." Further, when listening to a partner declines, it usually reflects not only growing distance, but also the inability (or lack of willingness!) to communicate on any level. Far too often, marital interaction is reduced to constant bickering and brief interchanges focused primarily on coordinating schedules and finances.

Further, a problem in listening may signal difficulties stemming from either *what is being said* or from *what is being responded to* by a partner. These represent two very different sets of issues. Let's consider each of these two problems separately. First, it would also be a mistake to assume that the primary problem is one partner in a marriage not willing to listen to the other. Not necessarily so. While this occurs on occasion, much of the time one partner has shut down the other because of *what* is said and how it is said. Unfortunately, negative communication can easily grow to become the dominant theme in marital interaction. It is instructive to understand how this unfortunate state of affairs develops.

The first step is life becomes more hectic and pressured as the years roll by. The result is that stress goes up for both marriage partners and, as it does, positive feelings are more difficult to maintain. In addition, it seems to be true that perceptions tend to reflect personal feelings. That is, it's very difficult to see the good and the positive when you're feeling stressed, pressured, depressed, and discouraged. The end result is that the individual begins to focus on what is wrong and what needs to be corrected.

Communication then follows perceptions, with the relationship between partners becoming increasingly negative and critical as conversing is progressively impaired. The end result of this process is that two once-close partners stop listening to one another. Why? Because all they hear from one another is negative remarks and criticism. As this pattern develops, a vicious circle often emerges. That is, as communication becomes more critical, it invites a negative response. Such responses increase negative feelings in a partner, and more critical comments ensue as a downward spiral is created.

The second problem with listening involves what is being "heard" by a partner and is reflected in the common complaint that "My spouse just doesn't understand what I am trying to say." In one sense, the problem here is quite simple. In any kind of marital communication, and particularly when there is discussion about a problem, the listener has a choice to respond at one of two levels. That is, the listener can respond at either an *informational level* or at a *feeling (or affective) level.*

The problem arises when one partner wants to communicate feelings and is responded to by the listener at an informational level. This results in a sense of not being understood or listened to. Let's take a moment to put this into practical context by using an example. Let's say a husband or wife has been mildly reprimanded by a supervisor at work during the day and that evening says to a spouse:

"Honey, I had a problem today at work. Andy, my boss, really called me on the carpet for not getting some paperwork done and that's not even my responsibility."

Now, the partner who is listening can respond to this stated problem at either an informational level or a feeling level as follows:

INFORMATIONAL LEVEL: "Well, who was responsible? Find out who was guilty and go and tell Andy about it right away. Then your problem will be solved."

FEELING LEVEL: "You must have felt awfully hurt and resentful to be unfairly accused of neglecting something that wasn't even part of your job."

The bottom line is that poor listeners either do not take time to listen at all or that they respond only at the informational level to what a spouse is saying. And, when responses are consistently at an informational level, too often feelings are neglected (or subtly denied) because of the tenor of the interaction. In addition, informational level responding often prompts unsolicited advice. This occurs even when a partner has not asked for advice or problem solving responses. The real request by a partner may be only to "listen to me" or "respond to my feelings," not "solve my problems."

It should also be understood that some listeners say too much. In some men and women, excess verbiage is driven by a need to take over or dominate the exchange. In others, attempts to empathize inadvertently cause the same problem. In still other men and women, a shift occurs in which an individual begins to respond to personal needs and perceptions rather than those of their spouse. You've heard the adage that "You have two eyes and two ears, but only one mouth. Therefore, look and listen twice as much as you speak." This maxim is nowhere more helpful than when empathically listening to your partner.

To improve your listening, you need to practice a number of communication skills. They have the double-edged benefit of maximizing the chance that your spouse's real message—the feelings—will get through, along with conveying interest and empathy. Here are six of the most important. Good listeners usually respond with a blend of different kinds of encouraging responses. None of them requires use of direct questions.

A. EMPATHIC LEADS. These kinds of comments communicate personal sensitivity along with encouragement to continue. They are usually short and are doubly effective when combined with interest expressed through good eye contact and an occasional nod. Further, empathic leads acknowledge either the feelings being conveyed by your spouse or the understanding of the listener. Such comments encourage your partner to continue because the responses convey that the listener is there emotionally.

Examples: "You must have felt terrible." "I really do feel for you." "That must have been a very embarrassing situation to deal with."

B. RESTATEMENT/PARAPHRASING. This kind of response helps both speaker and listener by simultaneously encouraging more interaction and checking the accuracy of what has been heard. Both restatement and paraphrasing simply repeat what has just been said. The difference is that restatement uses the speaker's words almost verbatim while paraphrasing restates the same things in the listener's words. To make the response smoother, a short introductory phrase is often added.

Example: A Husband or wife says: "I was really scared to death when I had to give that talk at the school." *Restatement:* "You were really scared to death when you had to give that talk." *Paraphrasing:* "It sounds as if that talk just about gave you a heart attack."

C. PROMPTS. These are simply direct comments that encourage your partner to continue. Generally, prompts are very short and tend not to reflect feelings as do empathic leads. Instead, they communicate that the listener is interested and therefore encourage further discussion. As with empathic leads, good eye contact and facial expressions that reflect interest help convey the listener involvement that make prompts more effective.

Examples: "Tell me more." "Go on." "Please continue; that's so interesting."

D. SELF-DISCLOSURE. This occurs when one spouse conveys sensitivity to the other's comments by disclosing a related personal experience or feelings of a similar nature. However, self-disclosing statements must not be overused. When this happens, focus shifts away from the speaker to the listener. Second, self-disclosing statements should be short and to the point rather than related as long and involved stories. Remember, in empathic listening, the aim is to affirm an emotional connection to your spouse and not to get equal time to tell your own story.

Examples: "I had the same uncomfortable feelings last year when my gift wasn't acknowledged." "You know, when I was put down at work, I felt just horrible and it lasted for a week."

E. CLARIFYING. This kind of response has as its goal to directly clarify what and check what has been said. Somewhat close to paraphrasing, clarifying also prompts the speaker to continue. A clarifying remark is simply an introductory statement followed by the specific point the listener wants to check. Taking the time to clarify is especially helpful when your partner is upset and hence may not be communicating clearly. Further, under such conditions, clarifying feedback may help the speaker to define feelings and perceptions.

Examples: "It sounds as if you are saying that. . . ." "Do you mean to say that. . .?" "Let me clarify something. As I listen, it's my understanding that. . . ."

F. VALIDATING. Affirming remarks by the listener encourage your husband or wife because they acknowledge and positively reinforce the validity of what is being said. As such, these kinds of comments let a partner know that you have heard, understood, and accepted as valid what your partner related to you. At times, validating remarks also include directly affirming the speaker as a person. These complimentary remarks help a spouse to continue, even though emotionally troubled or when thoughts and feelings are difficult to articulate.

Examples: "I see exactly what you are saying." "You know, no matter what, you're the kind of good person who is always willing to help." "What impresses me is how sensitive you are to other's feelings."

No question about it—it is a tremendous compliment to be labeled a "good listener" by others, especially by a spouse. It is also one of the key communication skills that keeps a marriage strong and healthy. By extension, the quality of being able to listen and really "hear" what a partner is saying is extremely helpful in raising healthy children who have great need to talk to adults who are accepting and understanding. To further develop listening skills in your marriage, here is a recap of some key points and a few additional suggestions to consider.

Listening Do's and Don'ts

1. DO GIVE YOUR PARTNER YOUR FULL AND UNDIVIDED ATTENTION when there is a need to talk. Make sure you won't be interrupted. It's only courteous. Sit where you can maintain good eye contact. Make it a point to turn off the television set and put down the newspaper.

2. DO NOT TRY TO CONTROL, DOMINATE, OR DIRECT the interaction with your spouse. If your partner expresses a desire to talk, let your spouse take it where it needs to go. Taking over or dominating only tends to shut down communication.

3. DO RESPOND TO THE FEELINGS reflected in your spouse's statements. Keep in mind that helping your spouse deal with hurt feelings, frustration, or anger is a necessary first step before any kind of meaningful problem solving can begin.

4. DO NOT GIVE ADVICE unless directly asked for by your spouse. Remember, respond at the feeling level first. Then, instead of direct advice, help your partner clarify the problem situation and develop options for response.

5. DO TALK WITH YOUR SPOUSE FREQUENTLY. Ironically, many marital conflicts can be entirely prevented if husband and wife take time to talk regularly. It takes very little time, but touching base with one another daily does keep you together.

6. DO NOT DENY A PARTNER'S FEELINGS when they are expressed. To be told that "You shouldn't feel that way" or "Those feelings are inappropriate" is not going to be helpful. And, don't put down what your spouse is saying as "dumb," "stupid," or "crazy."

7. DO ENCOURAGE YOUR PARTNER TO EXPRESS THOUGHTS AND FEELINGS with verbal expressions of concern ("That must be hard to take" or "You must have felt just terrible") or with encouragement to continue ("Tell me more about what you are feeling").

II. Apologizing: Admitting Your Imperfection

It is beyond dispute that no one is perfect. Everyone makes mistakes whether as a child or as an adult. And, most reasonable men and women would acknowledge the reality of human imperfection.

On the other hand, it is surprising how many adults *act* as if they are perfect with no faults and no mistakes. Deep down, each and every one knows better. The problem with such men and women is that they refuse to acknowledge their fallibility to themselves and to others. Seen from a psychological perspective, doing so is a blatant denial of reality.

More important, when such denial occurs within a marital relationship, it is a sure sign that that relationship can stand improvement! "My husband/wife never apologizes" is one of the most common complaints heard in marriages that have problems with intimacy and where there is impaired communication. Sadly, sometimes one individual hides behind such a strong false pride that the marital relationship is allowed to deteriorate and even end in lieu of admitting personal mistakes.

It is ironic that this lack of willingness to admit error often occurs with little things that really don't matter in the great scheme of a relationship. In this sense, refusing to admit fallibility is a defensive pattern in an individual's life, often extending to practically everyone with whom that man or woman has a relationship. Furthermore, it is axiomatic that the inability to apologize reflects deep personal insecurity. The fears that lie behind this insecurity are many: fear of being vulnerable, fear of being punished, fear of damage to personal image, or fear of what others might think.

On the other hand, in many marriage relationships, one partner does apologize to the other (although sometimes reluctantly). When such an apology doesn't seem satisfactory, the basic problem may lie not in the absence of apology, but rather in the *nature* of the apology. Typically, such apologies are not communicated in ways that reflect sincerity or true remorse for the mistake that has been made. Again, as with total lack of apology, these maladaptive styles of apologizing reflect personal insecurity, lack of interpersonal closeness and trust, and problems in marital communication. Here are a number of inappropriate styles of apology. Eliminate each and every one to make your marriage strong and healthy.

A. PERFUNCTORY APOLOGY. Here the intent of the apology is solely to pacify a partner. The apology comes too quickly and too often: "Oh, I've goofed again. Sorry." By quickly admitting fault, conflict is defused and discussion of issues is avoided.

B. INDIRECT APOLOGY. This very common kind of apology is never said in words. Rather, the individual is extra nice to a partner or may bring that spouse a gift. It is a way of "making up" without admitting error or talking about what happened.

C. SPLIT APOLOGY. Here, the apology is only partial: "I'm sorry if your feelings got hurt, but I still think I'm right." It comes across as a sop to a husband or wife while holding to a personal viewpoint or defense of personal behavior.

D. CONDITIONAL APOLOGY. By insisting on reciprocity, a conditional apology reflects game playing: "I'll apologize if you do (or when you do)." This ploy sets the stage for a power play if there is not willingness to unilaterally admit fault.

E. PUNITIVE APOLOGY. In this situation, an apology is used as a way to launch an attack: "I'm sorry that happened, but here's what you did to me." Then, conflict is reopened and typically results in more hurt feelings and loss of trust.

F. BLAMING APOLOGY. Here, every possible excuse is used to justify an inappropriate personal behavior or response. Instead of "I'm sorry. I really goofed," the message becomes "I'm sorry, but I'm a victim of circumstance. Here's why you can't blame me."

To round out your understanding of the importance of apologies, several additional points must be made. First, a sincere apology means much more than "I'm sorry." At best, it communicates an openness to more self-awareness and understanding. Further, when given with caring intent, an apology carries with it a commitment to change those responses that are hurtful or inappropriate. The end result is personal growth that over time improves a relationship. Paradoxically, self-awareness and positive change reduce the number of times when an apology to a partner is needed!

Second, for an apology to be forthcoming from a husband or wife, it is extremely important to receive it in a kind and gracious manner. In other words, if you want a partner to apologize again, the receiver must do his or her part to make it an experience that reinforces closeness and understanding. This is particularly important if a partner is just beginning to learn either to apologize or to do so in better ways. At all costs, avoid denying the sincerity of the apology ("You really don't mean it"), using that apology to reopen a conflict, or battering your partner's self-esteem. A simple, sincere response will usually suffice: "Thank you so much for saying that. I really do feel better. Now, let's both put this problem behind us."

A third point is often missed by parents. It is obvious that children must learn to sincerely apologize to others, including parents, when they have erred. Not so obvious, however, are two additional aspects of apologies and parenting. First, children need to see healthy apologies modeled by their parents so that they can learn not only by doing, but by seeing how mature parents do it. Further, since no one is perfect, including parents, they must be mature enough to apologize to their children when the need arises! These failures in parenting are one major reason why apologies cause so many problems in marriage relationships.

Some Do's and Don'ts for Apologies

1. DO MAINTAIN GOOD EYE CONTACT when you apologize to your partner. Looking into your partner's eyes communicates deep caring and regret for the actions that hurt. Conversely, avoiding eye contact implies insincerity or lack of caring.

2. DO NOT DELAY MAKING AN APOLOGY to your partner. In fact, as soon as an error or *faux pas* has been recognized, an apology should be made. The more time that passes between an action and an apology, the weaker the positive impact on a relationship.

3. DO TAKE THE INITIATIVE TO MAKE AN APOLOGY whenever possible. When you take the first step to apologize, it conveys personal strength and a desire to do the right thing. Conversely, an apology prompted by others detracts from its positive impact.

4. DO NOT MAKE AN APOLOGY UNDULY COMPLICATED. In fact, the best kind of apology is not only sincere, but also short and to the point. Take full personal responsibility without excuses: "I'm very sorry and I'll do my best not to let this happen again."

5. DO AFFIRM AN APOLOGY with a big hug. Adding a sincere "I love you" doesn't hurt a bit, either. These actions reflect and affirm deep caring for a partner. They also help both parties to remain close and truly put the problem behind them.

6. DO NOT CONTAMINATE AN APOLOGY WITH NEGATIVE FEELINGS. In short, an apology reluctantly made through gritted teeth is not usually sincere. Make it a point to express an apology openly with warmth and sensitivity to your partner for best results.

7. DO FOLLOW THROUGH BY MAKING APPROPRIATE CHANGES. By thinking about an error you made, the probability increases that it will result in more personal awareness, interpersonal sensitivity, and a better response next time.

III. Supporting: Sharing Your Commitment

When two people marry, they join legally and emotionally to

experience all the joys and sorrows of life together. Sharing their lives is what marriage is all about, and a husband and wife doing so create the core of the family. In fact, the ability to support one another is absolutely critical in any good marriage relationship. Early in a relationship, a couple's togetherness and mutual support are there simply because they are in love and because life is still relatively simple. And, togetherness is easy because there is plenty of time to have fun, to talk, and to share thoughts and feelings on a daily basis.

However, while legally creating a marriage is relatively easy, building an emotional partnership between a man and a woman that lasts and grows stronger with the years is a much more arduous task. Further, once established, that emotional partnership with all its benefits becomes increasingly difficult to maintain once responsibilities begin to grow and life becomes complicated. It is at this point, when living each day is hectic and intense, that husband and wife either become closer and stronger or begin to grow apart while living under the same roof.

Further, it is a mistake to think that providing support in a marriage means only "being there" when a partner is experiencing problems. While providing support for a husband or wife who is emotionally upset is certainly important, being supportive of a partner is really much more. Basically, supporting your partner and sharing your strength involves a way of thinking about a marital relationship. What is necessary is to develop a "couple's mentality."

When a couple's mentality is present, a husband or wife begins to think constantly in terms of "we" or "us." A problem is perceived to impact on both partners. News is shared with a partner because of a strong desire to do so. When problems arise, one's partner is the first one sought out both for emotional support and for a different perspective.

In short, a couple's mentality insures that a husband and wife automatically think in terms of one another because at a deep level, they are partners and they are together emotionally. Further, this emotional joining does not detract from the individuality of each one. In fact, each partner's individuality is not only valued, but each spouse encourages personal growth and change in the other. It is a way of really being together without giving up much in the way of personal identity at all.

Given the many benefits of this kind of emotional mutuality, it is legitimate to ask why so many couples have never developed it or have lost this kind of closeness. In fact, a number of reasons causes this kind of mental separation in a marriage. Each one of them represents a personal issue for that husband or wife that must be resolved before true support and closeness can develop.

A. FEAR OF DEPENDENCY. A surprising number of men and women can't become close to a partner because they fear losing autonomy and independence. In fact, being truly together really means becoming interdependent in a way that preserves personal identity.

B. SEXUAL STEREOTYPING. Men and women often play out stereotypical sex roles. "I'm handling things" is a message that precludes sharing with a spouse. Sometimes one spouse plays a helpless, dependent role with its implied message of "Take care of me."

C. DISTORTED PRIORITIES. It's a sad commentary on modern life that over time, as life becomes more complicated, a marriage relationship begins to inadvertently fade in importance. Because everything else comes first, mutual support disappears.

D. LACK OF SEPARATION FROM PARENTS. Lack of support for a spouse sometimes results when an adult child has not emotionally separated from one or both parents. Then, primary emotional support and sharing goes to a parent, not a spouse.

E. INAPPROPRIATE MODELING. Many young men and women these days grew up in households where highly-stressed parents provided little emotional support or togetherness for each other. As such children became adults, they follow the same patterns in their marriages.

F. NEED FOR PEER APPROVAL. Because of a strong need for both approval and acceptance from a peer group, a husband or wife can easily adopt standards of behavior toward a spouse that are not only nonsupportive, but are often downright degrading.

G. STRESS AND ANGER. As chronic pressure from busy lifestyles builds over the years, personal emotional needs are not met. The resultant stress is often transformed into anger. Then, constant angry outbursts push a couple apart.

H. AN EMOTIONALLY DIFFICULT CHILDHOOD. Absence of support for a spouse can result from childhood trauma. Closeness may be associated with punishment, or a pattern of passivity or aggressiveness may develop that prevents supportiveness.

In a nutshell, support for a spouse is reflected best in an attitude that conveys "We're together" in every facet of a relationship. At a deeper level, it communicates that "I love you. I like you. I care about you deeply and I want to live the good life with you." Again, this is a very precious feeling that is communicated more powerfully by little actions every day than by words alone. When this sense of togetherness and mutual support disappears, it is a sure signal that a husband and wife are emotionally separating and their long-term relationship is being jeopardized.

Support Do's and Don'ts

1. DO PAY ATTENTION TO AND INCLUDE YOUR PARTNER when socializing with others. For example, in a group be sure to include your spouse in conversations. At social events, introduce your spouse with pride and make it a point not to disappear the whole evening.

2. DO NOT ALLOW OTHERS TO PUT DOWN OR DIMINISH YOUR SPOUSE. It signals lack of support when children, parents, in-laws, or friends are allowed to make snide remarks about a spouse or to respond in other disrespectful ways. Step in and stop it at all costs.

3. DO ACCEPT THE IDEAS AND VIEWPOINTS of your partner as valid and legitimate. Get beyond the "If it doesn't come from me, it's no good" attitude. Instead, value your spouse's perspectives by encouraging discussion of ideas and then responding positively.

4. DO NOT GOSSIP NEGATIVELY about your partner. It is easy to "badmouth" your partner after a fight or complain to others about a spouse's behavior. Such nonsupportive responses usually are an attempt to justify personal behavior.

5. DO ADMIRE THE ACCOMPLISHMENTS OF YOUR SPOUSE no matter how mundane. Do not begin taking your partner for granted. Because recognition for what someone has done is tremendously reinforcing, it is vitally important that positive comments come from a spouse.

6. DO NOT SABOTAGE YOUR PARTNER'S ATTEMPT TO REACH PERSONAL GOALS. For example, bringing sweets to a partner attempting to lose weight is simply not supportive. Undermining a spouse in this way may be inadvertent, but it is very destructive.

7. DO BE THERE FOR YOUR PARTNER DURING TIMES OF CRISIS or emotional distress. It's easy and more comfortable to avoid such situations. But, if you aren't there emotionally during the tough times, your partner has a "fair weather spouse" in you.

IV. Touching: Providing Physical Affirmation

Take a moment to think back to the good old days when you and your spouse were lovers. Remember the closeness, the good feelings? You embraced frequently. You went for walks hand in hand. You always sat close together so you touched. And, there were those wonderful kisses when you departed—not to be together again for as much as 12–15 hours! Ah, the good old days when life was not so complicated. You and your husband or wife were lovers—two among millions and easy to spot the world over. To observers the two of you looked like a pretzel with legs. You both made it a point to stay in constant touch, literally and figuratively.

Now, years later, things have changed dramatically as far as all that affectionate touching goes. You both have taken to rushing about from morning to night getting done all that needs to be done. And, while you're both very productive, you don't take the time to be physically affectionate anymore. You might get a perfunctory peck on the cheek now and then. When you want a big hug, you have to ask for it. Holding hands and sitting close have gone the way of the dinosaurs. With lots to do every day and a pressured lifestyle, you've let affectionate touching diminish, if not entirely disappear. Now, affectionate touching is reserved for special occasions (if at all!), and you both are beginning to realize that something important has died in your marriage.

While it is true that affectionate touching is one of the most critical elements of a strong and healthy marriage, it is also one of the easiest to neglect. Furthermore, it is very difficult to sustain the emotional closeness needed in a marriage relationship without regular, sincere, spontaneous, nonsexual affection. In fact, the degree of affectionate touching in a relationship is very diagnostic. If it is present and reciprocal, then the relationship is usually close and fulfilling. Conversely, if there is little affectionate touching, it signals a growing emotional distance between that husband and wife.

Beyond the bottom line reality that regular touching is important in any good marital relationship, the fact is that physical touch serves a variety of emotional needs present in any relationship. Here are seven of the most important forms of touching. The more of them that are present in any marriage relationship, the stronger and more fulfilling that relationship is likely to be.

A. SOCIAL. This kind of regular touching helps to make social transitions easier—not only a must for marriage relationships, but also among good friends. *Examples:* A hug when greeting, a fond kiss goodbye.

B. SUPPORTIVE. This communicates togetherness and shared strength in times of problems or emotional upset. Examples: Holding a husband or wife who is crying, giving a pat on the back for encouragement.

C. FRIENDSHIP. This form of touching is very casual and easy. It occurs between husband and wife who are good friends and says that "I really enjoy being with you." *Examples:* Holding hands while taking a walk, gently massaging a spouse's neck after work.

D. TOUCH IN PASSING. Touching here is usually very brief, but full of meaning. Nonverbally, it says "I'm aware of you and I care." *Examples:* A light touch on the shoulder when passing, a gentle squeeze on the arm as a partner is working.

E. ROMANTIC. Often neglected in marriages, romantic touching is close and communicates emotional intimacy. However, it has no necessary sexual connotations. *Examples:* Slow dancing cheek-to-cheek, snuggling on the couch with the lights turned low.

F. RITUAL. This special form of touching develops within a relationship and is repeated in particular settings or circumstances. It symbolizes something special for the couple. *Examples:* A kiss for each year on a birthday, a hug in bed before going to sleep.

G. SEXUAL. Often overused in marriages, the explicit intention is to sexually arouse a partner. It is destructive to substitute sexual touching for other kinds of touch in marriage. *Examples:* Constantly grabbing at a partner, pushing a partner down on the bed.

The importance of touching in a relationship cannot be underestimated. The best way to look at touch is as an affirmation of the bond between a husband and wife. And, those affirmations must be regular and meaningful to maintain the closeness in a marriage. On the other hand, when touching is neglected, the distance created between two people leads to a sense of estrangement or outright loneliness. Unfortunately, as emotional distance is created and becomes the status quo in a relationship, everyone begins to suffer—even the children.

Two final points are worth making about the importance of touch in a marital relationship. First, it is true that different individuals have different levels of need for touch. Further, most men and women tend to *give* touch at the level they *need* touch. This may create a problem because one spouse's needs may be much more or much less than the other's. Committed marriage partners understand the differences between them in their need for touch. Further, they strive for a level of touching that is comfortable for them both. To attain tactile compatibility, each spouse must be willing to transcend personal needs to make sure a partner's needs for touch are met. After all, that's what love is all about.

Second, some men and women are extremely uncomfortable with touch. They visibly shrink from affection and touch others only with reluctance. Typically, such individuals come from emotionally cold and distant families. However, family heritage is no excuse. *With a little effort, every man and woman can become comfortable with the basics of touch needed to sustain a close and loving relationship!* The question is whether the effort will be put forth. With practice, touching becomes easier and everyone wins. A marriage partner feels closer and more fulfilled. Equally important, a man or woman who learns to touch becomes more open and expressive rather than emotionally withdrawn. A sense of personal well-being and life satisfaction usually follows.

Touching Do's and Don'ts

1. DO MAKE IT A POINT TO TOUCH YOUR PARTNER REGULARLY. Sincere, spontaneous, and regular are the bywords here. Touch with meaning and feeling. Don't let your own stress cause you to withdraw. Some form of touching three or four times a day is certainly not too much.

2. DO NOT TOUCH YOUR SPOUSE ONLY IN SEXUAL WAYS. Touching may be overtly sexual even if there is no sexual intent. This bad habit usually reflects discomfort expressing tenderness and can cause one spouse to resent and avoid the touch of the other.

3. DO COMBINE TOUCH WITH VERBAL EXPRESSIONS OF AFFECTION. It is always better to express affection both verbally and nonverbally at the same time. This makes the communication of caring more powerful because it is meaningful and clear.

4. DO NOT USE TOUCH IN MANIPULATIVE WAYS. For example, some individuals touch only when they want to go to the bedroom. Or, they become affectionate only when they want something. This selective use of touch is obvious and breeds resentment in a partner.

5. DO LET OTHERS SEE YOU TOUCH. Without making a public spectacle of yourselves, some affectionate handholding, sitting close, or putting an arm around your spouse is entirely appropriate. It proclaims to all the depth of your caring.

6. DO NOT BE PUT OFF BY A RELUCTANT SPOUSE. Sometimes a spouse or partner, under stress, withdraws from touch. Give hugs and pats anyway! Although hard to do, giving your husband or wife needed touching support is very important.

7. DO TOUCH YOUR PARTNER IN A VARIETY OF WAYS. In the best relationships, the importance of touch is understood and consistently practiced. Further, both partners touch in a variety of ways to meet a broad spectrum of emotional needs.

LASTing Love Has Benefits

These four relationship skills, the LAST factors, are absolutely necessary to gain all the fulfillment that marriage can bring. For best results, these qualities must be reciprocal in a marriage. That is, there must be give and take—literally and figuratively. But, as the years pass and daily life gets busier, it's easy to distort the healthy "give and take" in a relationship. That is, marital interaction can degenerate to become either very perfunctory and sterile or full of conflict. At this point, marriage partners have let the key relationship in their lives deteriorate into giving little of themselves and taking their spouse entirely for granted!

Furthermore, it is a sad commentary on contemporary society to observe how many adults were raised in families where these critical relationship skills were not modeled for the kids. Then, despite being bright and educated, as adults they have no healthy foundation learned at home on which to build loving and lasting relationships for themselves. It is even more striking to note how many of these children, now adults, came from economically successful parents. They were raised in nice homes with well-intentioned parents who let their life priorities become completely distorted.

Over the years, many such homes became emotional pressure cookers filled with stress and tension that diminished fulfillment and positive relationships for all family members. The bottom line here is simple: Make positive changes in your marriage not only for you and your spouse, but also to provide healthy modeling so your children will follow in your footsteps. It goes without saying that children need to be on the receiving end of all the LAST qualities from their parents. But, remember, for the good life to be theirs, they need to consistently *observe* the LAST factors in their parents for at least eighteen years before they leave home!

When you both begin to make consistent efforts to change, you will be on your way to the good life because you will be on your way to really being together again. The benefits are wonderful. Here are just a few of them.

1. TRUST AND COMMITMENT ARE STRENGTHENED. To bring the LAST factors into a marriage requires that a husband and wife place their relationship at the highest priority level and keep it there. As a result, problems get resolved, and a couple can relax and enjoy one another because they are close and trusting.

2. CLOSENESS AND INTIMACY ARE DEEPENED. By definition, it is virtually impossible to have a truly close relationship without the LAST factors. For emotional intimacy to develop, these key relationship skills require the ability to respond to a spouse as a personally-secure and emotionally-expressive mate.

3. CONFLICT RESOLUTION IS EASIER. When the LAST factors are present, many conflicts are avoided because of the shared closeness and understanding. And, because partners are willing to give one another the benefit of the doubt, conflicts that do arise are more compatibly resolved because of high levels of mutual caring.

4. A PHYSICAL RELATIONSHIP IMPROVES. For the best and most fulfilling sexual relationship possible, the LAST factors are absolutely essential. To put it briefly, for the best bedroom relationship to develop, begin in the living room. Bringing back closeness and trust will evolve into a renewed sexual relationship.

5. GOOD TIMES TOGETHER GET BETTER. Interestingly, the LAST factors are also important in the ability to "let go" together and have fun. To once again be spontaneous and joyful together and to create good memories as a couple, Listen, Apologize, Support and Touch. You'll see a positive difference almost immediately.

Once you've created a LASTing relationship with your partner, there's a wonderful personal benefit for you. You will be more personally fulfilled because you will be more complete. By extension, relationships with others—friends, children, relatives—will grow and become more satisfying. One of life's great truths is that being rich has little to do with your income or what you possess. Rather, the real riches that life has to offer lie in the quality of your relationships with loved ones. On reflection, perhaps it's time to "get rich" with your spouse and together start enjoying life.

Chapter 14

Steps to Romantic Recovery: Re-creating the Experience of Love

For young couples in love, romance is always in the air. It creates a wonderful feeling of exhilaration. Do you remember it? It is wanting to be close to that special person in your life. It is a yearning to spend time with a lover—a yearning that can never be completely satisfied. In fact, the highest priority of young men and women in love is to spend romantic time together. They live in a world all their own and little else really matters.

These are the wonderful days and nights of youthful love. To young lovers, intense feelings brought by the closeness of romance will go on forever. Virtually every couple has special memories of romantic times spent together way back when.

Paul and Glenna: "When we first fell in love, we used to sneak away from the family to just walk in the woods together hand in hand. Then we'd find a quiet place to hold one another and talk. It was so quiet and beautiful. We would spend hours there."

Walt and Chelsea: "I remember when we used to sit close and hold hands no matter where we were. Even sitting on the back porch was special as long as no one else was around. We would talk constantly about our feelings for one another and what we wanted out of life."

Avi and Fran: "We loved to dance when we were young and I especially enjoyed slow dancing. It was dreamy. We'd be there on the dance floor, and it was as if we were the only ones who existed in the whole world."

Les and Felicia: "Lying on the beach together in the moonlight is our most romantic memory. It was so beautiful there and every-thing seemed different and new because we were together. Sometimes we'd even get carried away and make love there."

Elton and Danita: "Friends and family used to tease us when we'd just look at one another with moonstruck eyes. I guess it was a bit silly, but at that point it didn't matter. We were in love and all that mattered was each other."

These are the romantic memories of young lovers totally infatuated with one another and, in some respects, completely out of touch with reality. In one sense, these memories reflect the intense feelings of youth when life was simple and the world was brand-new. An entire lifetime together stretched out into the future. Because of romance and closeness, no obstacle was too formidable to overcome, no hurdle too high to leap. These early romantic experiences became fond memories that helped bond a man and woman together for a lifetime.

Then, as time passes, the mundane realities of life set in. It is truly unfortunate that as life becomes busier, the responsiveness of a husband and wife to one another frequently declines and romance often disappears entirely. Now, years later, let's take a look at how the romantic experiences of these same couples have changed.

Paul and Glenna now: "We're never alone anymore. When we go out, it's always with friends and never by ourselves. It's almost impossible to feel really romantic and close when you're in the middle of a group of friends who are joking around and carrying on all the time."

Walt and Chelsea now: "We hardly ever touch one another these days. We used to be so affectionate. It's like a big void has grown between us. When we go out together—to dinner or a game—we just sit there. There doesn't seem to be anything to say."

Avi and Fran now: "I hate to say it, but the only time we're even slightly romantic anymore is when we've both had a few drinks. It starts out wonderfully. Then one of us says something that is taken the wrong way by the other, and a fight usually ends the evening on a terrible note."

Les and Felicia now: "We just don't seem to know how to be romantic anymore. When we have the opportunity for a romantic evening, it gets sexual right away. Maybe we've confused romance with foreplay but there isn't even much of that anymore. When the sex is over, we seem to lose interest in one another."

Elton and Danita now: "We have great careers and wonderful kids, but there just doesn't seem to be time for us anymore. In the past few years, whenever we try to make time for romance, we're so tired one of us usually falls asleep right in the middle of it. Sometimes we come home early because we're both so worn out."

As romantic interludes become less frequent, an extremely important part of the overall intimacy in a relationship begins to fade and eventually disappears. At this point, to avoid confusion, it is time to define romance.

ROMANCE: *When a man and woman are simultaneously experiencing one another in an open and intimate way that affirms their emotional bond and the physical attraction between them.*

In other words, romance is sensually relating to one another in a way that might well be termed lightly eroticized intimacy. Make no mistake about it. Part of romance is an underlying sexual responsiveness between a husband and wife that is deepened and made more meaningful by their emotional sharing. Furthermore, romance is a unique and very sensual experience that is created by a couple in love and, in that respect, stands alone. It is simply not part of anything else.

Sometimes couples ask themselves whether the naive, infatuation-oriented romance that existed when they were very young can be re-created after they've been married for a number of years. The answer is "Probably not, at least in that intense form." You're older and wiser now and you have years of the ups and downs of life behind you. All is not lost, however, because romance during later years can be even better than when you were young. The decline of the hormonally-driven infatuation characteristic of your youth will be replaced with a deep and comfortable security, along with a freedom to share romantic experiences in deeper ways not possible before.

In the end, it must be said that romance is wonderful. It is fun. It's meaningful. And it's a given that romance is part of every good marital relationship. Don't make the grievous mistake of thinking that romance is only a part of courtship and isn't needed once you are married. It's also an easy error to narrow romantic interludes to special obligatory dates, that is, your anniversary and your partner's birthday. At its best, romantic interludes should be regular and for no reason other than that you care about one another. Their purpose is to make your lover feel loved in a special way.

The fact is that romance is needed even more after you're married than before! Furthermore, experiencing together romantically is an important part of what separates marital best friends from a good (but platonic) friendship. In the end, romance is essential to getting better together because it's a key part of living the good life—together.

If you both let romance slip away with the years—and it's very easy to do—it's past time to re-create these very special feelings once again. Here are five steps to help you both on the road to romantic recovery.

Step I: Get Rid of Your Excuses

When it comes to bringing romance back into a marital relationship, some men and women become apprehensive. Such apprehension in turn creates resistance to the openness and vulnerability that romance entails. Overcoming such resistance is the first step in bringing romance back into your lives. True, some men and women have a natural knack for creating and enjoying romance. For others, learning romantic responses may be a bit more difficult. However, as with many marital skills, practice pays off. The more you try, the easier romantic responses become.

When resistance to romantic recovery is encountered, a number of excuses (really fears) lie at the basis of reluctance to try. Sometimes these are expressed out loud; just as often they are felt but left unspoken. It helps for both marital partners to review each one of these sometimes hidden fears and to reassure each other. Here are the five most common sources of resistance to becoming more romantic.

A. FEAR OF CHANGE. *Apprehension:* "I won't feel comfortable if I respond that way."

This perception is absolutely true. As marital distance has grown between you, you each have established a comfort zone. This more distant way of relating may not be fulfilling, but at least it is familiar and therefore secure. To bring new life back into your marriage, particularly romantic sharing, you will both have to push yourselves to respond in ways that are new and therefore uncomfortable. Keep in mind that you weren't comfortable when you first picked up a golf club or a tennis racquet either. However, by pushing yourselves a bit, romantic responses will become your new comfort zone. Then, you will both feel uncomfortable when romantic interludes aren't present!

B. FEAR OF VULNERABILITY. *Apprehension:* "You will make fun of me when I try to change."

This very common discomfort with romance reflects a fear of ridicule or a put-down by a spouse. Unfortunately, in many marriages there may be some element of validity to this source of anxiety. If things have not been going well, a husband or wive often resorts to sarcastic remarks or put-downs or even to making a partner the object of hostile humor. Being romantic involves letting down defenses in order to become closer and enjoy one another, but this also exposes a vulnerability to being deeply hurt by a partner's unkind remarks. Reassuring a spouse that "We will both be encouraging and supportive of one another as we relearn how to be romantic together" is the best antidote.

C. FEAR OF PEER REJECTION. *Apprehension:* "No one else I know does these things."

At times, peers can play a very positive role in bringing romance back into a relationship. On the other hand, friends, colleagues, and relatives can also reinforce resistance. Lack of self-esteem, fear of being manipulated, power dynamics in a relationship, and lack of trust can all become barriers to romance that can easily be reinforced by peers. While the advice or comments of others may be well-intentioned, they can also be destructive to a husband and wife struggling to recover this extremely important part of their marital relationship. The remedy here is quite simple. Gravitate toward those friends who are very encouraging and who are unself-consciously romantic in their relationships. Avoid bringing up the subject with those who are negative. Don't forget to talk about how you're doing romantically with one another.

D. FEAR OF CONSEQUENCES. *Apprehension:* "If I do it once, he/she will expect it all the time."

Well, holy cow! A spouse who wants romance on a regular basis? How bad is that! Better not do it at all because you both might like it. Just kidding, of course, but it certainly is a strong source of resistance in some men and women. There is no question that creating romance takes some time and effort. However, there are few other places in a marriage where that time and energy is better spent. Romance is one of the most powerful affirmative experiences possible in a marital relationship. Don't fall into the trap of needing tangible benefits to justify time spent. It doesn't work that way. The real benefits are a new closeness that develops between you as well as the personal uplift that comes from experiencing in ways that haven't been there for years.

E. FEAR OF FAILURE. *Apprehension:* "If I try, I just won't be good at it."

Of course not. You're out of practice and your romantic skills may be very rusty. If there has been no opportunity to be romantic with one another for years, why should you be good at it the very first time you try it again? In the intervening years between the romantic days of your youth and right now, you have also changed. You will both have to experiment a bit to find what kind of romantic experiences make you both feel good. Remember that you're developing new skills and bringing out a part of yourself that has been put aside for years. To the extent that this has occurred, you may have to put forth extra effort to relearn the basics. In either case, with practice and an upbeat attitude, you'll both get better together—romantically.

Step II: Some Points About Romance

There are many misconceptions and erroneous ideas about romance that can create serious barriers to romantic recovery in your marriage. In other words, you must both understand what romance is all about and not fall into the easy traps that can create problems. Even if only one of you has an erroneous idea or two about romance, it can be inhibiting or even sabotage the whole effort. Step Two is to develop a broader framework helpful for bringing the wonderful feelings of romance back into your life. Here are a number of points to help you do just that.

A. EVERYONE CAN LEARN THE BASICS. Individuals of both sexes, but more men than women, often complain that they can't be romantic because they were raised in emotionally distant and nonaffectionate families. Not so. Granted, you may never be Cassanova, but everyone can learn the basic elements of romance. Learning to be romantic, even for the first time, breaks the generational chain where one family sets the stage for distant marital and family relationships in the next. Granted, learning to be more romantic may create some discomfort, but it helps individuals and, by extension couples, break out of the lonely shell within themselves to which they've retreated.

B. INDIVIDUALS DIFFER IN THEIR RANGE OF ROMANTIC POTENTIAL. It's a fact that some men and women can be romantic virtually anywhere. For them, the ability to create a romantic mood lies within them and is almost completely independent of the environment. At the other extreme, many husbands and wives find that becoming romantic is possible only in very specific settings. If you find that your romantic range is too narrow, widen it by taking more initiative to create the mood for both of you no matter where you happen to be. It need not take much time and, as you do this, enjoying romantic interludes becomes easier because they can be created more often in more places.

C. COUPLES MUST LEARN TO BE ROMANTIC AT HOME OR CLOSE BY. Some husbands and wives relate that they feel romantic on the deck of a cruise ship, holding hands while waves shimmer in the moonlight. Or sitting together whispering sweet nothings in front of a crackling fire in a rustic mountain cabin. True, these are very romantic settings, but they're not practical on a weekly basis. To get better together romantically, it's necessary for you to find romantic opportunities in your community. They're all around and they're waiting for you to discover. Furthermore, it helps immensely if you practice being romantic right in your own home.

D. ROMANCE IS A GIVING EXPERIENCE. The best way to approach romance is to see it as a way of giving of yourself to a husband or wife. Too often, romance is mistakenly seen as getting something for oneself. For your romantic time together, use as your sole guide an intention to make your partner feel very special to you. After all, that's what romance really is: a special feeling of being loved and desired experienced by a husband and wife who are attractive to one another and who share a deep emotional bond. When you both share this mindset, romantic feelings of closeness fall into place almost without effort.

E. TRUE ROMANCE DOES NOT COST MUCH MONEY. Husbands and wives who recall their fondest memories of romance during their youth find that these experiences were by necessity inexpensive because they had little money. What was important was being close and experiencing special feelings together. Keep this in mind as you move toward romantic recovery in your marriage. To think of romance in terms of financial expenditure and impressing your spouse gets you off on the wrong foot right away. The same is true for a spouse who expects heavy spending as part of romance. Look at it this way. The more economical you make romance, the more opportunities you will have to experience it!

F. ROMANCE IS NOT SEX. It is an easy and common mistake to confuse romance and sex. Romance is not foreplay, and to treat it as such plainly diminishes the experience. As already mentioned, romance is an experience that can and should stand alone. True, romance is very sensual, but it does not necessarily lead to a sexual encounter (although it sometimes does). To make romance overtly sexual often creates discomfort. It can kill the mood entirely if one partner perceives "romance" only in terms of a partner's sexual agenda. Ironically, if you both focus on romance and forget about sex, it often happens naturally. Then, when you do get to the bedroom, you'll find that you'll be making love again instead of having sex.

G. ROMANCE TAKES ENERGY AND PREPARATION. Unlike the days of your youth when life was simple, it's not as easy to shift into a romantic mood when you have a busy career, a home to maintain, community responsibilities, and children who need attention. In addition, romance simply can't be treated as an "extra" in your life that you do after everything else is done and you're exhausted. To remedy these problems, begin to treat these special times as a high priority in your marriage. Then, one or both of you must take some initiative to plan so that the romantic experiences you share are as wonderful as they can possibly be.

H. IT'S DIFFICULT TO BE ROMANTIC BY YOURSELF. If one partner in a marriage responds in a romantic way and the other one ignores these attempts, the experience is diminished for both. Eventually, if a partner persists in not responding, the incentive to make romantic overtures will surely die. For romance to become part of the good life together, you must both be ready to relearn how to create these feelings for yourselves as a couple. By keeping yourself receptive to such experiences, regardless who initiates them and when, romance grows emotionally deeper, more fulfilling, and certainly more fun.

Step III: Romance Begins in the Living Room

One of the strongest characteristics of youthful romance is complete comfort with a partner and in the relationship. This basic trust allows each partner the freedom to respond in open and caring ways. The result is a delightful and uninhibited way of relating without any self-consciousness whatsoever. It is experiencing the moment with complete freedom to be oneself without fear of censorship or criticism by a partner. Under these conditions, romance becomes an intense and emotionally uplifting experience.

Unfortunately, as life becomes busier and more hectic. There is no time for romance, sometimes not even for sex. Because there is so much to do each day, meeting responsibilities takes priority over all else. As you already know, often accompanying the stress of this work-driven lifestyle are a negative outlook and critical ways of communicating. The end result is a husband and wife living under the same roof who don't feel close anymore. They may still love one another, but they may not like one another anymore.

Under these conditions, it is very difficult to be romantic. Why? Because walls have been put up as husband and wife take one another and their relationship for granted. Both spouses are guarded because an irritable comment, a critical remark, or a sarcastic statement can come out of nowhere at any time. Bickering, arguments, or fights become commonplace. With these expectations, sometimes based on years of living together, neither partner feels good personally. Nor are a husband and wife drawn to one another by positive feelings about their marital relationship.

This brings us to Step Three: understanding the psychological foundations of romance. These are ways of relating that help each partner to relax and enjoy one another during day-to-day living. These ways of relating also bring enough trust back into the relationship so that the next step, becoming overtly romantic, is not only easy but also more natural. All have been previously mentioned in other parts of *Getting Better Together*, but they are so important in so many ways it is worth emphasizing them again in this chapter on romance. In short, *the foundations of romance are built—every day—in the living room and not in the bedroom.* To set the stage for bringing romance back into your relationship, prepare by making it a point—every day—to practice these kinds of responses with your partner. All of them communicate through your actions a simple message that means everything: "I deeply care about you."

A. START BEING MORE AFFECTIONATE. There are few stronger indicators of marital distance than the absence of sincere, nonsexual affection in that relationship. Begin to bring back closeness right away by reaching out to your spouse with regular physical expressions of affection. A big hug, a touch, a pat on the back, and holding hands all begin to lessen the distance between you. In fact, with just a bit of tongue-in-cheek, someone has said that hugs make the perfect gift: one size fits all and they're easy to exchange!

B. BEGIN TO CONVERSE MORE. Too often, husbands and wives become totally immersed in their own hectic worlds and talk very little. And when they do talk, it's about problems, hassles, schedules, kids, and money. Not much stimulation there. Make it a point to regularly find a few moments of quiet time for some easy conversations. Regular chats about interesting topics, or about nothing in particular, help you become closer.

C. BECOME MORE SUPPORTIVE. Be honest about it. Since you became so busy, you haven't been very supportive of one another. Taking the time for sincere compliments, expressing appreciation of what your partner has accomplished, and providing a shoulder to lean on when problems occur all affirm your togetherness. These are all ways of saying "I care about you," and such support is one of the bedrocks of trust that make romantic responses very easy.

D. ADOPT A POSITIVE ATTITUDE. With chronic stress and pressure, negative attitudes grow and critical remarks are easily and openly directed toward loved ones—especially a spouse. Reverse this trend by shifting out of that complaining victim role; instead begin to consistently comment on the bright side of things. If you take the initiative to become upbeat, you both will soon feel more comfortable with one another.

E. BE MORE SPONTANEOUS. As life has become dominated by schedules and routines, the spontaneity of your youth has probably diminished, perhaps even disappeared. Begin to take small fun breaks on a regular basis. On the spur of the moment go out for an ice cream cone, take a few minutes for a short walk, or stroll over to visit a neighbor. For best results, keep your fun breaks lighthearted and easygoing.

F. INITIATE CARING GESTURES. Those creative gestures that said simply "I'm thinking about you and I care" made when you were young often disappear with the years. You remember! Romantic notes left for one another, bouquets picked by the roadside, smoochy telephone calls, a small surprise left under a pillow. These small gestures, creatively expressing your caring, are not only fun and set the stage for romance to bloom, but also keep life interesting.

Step IV: The Characteristics of Romantic Experiences

What is really going to make romance deeply fulfilling is your understanding of one another's needs and your creativity in finding interesting ways to meet those needs. This is Step Four in romantic recovery. Remember that romance is primarily a positive emotional experience and that is the essence of what must be re-created. As with virtually all facets of the good life, romance isn't measured by how much you spend as much as it depends on being there emotionally with your partner.

In the beginning, it may take a bit of experimentation to discover what works for you both romantically. Once you know the basics, then you can add imaginative twists on such experiences. It won't be long before you'll both look forward to romantic interludes and you'll wonder why you let them disappear from your life in the first place. To get started on bringing back the excitement and fulfillment of romance in your marriage, concentrate on these basic components of romance. Try to bring as many of them as possible together in the romantic experiences that you share with one another.

A. MAKE YOURSELF VERY ATTRACTIVE. Romantic experiences are always enhanced when husband and wife take a bit of time to "spiff up" and make themselves look their absolute best. This welcome change from routine attire is stimulating, particularly when it accentuates your masculinity or femininity. This does not necessarily mean dressing expensively and to the nines. It does mean making yourself look very special for your partner. Don't forget to dress attractively whether going out or staying at home when you're going to be together romantically.

B. FORGET ABOUT EVERYTHING BUT YOUR PARTNER. When romance is in the air for young lovers, nothing exists but one another. And, that's exactly the way it should be for adults as well. During romantic interludes, make it a point to drop all references to work, the kids, money, schedules, and other problems. No beepers or telephone calls allowed. Negative comments should be completely taboo. The focus should stay entirely on a man and a woman, in love and attracted to one another, experiencing fun times and closeness in a world of their own.

C. MAKE SURE THAT YOU CAN BE ALONE. As the kids age, it becomes at once very difficult and more necessary to find time to be alone together. In the beginning, it helps to spend romantic time outside the home where work that "needs to be done" can't be seen. Finding a baby-sitter regularly for time away from the kids to renew your marital relationship is a must. Another mistake, particularly in the beginning, is to always be in the company of other individuals or couples so a completely romantic mood is difficult to create and sustain.

D. CREATE A SENSUAL ATMOSPHERE. In other words, for romance to be most interesting and fulfilling, the setting must be conducive to it. There are no rights and wrongs here—just what works for two people in love. Bring in as many romantic sights, sounds, smells, gentle touches, and kind words as you possibly can. A quiet dinner at home (or on the patio) is much more romantic with candlelight, pleasant music in the background, flowers on the table, and a special cologne or perfume wafting through the air. The more sensual the ambience, the easier it becomes to slip into that special closeness that is the essence of romance.

E. AFFIRM YOUR TOGETHERNESS. If romance can fairly be called lightly eroticized intimacy, then both components must be present. However, it is necessary here to reiterate a point already made. With busy couples, it is all too easy and a serious mistake to see romance only as a prelude to sex. Such slippage definitely detracts from the real meaning of romance. In fact, the most critical part of romance is the emotional affirmation of the bond between you as you sensually experience together as a man and woman. Communicating through kind words and gentle touch how much you care about one another is the true foundation for romantic love.

F. GO WITH THE FLOW. The best way to be romantic together is to have no set agenda. Try not to create any kind of "schedule" in your mind. Granted, some time boundaries must be respected: for example, when a play will begin and what time you must be home. However, within those outside limits, romantic experiences are best left relatively unstructured. Further, don't set goals and don't hurry. Adopt the attitude that "what will be will be" as you both go with the flow of your experience together. Being very flexible and just enjoying one another by doing what feels good is the best way to approach romance.

G. STIMULATE YOUR PARTNER'S HEART AND MIND. Basically, the essence of romance is emotional and mental stimulation. Appreciating your partner as an attractive man or woman, creating a relaxed mood, and affirming the deep caring bond between you all serve to stimulate the mind and the emotions. Remember, your primary focus is to make your partner feel deeply loved and very special to you. When you do so through your words and your actions, the erotic part of romance usually falls into place naturally and without effort.

H. CREATE DELIGHTFUL SURPRISES. The pleasantly unexpected is always fun and can contribute heavily to a romantic mood. The possibilities are limited only by the creativity and imagination of a husband and wife. Remember that couples are used to being around one another so surprises are very appealing. For example, bringing flowers to your spouse, wearing dainty underthings, or arranging a special meal at your favorite restaurant are all great fun and extremely pleasant. Make sure your romantic surprises are what your partner will enjoy, and let your special present be fun without spending much money.

I. "BE THERE" EMOTIONALLY. A common romance killer is a spouse who goes through the motions, but who is distracted and not emotionally "there" experiencing with a partner. Constantly thinking about other things, turning romance into an overtly sexual and goal-directed experience, and hurrying it along all detract from romance. Being there emotionally, in the moment, requires shifting out of your "getting things done" mode of functioning. It may take some practice, but psychologically "letting go" of your day-to-day responsibilities is a necessary requisite for romance and for making love. Remember, your partner can intuitively feel whether you're there or not.

J. VARIETY IS THE SPICE OF LOVE. In other words, keep romance interesting. Without intending to do so, couples can allow romance to become monotonous just like the other routines that rule their lives. For most busy men and women, the more routine romance becomes, the stronger the perception that it's just not worth the effort. Today, romance can be playful; tomorrow, languorous and dreamy. It can be a few stolen moments or an entire day to enjoy one another. Romance can be indoors or out and be active or relatively sedentary. Good lovers leap from a foundation of deep trust to keep romance stimulating because it is always a bit different and so very creatively stimulating.

Step V: Developing Your Romantic Potential

You now understand what romance is really all about and you're ready for Step Five: putting what you know about romance into practice. For you and your partner, it's going to take a bit of thought, some discussion, and a willingness to experiment. Do keep in mind that you can't be kids again exactly like you were way back then. Instead, strive to create new romantic experiences that will be deeply fulfilling right now.

There may be many ways to go about actively bringing romance back into your lives. However, you may find that going about this in a somewhat structured way will make the process easier and help you both by-pass some easy mistakes. Here's one way to go about it. It's fun and it can help you learn more about yourself and your partner's romantic needs. Using this structure will bring you closer together as you learn how to meet one another's romantic needs in more sensitive ways.

A. REVIEW ROMANTIC INTERLUDES FROM YOUR PAST. If you haven't had much romance in your life recently, it's helpful to recall what made romance so wonderful way back in the good old days. When you're by yourself or, if you're comfortable with your partner, take a moment to lie back, close your eyes, and let memories of romantic experiences from your youth flood back. Feel the feelings. Experience through all your senses as you take yourself back in time to some of the good times you've had together. Share these memories with your partner. Include your feelings, what happened, and all the sensations that are part of your romantic memories.

B. OUTLINE A FANTASY ROMANTIC INTERLUDE YOU WOULD ENJOY RIGHT NOW. Recognizing that you are not the same person as you were years ago, use your past experiences as a foundation to create a romantic interlude that you would enjoy right now. Make it an evening or several hours of togetherness. Create your fantasy in some detail and write it out. Make sure you include the sensual aspects of the setting. Be specific about an activity that you and your partner would enjoy together. Your fantasy should be realistic enough that it would be possible to carry it out right now— today—without spending much money and without leaving your community.

C. OUTLINE A ROMANTIC INTERLUDE YOU BELIEVE YOUR HUSBAND OR WIFE WOULD ENJOY RIGHT NOW. Now comes the hard part. Without talking it over first, create the same kind of romantic fantasy that you believe your spouse would enjoy. This may be difficult, but the difficulty you encounter may simply indicate just how far you've both let romance slide in your relationship. Don't make the error of projecting your own romantic needs to your partner. After all, you're two different people and what is romantic to you may not meet your partner's needs at all. Again, make it an economical possibility in your own community. As with your own romantic fantasy, make it as detailed as possible and describe it in writing.

D. EXCHANGE ROMANTIC FANTASIES WRITTEN FOR YOUR PARTNER. In other words, compare what you have written for yourself and what your spouse has written for you. You may find them in close correspondence or, more likely, you will immediately see striking differences. To the extent that there are strong similarities, it indicates that you and your husband or wife know one another and your respective romantic needs quite well. However, strong and consistent differences indicate just how far you've grown apart. These signal lack of awareness of one another's needs as well as missing communication about this important part of your lives together.

E. DISCUSS SIMILARITIES AND DIFFERENCES WITH YOUR SPOUSE. This part of the process is absolutely crucial although it is sometimes difficult because you are revealing a deeper part of yourself. By sitting down and talking about what you each need romantically, you learn more about one another. Perhaps you've just assumed you knew what your husband or wife desired. Remember to keep sex out of it. Maybe there were critical misconceptions that have created problems in the past. Or, you may have used past information valid years ago that just isn't up-to-date. By talking about your specific likes and dislikes, your romantic desires and fantasies, you set the stage for putting it all into practice. It helps to keep all your comments about what you need romantically from your partner as positive as possible, very tactful, and always encouraging.

F. DECIDE WHO WILL BEGIN TO CREATE ROMANTIC INTERLUDES. The fact is that if romance is going to become part of the good life you share together, one of you must take the initiative to begin. If you can't decide, flip a coin and the winner can begin the first week. The next time, the other spouse can take the initiative. Use the information you gleaned from your partner to plan an interesting and romantic evening that you both will enjoy. Take turns creating romantic experiences that you share together until husband and wife have each created three romantic interludes. As you start, don't try to do too much too quickly. One romantic experience a week or once every other week is a good interval to begin. If needed, create a small budget for each of you to use.

G. TALK ABOUT HOW TO MAKE YOUR ROMANTIC TOGETHERNESS EVEN BETTER. Later, after you've spent a romantic evening or afternoon together, take a few moments to tell one another about what you really enjoyed about those hours. For best results, eliminate all criticism from your remarks because that's exactly the kind of negativity that has created distance between you in the first place. Focusing only on the positives is not only complimentary and makes your partner feel good, but it also helps you both learn how to become even better together romantically. By now, letting go romantically to really enjoy one another should be easier and more natural for you both. From the living room to the bedroom, you'll see every part of your relationship begin to benefit.

Romantic Recovery Feels Wonderful

Someone has said that romance is characteristic of youth, and it is certainly so. In all likelihood, you were probably much more romantic when you were young than you have been in recent years. On the other hand, romance in adulthood is the kind of experience that keeps you youthful. But, keeping romance alive takes a husband and wife who recognize the value of this kind of special experience. Romance bonds a husband and wife together in a way that no other kind of experience can possibly create.

It's also a grave mistake to think that romance inevitably dies with age or with the stresses and strains of a busy lifestyle. It never has to disappear, but you know personally that it often does. Without thinking about it, romance is shifted to the back burner of your lives as other priorities take over. When examined, the reasons for the demise of romance are many: lack of practice and neglect, a cynical attitude, personal hurt by a partner, misperceptions ("He/she doesn't love me anymore"), excessive drinking or use of drugs, chronic stress, physical and emotional exhaustion, and inability to shut off work-related concerns, just to name a few.

When romance is allowed to die in a marriage, it is often accompanied by "dead feelings" within a husband or wife or both. If two partners haven't had much fun or closeness in their marriage for a long period of time, sometimes they learn to get along without these kinds of experiences. Husbands and wives then get to a point where doing anything together, much less anything that smacks of romantic intimacy or fun, just doesn't matter much anymore. Most of the time though, deep down, such men and women are lonely and long for something better.

Sometimes husbands and wives believe that romance takes a lot of time and that's just not so. A romantic interlude may be an evening or a day, even a weekend spent together. On the other hand, a romantic experience may be just a few minutes of special intimacy spontaneously created and shared by a husband and wife. Once you both break through the barriers (read excuses) that have been created with the years, romance becomes an important part of the couple's mentality that keep you in one another's thoughts every day. Beyond its intimate aspects, romance should be fun so make it fun. As such, these experiences are an essential part of the good life that you are creating together.

To personally prepare yourself for romantic recovery, you may each have to confront some issues within yourself. The more hurt or neglect there has been in your relationship over the years, the more important these personal issues become. Left unresolved, they can completely block any efforts made by you both to bring romance back into your relationship.

1. FORGIVENESS. Part of the readiness to become romantic once again is to forgive the past. Perhaps you and your spouse have allowed your relationship to become strained and distant. By forgiving yourself and your husband or wife for what has happened in the past, you set the stage to begin creating romance and, by extension, the good life for yourselves right now with a clean slate.

2. OPTIMISM. Dovetailing with forgiveness is an optimistic attitude. This counters the discouragement and unhappiness, even depression, often found when life gets too busy. Even worse, some men and women give up on their mates and themselves. By adopting a persistently optimistic attitude, you keep hope alive. You believe that things can get better between you with some effort and, armed with some know-how, you will make it happen.

3. INITIATIVE. A willingness to put forth some energy to re-create romance in your marriage reflects the knowledge that you can exert some control over how you relate to your partner. Conversely, by waiting for your partner to begin, helpless out-of-control feelings grow dominant and are often accompanied by resentment. By making a commitment to change yourself and to take some romantic initiative while doing so, you make it easy for your partner to follow.

4. PERSPECTIVE. Driving the need to bring back romance to your life is a changed, long-term perspective on what is really important in life. There is recognition that you can't wait for the future because you're living it every day. To your credit, you have started to realize *now* that when you reflect on your life in the future, you're not going to wish you had worked more or spent more time getting things done.

In the end, when you look closely, you will find that you've lost a lot as life has gotten busier and more hectic with the years. Romantic experiences rank right up there with having a bit of time for yourself to relax, positive experiences with the kids, good friendships, and fulfilling leisure activities. It's part of the Quality of Life that you're struggling to regain. As you reorient yourself to pursue Quality of Life instead of an enhanced Standard of Living, with a little effort romance will bloom and you'll be together again—literally and figuratively—in a way that you haven't experienced for years. And, there's a wonderful bonus that you simply won't believe until you experience it. When you're romantically together, no matter what your age, you'll both be young again.

Chapter 15

Your Urge to Merge: How to Make Love Instead of Having Sex

As the song says, love is a many splendored thing, and it has many different facets in a marriage relationship. Not the least of these is the sexual part of love. Few would argue that making love is one of the most fulfilling and validating parts of the total relationship between a man and a woman who deeply care about one another. At the same time, many would also argue that the fulfillment of sexual relating can not only disappear with the years, but can also become entangled with conflict and other mixed feelings that have no place in the bedroom. Without even realizing how it happened, a husband and wife can become as emotionally distant in the bedroom as they are in the living room.

For many couples, the decline of a once-good physical relationship signals personal unhappiness and a lifestyle not conducive to emotional intimacy, fulfilling friendship, or the close partnership on which a good marriage is based. Here's a provocative question to ask yourself and answer—truthfully. Then, ask your spouse to answer the same question.

THE BIG BEDROOM QUESTION: "These days, do we really make love or are we just having sex in our bedroom?"

When you're completely honest with yourself, the answer may be a clear and unequivocal "No, we don't make love anymore." Or, while you may have sex fairly frequently, you find yourselves making love only once in a great while and then only under special circumstances. Perhaps your response is that you don't really know because you hardly have any sexual relationship left, much less lovemaking, except on widely spaced and sporadic occasions.

When your husband or wife answers the same questions and is also forthright about them, the answers are likely to be similar because it takes two to make love. And, when the answers of a husband and wife reflect having sex but not making love, it is a sure signal of an important emotional disconnection between a man and woman who used to frequently make mad, passionate, fulfilling love early in their relationship. And, at that time, a freight train couldn't stop them from finding that special time to be together! My, my, how things do change with the years.

Perhaps at this point it would be useful to define these terms.

HAVING SEX: *Engaging in sexual acts for personal physical release or doing so primarily in response to a partner's needs.*

Notice that having sex is a physical act and little else. It stands in stark contrast to making love. It may be relaxing and pleasurable and sometimes even fun, but it lacks the deep emotional meaning of making love. Why? Because, for whatever reason, the emotional sharing that is the core of making love is not present. The fact is that anyone can have sex, but making love is only possible when a husband and wife are emotionally together.

MAKING LOVE: *A sensual union in which caring partners together experience an emotional closeness that is deepened and made more meaningful through physical sharing.*

Now you can see the difference. In short, making love begins with an emotional intimacy which then extends to involve sexual relating. You can feel your partner emotionally experiencing with you. Making love validates the total relationship between a husband and wife in a way that having sex can never do. Making love requires trust and openness and caring. And, it means making your relationship together a top priority. Unfortunately, these are the very qualities that are often lost as life becomes busier and more intense. Too many once-close couples now live together but have grown apart. It's a telling sign that they have sex now and then, but making love has gone by the wayside.

However, all is not lost. You are both perfectly capable of making love again. To set the stage for this to happen, it may help to outline more specifically some of the qualities that define the difference between making love and having sex. Remember that you have sex below the waist, but you make love between your ears when you mentally and emotionally merge to experience as one. When both levels are intimately entwined, it's a special and wonderfully affirming experience. For this to happen, several relationship qualities must be present.

1. TRUST IN YOUR PARTNER. Part of making love is allowing yourself to become emotionally open and therefore vulnerable. For such closeness to develop, you must trust your husband or wife to accept and respect that vulnerability. Further, there must be trust that your spouse deeply cares about you and that your love will endure. In other words, you trust that the bond between you will always be there and your relationship will continue because there is a deep commitment to one another.

2. SENSORY INVOLVEMENT. Making love does not occur in a sensory vacuum. In fact, making love at its best is a total sensory experience in which you both become completely immersed. Sight, touch, smell, and hearing are all important parts of making love. For best effect, sensory involvement must be built slowly; that's what romance is all about. It creates and deepens the desire to make love and stands in contrast to the "Do you want to do it?" approach that reflects a need for sex, but not much else.

3. EMOTIONAL TOGETHERNESS. This third characteristic is at once an extremely important but difficult-to-define quality for making love. Basically, emotional togetherness is an intuitive knowledge that your partner is right there, experiencing at an emotional level with you when you are making love. You feel this emotional union clearly when it is present and are acutely aware when it is absent. This emotional togetherness is an experience that bonds a couple together and is the heart of making love.

4. RECIPROCAL GIVING. If making love is significantly skewed in the direction of either taking from your partner or giving excessively to your spouse, then it's not making love anymore. Somewhere between selfless and selfish lies an easy and reciprocal giving to one another. Further, giving to your spouse must be at both emotional and physical levels. You give to your partner because you want to give of yourself and to pleasure your partner. When such giving goes two ways, you're making love.

5. A FLOW EXPERIENCE. A flow experience occurs when being in the moment is paramount. You are experiencing pleasure moment-by-moment with nothing else—no past, no future, no time consciousness—to distract you. Nowhere is the ability to experience flow more important than when making love. Lovemaking requires no goals, no ego involvements, nothing to prove. It's only the two of you, existing in the moment, emotionally connected and immersed in the pleasure of experiencing one another.

6. LACK OF SELF-CONSCIOUSNESS. This is a special kind of trust that you must have in yourself. It's a basic trust that you are an attractive man or woman and that your spouse is responding to you at that level. This trust eliminates negative self-talk: "What's he thinking?" "Am I doing okay?" "What's going to happen next?"

The variety of questions is endless, but all reflect a self-consciousness that not only forms an emotional barrier, but also prevents you from really making love.

It's true that any two consenting adults can have sex. However, it takes two people with special caring and a deep bond between them to make love. It's precisely these qualities that are lost as life becomes busier, as healthy priorities in life disappear, and as distance grows between a husband and wife. What sex gives you is physical release, and sometimes not even that. Making love gives so much more at every level in your relationship. It's past time to start making love again because it's an essential part of getting better together.

Some Questions and Answers

Keeping your sexual relationship alive and well over the years is not only entirely possible, but is a desirable part of a total marriage relationship. However, with the years and the cumulative effects of pressure, conflict, parenting, and other responsibilities, making love can easily deteriorate into having sex now and then when time and energy permit. While the days of the hormonally-driven, high-energy lovemaking of a twenty-year-old will inevitably pass, when there is a good relationship between a husband and wife, lovemaking gets even better with the years.

When it comes to how two people relate in their bedroom (or wherever!) during a sexual encounter, no hard and fast rules exist. In short, how to make love in the most satisfying way is defined by the couple through their experiences with one another over the years. What is right for a given couple is making love how they want, as often as they want, in ways that are mutually fulfilling. However, it must be understood that some changes will occur in personal sexuality and lovemaking as a relationship matures, as life circumstances change, and as a husband and wife grow older.

Often, however, questions arise in either one partner or both that lead to personal doubt and insecurity in a husband or wife. These questions often reflect lack of understanding or blatant misconceptions about long-term sexual relationships. To allay such needless apprehensions, here are some often-asked questions and answers about marital sexual relating as it evolves over the years.

1. DOES THE IMPORTANCE OF SEXUAL RELATING CHANGE WITH THE YEARS? In a word, yes. Remember back when you were in love in your late teens or early twenties; sexual relating was probably the number one priority in your relationship. However, as the years pass, the overriding importance of the sexual aspect of a relationship slowly falls. Priority-wise, it typically drops somewhat to stand alongside companionship, sharing fun times, emotional intimacy, and communicating well. In short, as the years pass, sexual relating remains a very fulfilling part of most good marriages, but it becomes integrated into the totality of the relationship as one important part of a whole.

2. DOES SEXUAL RELATING CHANGE QUALITATIVELY AS TIME PASSES? Young lovers, with hormones throbbing, make mad passionate love as often as they can. A sexual encounter, though certainly involving intimacy and closeness, is often an intense experience, but quickly over. As a man and woman and their sexual relationship mature, sex gets better as it slows down. It becomes more loving with the addition of romance, foreplay, tenderness, and caring responsiveness to one another's needs afterward. It simply doesn't have that driven quality anymore as a couple develops the ability to make love in ways that are easy, comfortable, and deeply satisfying to them both.

3. IS FREQUENCY OF SEX RELATED TO THE DEPTH OF THE BOND BETWEEN A HUSBAND AND WIFE? In a very broad sense, no. Frequency of sex is relatively independent of how deeply and positively a husband and wife feel about one another. What is important is how comfortable a husband and wife feel about how often they have sex. If they make love once every couple of months, or every other day, it's okay as long as they both feel good about it. However, frequency can become a huge problem and a source of significant conflict if *both* partners don't agree on how often to have sex and fail to reach a level of sexual relating comfortable to both.

4. DOES SEXUAL DESIRE WAX AND WANE? Absolutely! And, incidentally, so do feelings of love and emotional closeness to your partner. Sometimes days or weeks of deep and intense feelings of physical attraction and sexual responsiveness to your partner are followed by their diminution. However, in a good relationship, partners trust that those deeper feelings, while not paramount at the moment, will return. Furthermore, feelings of love, intimacy, and sexual responsiveness are very sensitive to stress and pressure and to how well partners are generally meeting one another's emotional needs. Mature couples realize this and strive to create a lifestyle where the sexual and emotional bonds between them remain strong.

5. HOW LONG CAN A COUPLE EXPECT TO HAVE A FULFILLING SEXUAL RELATIONSHIP? As long as they want. The belief that loving couples stop having sex when they get to retirement age is a myth. So is the misguided notion that older men and women shouldn't have sex after a certain age. The fact is that many couples in their sixties, seventies, and eighties have regular and very satisfying sexual relationships. On the other hand, many couples in these age groups (or younger!) stop having sex altogether. It's not because they can't or shouldn't—it's because they avoid or neglect that part of their relationship. It's their loss; it doesn't have to happen.

Diminished Sexual Feelings

It is certainly true that many couples experience a problem in their sexual relationship after a number of years of marriage. For some, their physical relationship remains emotionally healthy and strong; for many others, interest slowly begins to fade under the weight of daily demands, growing separateness between a husband and wife, and other life problems. More often than not, when a couple's sexual relationship begins to deteriorate, it is a signal that other important parts of their total relationship are beginning to fall apart as well. In other words, an unsatisfying physical relationship is often a symptom that reflects the state of a couple's total relationship.

Furthermore, the decline of a sexual relationship can cause other problems in a marriage because the bonding that making love provides isn't present anymore. Regardless of where and when it begins, a declining physical relationship is both a cause and an effect. And, once the decline begins, it becomes a vicious circle. That is, lack of or discomfort with sexual relating creates negative feelings or insecurities which affect closeness. Lack of emotional closeness then begins to create more problems sexually. This process, unfortunately, drives couples even further apart and creates great unhappiness for them both.

While these difficulties can certainly be manifested as problems while in bed, just as often they are expressed as a lack of desire to make love in the first place. In other words, there is a problem of inhibited sexual desire. Over a period of time, the importance of sexual relating declines because sexual feelings for one another just aren't strong enough anymore. Or, the emotional fulfillment of making love has diminished to the point where it's just not worth the effort. This gradual decline of desire, over time, can have serious effects on a husband and wife and on their relationship.

If lack of sexual desire is prolonged, a first step is to see your family physician to rule out possible physical causes for this problem. However, in the absence of physical factors, it can then be assumed that diminished sexual desire has psychological origins. In fact, sexual feelings can be psychologically suppressed at two levels. The first level may involve ignoring existing sexual feelings because of other priorities. The second and more serious level involves suppression of the sexual feelings themselves. Here, a husband or wife simply does not have any conscious awareness of sexual feelings toward a partner. When this happens to both of them, a couple can drift into an asexual mode of functioning which not only brings many personal doubts and insecurities about personal sexuality, but may also create apprehensions or fears about the status of their marital relationship.

Let's tackle problems of expression first. When sexual feelings are present but not expressed in the relationship, it frequently turns out to be a problem of priorities. Four excuses (and they are excuses!) are commonly heard. While all four have an element of truth, not one should stand in the way of making love regularly. And, all four reflect an unhealthy inversion of life priorities—work, children, spouse, self—in that order. This ranking of priorities must be modified for healthy marital relating, including making love, to blossom again. Here are the usual excuses.

1. "I HAVE TOO MUCH TO DO." There is no question that a busy lifestyle entails a million and one things to do. However, lack of time to make love may really reflect an inability to give to yourself and your relationship. Making love must be considered something that you do for yourself and for your relationship. It is not just another obligation, but a crucial part of affirming the bond between you both. As such, it must be considered an important part of sustaining your relationship and placed high on your priority list, not near the bottom.

2. "I'M TOO TIRED." Again, this problem reflects giving too much to others. Daily demands and responsibilities require external giving: to a home, to a community, to children, to a career. However, when you give everything you have to others and fail to nurture yourself and your marriage, you place yourself on dangerous ground in two respects. First, you inadvertently begin taking your marriage for granted, and, second, you fail to meet your own emotional needs. These two factors are prime ingredients for feeling bad and growing apart emotionally.

3. "THE KIDS ARE ALWAYS AROUND." When the kids were little, young parents could outlast them and have time for themselves after the kids went to bed. As children (and their parents) age, this can become a problem. Not only do the kids demand attention, but it's hard to find time alone in the house without them. The remedy here is to teach children to respect parents' needs to be left alone for periods of time, whether they are talking in the living room or making love in the bedroom. Most children learn to respect parents' privacy only if they are directly and firmly taught to do so over a period of time.

4. "THERE IS NO EMOTIONAL PAYOFF." When making love becomes a chore, it becomes having sex for physical release, but not much else. When this happens, the bond of intimacy between a husband and wife is not affirmed and validated at this deep level. Fortunately, this common bedroom malady is easily remedied. After placing making love higher on their priority list, a couple must learn (or relearn) to make their sexual encounters romantic and emotionally fulfilling. As this happens, making love will not only become attractive, but sorely missed if it's neglected.

When the above factors are allowed to become established as a lifestyle pattern, the net result is an avoidance of the sexual part of a relationship between a husband and wife. It just seems to be too much trouble. Everything else comes first and as their sexual encounters become more infrequent and less fulfilling, sexual feelings often begin to weaken and then fade. Then, there may come a time of literally no awareness of sexual feelings toward a partner at all. At this point, an individual or a couple usually begins to function in an asexual mode in their marriage.

Needless to say, this asexual mode of functioning creates great personal insecurity, as well as questions about the status of a marriage partner. "What's wrong with me that I seem to have no sexual feelings anymore?" is often followed by "What's wrong in my marriage that I have no sexual feelings anymore toward my partner?" Certainly, these are entirely legitimate questions and can create many marital problems (including the temptation of an affair) if the dynamics of what has happened are not understood.

It is an easy but untrue assumption to attribute this asexual state of affairs to the aging process. The fact is that sexual feelings stay alive and well far past retirement age if nurtured along the way. However, libidinal (*i.e.*, sexual) energy is very vulnerable. In many men and women, sexual feelings can easily become repressed when their overall feelings are preponderantly negative: fatigue, stress, resentment and anger, low-level depression, and a life filled with too many things to do and get done. Under the weight of these negative emotions, sexual feelings can easily become suppressed to the point where they are no long even in conscious awareness.

All is not lost, however. The suppression of sexual feelings is rarely permanent. When the overlay of negative feelings is removed, sexual feelings usually return relatively quickly. For example, take a couple on vacation; away from work, home, and the kids, the stress and pressure they feel are reduced. Then, romantic and sexual feelings begin to emerge again, usually within a short period of time. However, practically speaking, it's impossible for couples to go on vacation every week and even getting away for a weekend together isn't feasible except once in a while. Even then, it's a very complicated and time-consuming process.

What makes the solution to this problem most difficult is that coming home is no longer relaxing, particularly in two-career families. As is too often the case, evenings and weekends at home are used to take care of the kids and get everything done to maintain the household. The net result is that home provides no relief from the stresses and pressures of the day. The end result is that when a couple has no time to relax and enjoy one another at home, their once strong sexual feelings are suppressed and easily remain buried.

The fact is that the problem of weak or suppressed sexual desire can be remedied. The essence of the solution, though, is first to recognize that this problem can seriously erode a marriage relationship. Second, it is up to a couple to begin to place a high priority on one another and to begin to nurture their relationship at emotional, recreational, communication, and physical levels. Because it isn't possible to get away from daily responsibilities, a couple must learn to emotionally embrace one another at home which, ironically, has become the most difficult place of all to relax and enjoy one another.

Finally, there are steps each partner in a relationship can take personally to increase sexual desire. Not one of these changes depends on a partner; these steps are taken for oneself. Six interrelated factors have been shown to enhance personal sexual feelings.

1. BEGIN TO EXERCISE REGULARLY. A trend toward mental

work (in lieu of physical labor) along with busy lifestyles has often contributed to lack of time for physical exercise and active recreation. "Leisure" becomes very sedentary when a man or woman collapses after a hard day of meeting heavy demands, deadlines, and tight schedules. Becoming more physically active through exercise or recreational outlets not only keeps muscles in tone, but also contributes to increased sexual energy.

2. BUILD YOUR SELF-ESTEEM. Many busy men and women who once had relatively good self-concepts begin to experience negative feelings about themselves when under prolonged stress. When personal emotional needs are not met, self-esteem plummets and this may be accompanied by a decline in sexual energy and interest. To begin feeling good about yourself and enhancing your sexual energy, start doing small things for yourself regularly: take a bit of time to relax at home, meet a friend for a cup of coffee, or go for a walk with your spouse.

3. TURN OFF THE TELEVISION SET. Certainly, it is well-known that too much television negatively affects children. However, it is also true that massive television time also adversely affects adults. Coming home tired and becoming very sedentary by watching television during all available free time worsens the emotional fatigue that most adults feel these days. As lethargy breeds more lethargy, sexual energy often begins to decline. Conversely, turning off the television set in lieu of other interesting activities stimulates sexual energy.

4. MANAGE STRESS BETTER. As stress and pressure experienced by a husband and wife increase, so do negative emotions: a low level of depressive state (*i.e.*, burnout), persistent irritability, and chronic fatigue. Often these powerful emotions not only contribute to negative feelings about oneself, but also cause conflict and more distance from a spouse. The result is that sexual feelings are often diminished. Conversely, simplifying life and managing stress better help generate sexual energy.

5. ENHANCE YOUR BODY IMAGE. Several surveys have documented the fact that personal body image is highly related to sexual feelings. If you don't feel good about your body, it's psychologically much more difficult to enter into a deep and loving sexual relationship. Improving your body image certainly doesn't mean you must strive to be Mr. or Mrs. America, but losing a few pounds, toning up your muscles, and making yourself attractive as a man or woman does help create sexual responsiveness. When both partners do this for themselves, each partner benefits as well.

6. LEARN TO RELAX. Sexual feelings for most men and women frequently depend on being personally relaxed. When you are scurrying at top speed from one task to the next, stress builds and suppresses sexual feelings. Further, sexual feelings have no time to mentally and emotionally build in anticipation of making love. By learning to relax and psychologically "let go" of responsibilities and daily problems, the inhibiting effect of stress and pressure is lifted and sexual feelings emerge as you have more time to think about them.

Problems with Sexual Relating

On first thought, problems with sexual relating might be interpreted to mean overt sexual dysfunctions. However, while sexual dysfunctions (*e.g.*, impotence or absence of orgasm) do exist, many such problems resolve with the re-creation of a close, caring marital relationship and the addition of romance to making love. In other words, just having sex now and then with a spouse who is emotionally distant and who happens to live under the same roof can often create such problems. More often than not, such problems are temporary although they can cause great insecurity and distress when present.

On the other hand, many equally significant sexual problems exist that do not involve overt sexual dysfunctions. The base problem is that sexual relating can easily become an arena where all manner of nonsexual problems surface in a marriage relationship. In fact, as already stated, the only other area with as much potential for marital conflict lies in how a couple handles money. When these extraneous needs and conflicts are brought into the bedroom, they become easily entangled in lovemaking.

In other words, instead of a sexual encounter affirming the emotional bond between a man and a woman, these emotionally loaded issues lead to many negative feelings that can drive a couple further apart. In the end, and with repetition, such feelings create negative anticipation of sex. This then leads to emotional suppression of sexual feelings and, finally, either neglect or outright avoidance of this important part of a couple's total relationship. It is incumbent upon every couple to remove all such sources of potential conflict from their bedroom so that they are free to really make love once again.

To resolve these sources of sexual discomfort requires not only knowledge, but also personal security. That is, confidence in one's own sexuality unencumbered by sexual stereotypes and unhealthy attitudes. Here are some of the common problems encountered by couples after they have been married for a number of years. Each and every one of these problems is driven either by personal insecurity or a self-centered orientation toward sex. Talking about the problems and finding creative solutions or satisfying compromises can only help.

1. ABSENT SEXUAL COMMUNICATION. This may be due to excessive reserve or shyness on one or both partners' parts. A husband or wife is somehow supposed to know what is loving and arousing to a partner without any direct communication about it. When there is lack of such communication, sexually relating can easily become unsatisfying or an outright uncomfortable experience. This is especially the case when husbands or wives begin to project their own needs and desires onto a partner.

SUGGESTION: The best solution here is to directly ask a partner about what is comfortable and arousing during a sexual encounter. Sometimes, it helps to subtly guide a partner during lovemaking without direct advice which can sometimes be taken as rejection or failure. Don't forget to supportively reinforce your partner verbally and nonverbally for responding to personal needs in more loving ways.

2. INITIATIVE ISSUES. Not infrequently, as a couple drifts apart, one or both partners become apprehensive about initiating lovemaking because of so many past rejections. Often, these rejections have not been kind and have deeply hurt self-esteem. Or, there is an expectation that one partner always initiate (often male) and the other one (often female) never do so. Sometimes discomfort develops because one partner initiates so often that a spouse never has the chance to take the lead.

SUGGESTION: To break out of this self-created box, try taking turns initiating romantic and sexual encounters. At first, use a time frame in which alternating partners initiate lovemaking within one week of the last encounter. Further, if you're just not in the mood, make sure you are very kind and supportive in saying no and suggest an alternative activity or a specific later time.

3. STEREOTYPED SEX ROLES. Inappropriate perceptions of what males and females are supposed to do in bed are many. For example, it's okay for men to be sexually aggressive, but women are not supposed to be active. Or, to provide sex is a woman's obligation to a husband. If she enjoys it, that's just incidental. If a partner doesn't reach orgasm, that man or woman is sexually inadequate and has failed. These unhealthy perceptions all produce serious barriers to fulfilling lovemaking.

SUGGESTION: It is important to talk out these issues and, over time, free one another from these inhibiting bonds. Remember, making love and bonding at both an emotional and physical level is a gift that a husband and wife give to one another and to their relationship. For the good life, learning to freely enjoy yourselves and one another in the living room *and* in the bedroom is essential.

4. SEX AS A WEAPON. It is unfortunate that sexual withdrawal is often used in a punitive fashion by both sexes. Without realizing it, the possibility of a sexual encounter is used as both a carrot and a stick to control a husband or wife. If a partner is good, sex is available; if a partner "misbehaves," sex is withheld. Although an individual may not be consciously aware of this use of sex, nonetheless it creates anger and ultimately creates more emotional distance in a marital relationship.

SUGGESTION: It is extremely important to any loving marital relationship that sex not be used in any controlling fashion. The baseline of emotional and physical bonding must remain constant. The best solution is for both partners to make sure that they communicate well and resolve problems and differences in the living room. That way, this problem will not contaminate their bedroom.

5. TIMING OF SEX. As busy lifestyles develop for a couple, time is at a premium. Add to this reality that one partner may be a morning person and the other may be a night owl. The implications for a serious disparity in sexual relating are then obvious. The morning person may enjoy sex most early in the morning. Conversely, the other partner may want to initiate lovemaking late at night when a husband or wife is dead tired (or may awaken a partner for a sexual encounter in the middle of the night!).

SUGGESTION: Here, solutions that meet both spouses' needs seem to work best. For example, with advance knowledge, both partners can save time and energy for an evening encounter. At the same time, to suit the morning person, making love is arranged early in the day. Although sex must often be "scheduled," don't forget to reserve enough time to become romantically relaxed.

6. CRITICAL ATTITUDES. When this insidious and destructive problem is present, one spouse constantly complains to and about the other partner during lovemaking. The candle's too bright, the kids can hear, a spouse isn't responding exactly right, and for many other picayune reasons, everything isn't perfect. To make matters worse, every little thing evokes a comment. Sooner or later, a husband or wife begins to feel constantly criticized and put down, and then eventually avoids sex altogether in order to escape that growing feeling of failure.

SUGGESTION: Making love is relating intimately with great vulnerability on both a husband and wife's part. As a result, support for one another must be constant. Further, no situation is perfect, but it can become even better by commenting on and reinforcing the positive. What is really important is making love; let those little things pass.

7. WORKING AT SEX. When a man or woman is working at the office or at home, activity becomes very goal-directed and oriented to finishing. Often, a premium is put on getting work done as quickly as possible and anticipating what is coming next before the present task is completed. Sound a bit familiar? What productive workers may not realize, however, is just how easily this whole orientation to work can be applied to lovemaking. When this happens, sex becomes stressful and worklike. Consequently, it is not very fulfilling.

SUGGESTION: When you're making love, forget about goals and speed. Just going with the flow of relating sexually is in direct contrast to working. It will take some practice to learn to shift gears into a more relaxed mode of relating in bed. It often helps to first begin learning how to relax through easy conversations and fun leisure activities.

8. FREQUENCY OF SEX. Libido, or sexual energy, varies significantly from person to person. It is sensitive not only to situational factors (*e.g.*, stress and pressure), but may also wax and wane from week to week or month to month. Certainly, sexual energy changes in both sexes with age. For many reasons, a husband and wife may find themselves "out of phase" with one another in terms of their sexual energy and responsiveness. If not addressed, these differences can cause great conflict.

SUGGESTION: In a loving relationship, a husband and wife try to understand one another's needs and respond to them because each partner cares deeply about the other. This works well as long as lovemaking doesn't become selfish or "just sex." Often, even if one spouse is not really in the mood, going ahead with a bit of romantic involvement awakens the desire to make love to a partner.

9. SEXUALIZING ALL TOUCH. As life gets busier, affection between a husband and wife often begins to decline. No hugs, holding hands, or sitting close anymore. A perfunctory kiss on the cheek now and then becomes the norm and sometimes that must be requested. The next destructive step is that any affection that is offered becomes a sexual message: "I want to go to bed." Then the deep emotional bond between a husband and wife weakens with a perception that "My spouse only wants me for sex."

SUGGESTION: One of the best remedies for a declining sexual relationship is to bring back lots of regular, spontaneous, nonsexual affection in the living room. Such affection begins to rebuild closeness and intimacy in a relationship. It communicates responsiveness and appreciation of a spouse as a complete person. Then, receptivity to lovemaking grows quickly.

10. SEX AS STRESS MANAGEMENT. While most individuals respond to chronic stress and pressure with decreased sexual energy, a few men and women experience increased sexual needs under the same conditions. For these individuals (probably no more than 10–15%), sexual relating becomes a stress management strategy that truly relieves personal tension. A problem grows when both husband and wife are under stress and one spouse experiences a strong increase in sexual energy and the other's desire is correspondingly diminished.

SUGGESTION: The obvious solution here is for both husband and wife to manage stress more effectively. Then, their sexual needs will even out, and they can truly make love once again. When one partner has strong stress-driven sexual needs and then imposes that on the other for selfish reasons, it is imperative that alternative means be learned to reduce stress and to relax.

Becoming Friends and Lovers

When you and your husband or wife were young, you were friends and lovers. Now that you're an established couple with a home to maintain, children to care for, busy careers, and a few community responsibilities thrown in for good measure, your lives have changed dramatically. And, so has your physical relationship. Sadly, you have grown away from one another while living under the same roof. You started out in life as friends and lovers. Now you're neither. It's time to fix this unfortunate, but rather common, state of marital affairs.

Anyone can have sex, but relatively few couples consistently make love. Making love requires a bonding of your hearts and minds, as well as your bodies. To become friends and lovers once again, start with your friendship. Until your friendship is rebuilt, romance and making love will not mean much. In other words, good sex starts in the living room and in how you treat one another every day. As your guide, keep in mind that in contrast to the well-known comment, deep fulfilling love doesn't "go without saying" or doing or sharing.

It should not be surprising that when a couple focuses on their friendship and begins to live the good life together, their physical relationship improves almost without effort. Why? Because they are interested in one another. They trust each other deeply. And, they have their priorities in order. They are Number One for each other. For the same reason, personal insecurities decrease and stress diminishes. Because they have become close, giving to one another is easy and becomes reciprocal. Problems can be resolved in mutually satisfying ways because both husband and wife are willing to compromise. The good feelings of that husband and wife for their mates then extend into their bedroom, with the result that love and friendship begin to blossom once again.

In the end, however, becoming a close friend and lover to your spouse is not your partner's responsibility. It is up to you. You may have to strive to develop a stronger sense of your own masculinity or femininity. You may have to resolve conflicts or other issues that had their origins in early experiences or in parental teachings. Fundamentally, it is up to you to begin again to celebrate yourself as an attractive man or woman. When you confront your insecurities and overcome them, the efforts that you have made for yourself will soon become apparent to your spouse.

No matter what your age, you're never too old to love and to make love. To exist under the same roof and have sex occasionally isn't what the good life is all about. And, making love is part of what keeps you both young at heart and full of life. When deep and abiding love returns to your relationship, you will begin to see an inner beauty in one another that has been hidden for years . Sadly, as someone once commented, "In this world of give and take, only a few give what it takes." How true of love in the living room and the bedroom. Remember e.e. cumming's remark: "unlove's the heavenless hell and homeless home . . . lovers alone wear sunlight."

Chapter 16

Creating "Doubles Diversions": Having Fun Together Again

To the young, the whole world is brand-new and waiting out there to be experienced with a loved one. Starting off life together, a young couple in love finds every day full of interesting and stimulating things to do. Adventures they can share seem to be everywhere, and they have plenty of time to plan new ones. While certainly some work must be done, it is broken up by regular experiences that are not only fun, but help that young couple to relax and unwind. These are "the good old days," but the realization of just how good they are may not come for a decade or more.

Then, as life becomes busier, these same wonderful and fulfilling marriage relationships slowly change until a point is reached where very common complaints are heard:

"We just don't have any fun anymore. When we were young, it didn't matter what we did; we had fun all the time.

"It seems that every time we go out to have some fun these days, we wind up bickering, and that never used to happen."

"In the past, we used to do lots of things together. These days, we don't seem to have any interests in common."

"Sometimes we go out together and it's nice, but it's really hard to relax and 'let go' with one another like in the past."

"All we've done lately is sit around the house and watch TV, and that's not much fun. It's boring."

The themes of these complaints seem to be twofold. First, the couples used to spend lots of time together and have loads of fun, but that was in the past when they were young. Second, for one reason or another, the ability to "let go" and have regular fun together has disappeared over the years. The reasons for this common state of affairs are as many as they are powerful in their influence on how married couples live together. Because of this common state of marital affairs, a cynic might even come to believe that being married for a number of years and having regular, relaxed, fun times together are antithetical.

Let's cut right to the bottom line. Having fun together and being married for a while is definitely not an oxymoron, that is, a contradiction in terms. However, to redevelop the ability to "let go" and have fun again takes know-how and practice. It also requires that importance be placed on leisure activities and recreation. If you're not having much fun anymore, it is likely that work priorities have inadvertently come to dominate your life, and in so doing have eliminated relaxation time. These inverted priorities must be rolled back and replaced with healthier lifestyle and marriage values, not the least of which is regularly shared recreational experiences.

To begin to re-create the ability to have fun together, several points must be made to create the context for developing these skills once again. These ideas together form the rationale for bringing fun times back into your married life.

1. HAVING FUN IS MORE DIFFICULT TO JUSTIFY THAN WORKING. In childhood, men and women learn that work comes first and fun comes later. In other words, you must meet all your responsibilities first and only then can you justify having fun. These days, this "bonus" theory of relaxation is being replaced. Now, regular relaxation has become a health mandate and is justified on that basis regardless of whether you are "all caught up" or not!

2. LACK OF A SHARED RECREATIONAL OUTLET IS AN INDEX OF HOW FAR APART YOU'VE GROWN. There is truth in the axiom that "Those who play together, stay together." One reason marriages break up is because of too much work and no play, resulting in one partner eventually finding someone "to have fun with." Having fun and playing together cement togetherness—a connection that makes all the hard work worthwhile.

3. GETTING OUT AND HAVING FUN CONTRIBUTES TO QUALITY OF LIFE AND LENGTH OF LIFE. In short, "getting away from it all" mentally and physically to have some fun together is what makes all the hard work worthwhile. Furthermore, not only is active relaxation fun, but it also helps keep your body in tone. Evidence is steadily coming in that such activity, reflecting a balanced lifestyle, contributes to health and personal longevity.

4. IT MAY BE EASIER TO LEARN TO HAVE FUN WITH OTHER PEOPLE. There are several reasons for this distressing fact. Another fun-loving couple acts as a trigger for you and your spouse to do the same. When you are together alone, it's much easier to fall into old marital ruts: bickering, talking about work or the kids, or becoming defensive with one another and giving up. Joining with other couples helps not only to have fun, but also to develop friendships.

Perhaps at this point, it is important to define what "letting go" really means. In the best kinds of fun, an individual or couple is able to become so absorbed in an activity that work, responsibilities, or other concerns are completely forgotten for a while. That is, at a psychological level, they literally "let go" for a period of time. This kind of experience is not only pleasurable, but is also rejuvenating. It allows emotional energy to be regenerated after being depleted through constant mental work. Couples who have lost the ability to "let go" and have fun feel down, discouraged, tense, stressed, and, of course, distanced from one another.

Three Important Principles

In a broad sense, creating lifestyle balance means placing priority not only on work, but also on leisure interests, loved ones, and friendships. However, when it comes to developing fulfilling leisure activities, lifestyle balance has another more specific meaning. You already know that work has evolved in the direction of steadily becoming more mental in nature, quite sedentary, and often increasingly solitary. When these same qualities show up during time spent at home, that individual will often begin to experience all the dysphoric effects of stress overload, which in turn contribute to marital problems.

Because work activities with these characteristics absorb so many hours each week, they must be balanced with their opposites for an individual to remain healthy and upbeat. Here are three guidelines to use when choosing recreational outlets that help create this important balance. And, because they stand in direct contrast to work, they are often more stimulating and fun than those leisure outlets that are psychologically similar to work.

PRINCIPLE #1: THE MORE MENTAL WORK YOU DO IN YOUR CAREER, THE MORE IMPORTANT IT IS TO DEVELOP A "HANDS-ON" AVOCATION. One downside aspect of making a living doing mental work is that it all takes place "between your ears." Leisure activities that require at least moderate activity help focus attention away from thoughts of work or responsibility. Thus, they are more rejuvenating. Further, many men and women doing mental work see no direct cause-effect relationship in anything they do.

Many men and women develop a need to "make things happen" in very obvious ways. An active, hands-on avocation satisfies the desire to experience a cause-effect relationship.

PRINCIPLE #2: THE MORE SEDENTARY YOUR WORK, THE MORE NECESSARY IT IS TO DEVELOP PHYSICALLY ACTIVE RECREATIONAL OUTLETS. No one these days can dispute the benefits of regular physical activity. And, physical activity is becoming ever more important as work, because it is largely mental, has also become extremely sedentary. To make matters worse, many easy and seductive "leisure" activities after work are both sedentary and passive, like television and watching videos. To maintain both physical health and emotional well-being, it is extremely important for couples to develop physically-active avocations to enjoy together.

PRINCIPLE #3: THE MORE SOLITARY YOUR WORK, THE MORE CRITICAL IT IS TO FIND LEISURE ACTIVITIES THAT INVOLVE OTHER PEOPLE. Although not true across the board, information-processing technology, combined with intense pressure, has isolated many men and women from the collegiality once found in the workplace. At home, adults are often isolated from neighbors and have little time to spend with friends. To counter this negative trend, it is often helpful for couples to develop leisure outlets that involve other people, particularly good friends. While enjoying an activity together, couples can solidify friendships as well as relax and enjoy one another as people.

Get Out of the TV Rut

One of the big tasks for most couples wanting to have fun together is to move beyond their television habit. If the television tends to be on whenever anyone is in the house, it is very diagnostic for couples to ask themselves three questions:

1. "What do you spend most of your time doing when you're at home?" Most common answer: "Watching television."

2. "Is it stimulating and fun?" Most common answer: "No, it's often boring, but it helps pass the time."

3. "Do you feel close to your spouse when watching television?" Most common answers: "No, we hardly talk at all when the TV is on" or "Every time I say anything when my spouse is watching TV, I'm told to be quiet and come back later."

These answers reflect a serious problem for many married couples. Just flipping on the TV set is too easy. Particularly during the hectic parenting years, both husbands and wives watch television virtually nightly, but with consistent differences in their styles. During these busy years, wives tend to work while they are watching television. Men, on the other hand, tend to lie on the couch or in a recliner and watch in an extremely sedentary way. Not only are men more prone to become true "couch potatoes," but the vast majority of "channel changers" with the fastest thumbs around also are male.

The big question that must be addressed, however, is what the massive amounts of time spent watching television are replacing. Typically, it replaces healthier outlets like quality time with the family. Spending time with good friends. Or, involvement in quality leisure or recreational time. Look at the three principles above which help to create lifestyle balance in those individuals whose careers involve mostly mental work, and whose work is primarily solitary and sedentary. Television watching as a primary leisure outlet is but an extension of these patterns.

Furthermore, several other negatives accrue from spending massive amounts of time in front of the television set.

1. TELEVISION IS NOT USED FOR ENTERTAINMENT. Often, watching television is not stimulating, entertaining, or even fun. However, it does have some distraction effect on men and women who do mental work all day. When watching television, people sometimes think less about work and responsibilities. However, this is only a partial diversion because troubling thoughts keep creeping back into awareness. The result is that watching television as a way to "get away from it all" is only partially effective and therefore a poor substitute for more active leisure outlets.

2. TELEVISION IS NOT REJUVENATING. Because it is not fully effective in eliminating thoughts that reflect personal and career responsibilities, television often inhibits emotional rejuvenation. Remember that to recover from physical labor, it is necessary to sleep or rest. However, the remedy for mental labor is quality relaxation time with interesting diversions in your life. Thus, watching television while working (women) usually isn't helpful. Nor is dozing or reclining while watching television (men).

3. TELEVISION REINFORCES MARITAL ISOLATION. In other words, except under very limited and special circumstances, it is very difficult to feel close to your husband or wife while watching television. On a nightly basis, if she's working and he's reclining, the net effect of these activities is more isolation. The separation is even worse when he watches his shows on one set and she watches hers in another room on another set. When a couple hasn't been together all day and this is how they spend their evenings, isolation and loneliness begin to grow.

4. TELEVISION IS A POOR SUBSTITUTE FOR REALITY. Television often replaces personal and active interests. Watching a baseball or basketball game on television now and then isn't a problem. Nor is viewing a show depicting trout fishing on a beautiful mountain stream. Sitting down to a golf classic can't be faulted, either. That is, unless watching such shows on television becomes a complete substitute for actual experiences. In other words, if you once liked to fish and golf and now only go fishing or golfing via your television set, there is a problem.

5. TELEVISION CONTRIBUTES TO SLEEP PROBLEMS IN MEN. Your body needs some physical activity every day to sleep well. Men who work in sedentary jobs and then passively watch television at night often complain of tiredness and sleep problems. Sedentary home activities disturb sleep even more if high levels of stress or personal burnout are present. Such men may feel chronically tired and often sleep long but not well. Increasing activity levels helps produce a sounder and more refreshing sleep, with fewer hours of it needed to feel energetic the next day.

6. TELEVISION UNDERMINES MOTIVATION. A subtle but destructive aspect of a chronic television habit is lethargy. With a sedentary career, too much television, particularly if watched in a sedentary fashion, contributes to an amotivational state. A chronic tiredness develops so that it's difficult to get the energy to do anything else. A side effect of this lethargy is that sexual energy (libido) also frequently drops. This creates a triple marital whammy: too much isolation watching TV, persistent fatigue, and no sexual energy, which creates even more distance between a husband and wife.

The issue here is not that television *per se* is bad. It can be educational and entertaining. The problem is too much television which eliminates time spent in healthier recreational activities. To break this bad habit, here are some suggestions. And, make no mistake about it, overcoming your TV habit also helps develop better TV watching attitudes in your children.

1. DO NOT USE TELEVISION FOR BACKGROUND NOISE. It's a bad habit to walk in the house, turn on the TV, and then go to another room. You're not really watching or even listening to it. It's just noise. Instead, begin to train yourself to walk right past the TV set when entering the house. You'll both begin to enjoy the quiet which will facilitate talking.

2. BEGIN TO PLAN "TV-FREE" EVENINGS TOGETHER. That is, do other things at home for one night at a time without resorting to watching TV. This may seem difficult at first because a huge and uncomfortable void opens up on that evening. However, with a little forethought, all kinds of interesting activities to enjoy right around the house (or outside) can be found.

3. WHEN YOU WATCH TELEVISION, DO SO VERY DISCRIMINATELY. That is, when you are really interested in seeing a good show, turn the television set on. When that particular program is over, then turn the television off. It is interesting that when TV is viewed in this way, it becomes a much more interesting and personally satisfying diversion.

4. SIT DOWN TOGETHER TO WATCH SPECIFIC SHOWS. Watching a specific show now and then can be quality time spent together. It helps if this occurs after the kids are in bed or have gone out. This means don't lie down (unless together) or work while watching. Sitting close on a couch or sofa helps. Chat while watching the show and plan some good snacks to enjoy together.

5. NEVER LET TELEVISION INTERFERE WITH SOCIAL INTERACTION. Here, bad habits are rampant. Immediately turn the TV off when friends drop over. Never leave the TV on during meals. When your spouse wants to talk, don't try to do so with the TV set on. Beyond being discourteous, all of these habits create distance between you and those you love the most, including your spouse.

Note: A frequently-asked question is whether reading, using a personal computer, or playing video games is harmful as a leisure activity. On the positive side, these activities are interactive and therefore better than passively watching TV. On the downside, such leisure activities can be very isolating if too much time is spent on them to the exclusion of family and marital recreational activities. Further, if these are the only leisure outlets, lack of physical activity may eventually cause health problems.

Barriers to Enjoyment

As couples make a commitment to "the good life" and to finding interesting leisure activities to enjoy together, they usually find some strong initial barriers to enjoying such outlets. This is particularly true if a couple has given up virtually all recreational activities because of the busy lifestyles they have developed. A similar state of affairs also occurs when a husband and wife enjoy only separate recreational activities—that is, they enjoy no leisure activity as a couple. In other words, having fun together is actually a form of intimacy that has been allowed to erode in the marriage and now must be carefully rebuilt.

To put it bluntly, when a couple has allowed work demands to overwhelm their relationship and have grown apart while living together, they typically do not "snap back together" like two magnets just because they have decided to have some fun. Ironically, they are going to have to practice enjoying one another. They must also confront and work through a number of personal and psychological barriers that have grown over the years and that act together to prevent enjoyment of leisure activities.

Although it may require effort in the beginning, the results of committing yourselves to developing "doubles diversions" are eminently worthwhile, not to mention that living the good life together is virtually impossible unless you have regular fun together. Here are a number of the most common barriers that stand in the way of enjoying yourselves as a couple. Certainly not every couple is going to experience every barrier, but every couple is certain to encounter a few of them. As you face and overcome these barriers—together— you grow as individuals and as a couple.

1. THE "TRIGGER" PROBLEM. This occurs in relationships where one individual, early in a marriage, found it easy to let go and have fun. As such, this husband or wife's personality was a trigger for a more reserved spouse to do the same. However, with a pressured lifestyle and increased stress, this freedom to let go declined, and the initiative it created for a spouse was lost. The end result is that neither spouse can let go now because neither is able to initiate it.

THE SOLUTION: Begin by making regular time to be together. Then, one spouse must begin being lighthearted and open, even if it feels forced at first. Soon, the ability to let go together, never lost but emotionally suppressed, will "click in" and become easy again.

2. DISTRUST OF SPOUSE. The question here is whether a husband or wife can be emotionally unguarded with a spouse, even while having fun. Often, the question is "no." When put-downs, arguments, or angry outbursts occur during fun times, that time is usually ruined. After a few such experiences, the ability to have fun together is severely inhibited. Frequently, couples just eliminate joint recreational activities because they are so uncomfortable.

THE SOLUTION: Each partner must make a studious decision to avoid conflict at all costs during fun times. Problems and other irritations can be talked about later. If one partner goofs up, a sincere, quick apology should be made, and the issue completely dropped.

3. "BONUS" PERCEPTION OF LEISURE. This problem has its roots in one value of the work ethic: "You can only justify relaxing and enjoying yourself when your work is completely done and you are all caught up." The reality is that these days, one never gets completely caught up. When this value begins to drive one's life, then one of two things happens: either a heavy workload completely precludes having fun together or relaxation time is scarce because so much work must be done beforehand.

THE SOLUTION: First, justify regular fun times on the basis of emotional, physical, and marital health. Then make time to enjoy regular leisure activities regardless of whether you are caught up or not. After that, you can return to work more upbeat and with more energy.

4. WORK THAT CAN BE SEEN. This insidious barrier stems from deciding not to do work when it is right there in front of you and obviously needs to be done. The emotional association, usually learned during childhood, is that to actively decide not to do work that needs to be done is bad, immature, and irresponsible behavior and that one should feel guilty about it. Where does the problem show up? It tends to completely eliminate the possibility of relaxing together at home because there is so much work there that needs to be done and it's sitting right before your eyes!

THE SOLUTION: "Out of sight, out of mind" is the byword here. Begin the process of learning to relax and having fun together outside the house. It's mentally much easier to "let go" when work isn't seen. Later on, bring relaxation back home.

5. DIFFICULTY OVERCOMING ROUTINES. Because there is so much to do each day, life routines and daily goals are helpful. Daily lists, activity organizers, and notes to oneself all help in this regard. The net result is that daily life comes to be ruled by self-created timetables and deadlines. Often, particularly in dual-career families, structure and routines carry over into the weekend. The net result is that recreational activities require breaking a routine, which is very uncomfortable.

THE SOLUTION: The solution here is so simple it is often missed. Make recreational activities a high priority and then "schedule" them into your daily or weekly activities. However, be careful to schedule only times to start and stop. Avoid structuring your leisure activities themselves to keep them open and fluid.

6. LACK OF PRACTICE "LETTING GO." The fact is that all children have the natural ability to "let go" and enjoy themselves by becoming deeply absorbed in an interesting activity. As their lives fill up with work and home responsibilities, adults frequently lose this very important skill. The reason is lack of practice. They spend so little leisure time together that they can't "get into" the experience without distracting thoughts of work demands—what must be done and what hasn't been done yet.

THE SOLUTION: To bring back this skill, regular time spent having fun (preferably outside the house) is the antidote. Enough time must be allowed to become absorbed in the activity. Do not contaminate activity by bringing work along or verbalizing any work-related thoughts.

7. USE OF INTOXICANTS. Unfortunately, one of the most common problems with enjoying leisure activities is the chronic association of intoxicants with time spent together. This signals that the individual (or couple) has lost the ability to "let go" without chemical aid. Often, the habitual use of intoxicants (street drugs, alcohol, sometimes prescription tranquilizers) begins as a way to "unwind" after work and then carries over into recreational activities where it begins to sabotage real fun.

THE SOLUTION: To be healthy and well-adjusted, adults must relearn to have fun without any use whatsoever of chemicals to "loosen up." By making this commitment, a valuable skill is relearned and future drug or alcohol problems can be eliminated.

8. FRIENDS WHO MODEL INAPPROPRIATE RESPONSES. It is a truism that busy men and women gravitate to others who are just like themselves. Then, when they socialize or go out to have some fun together, they talk about work and its problems. Or, they begin to drink to "get away from it all." The consequence of contact with such friends is that quality relaxation and fun leisure times are contaminated. The beneficial effects are significantly diminished and true closeness is sabotaged.

THE SOLUTION: Make it a point as a couple to find friends who don't care what you do for a living, wouldn't understand if you tried to explain it, and don't want to hear about it. Such good friends just want to know and enjoy you both only as interesting people.

9. CHANGED INTEREST PATTERNS. As you have matured, your lifestyle has changed. And, it is entirely possible that your recreational interests have changed as well. At this point, those activities that used to be fun and pleasurable no longer have that effect. In fact, they may be sterile and unfulfilling. The same may be true for your spouse. It is certainly not uncommon to find both husband and wife who are more aware of what they don't like to do than what they do like to do to have fun together.

THE SOLUTION: The remedy is experimentation. Talk about possibilities that might be fun. Then, be willing to put forth some effort to try them out. It is helpful to accompany other couples who are already involved in that activity to show you the ropes.

10. SOCIAL OR SELF-IMAGE PROBLEMS. The theme of this problem is simple: "Married people don't do that. What would other people think?" Sometimes this reaction is focused on a recreational outlet that seems to be "kid stuff" or beneath the decorum of a couple married for some years. At other times, this barrier prevents an individual or couple from "letting go" to be light-hearted, impulsive, and spontaneous. This difficulty results from constant training to carefully monitor personal behavior to make sure of its social acceptability.

THE SOLUTION: Who really cares what you do to have fun? Recreation is something you and your spouse do for yourselves and for no one else. If it's fun and healthy, then do it. The sheer enjoyment then will override your unduly restrictive self-image.

Suggestions for Re-creating Recreation

Now you realize just how much of your life together has filled with responsibilities constantly bombarding you from every possible direction. And, realizing that life has become more intense and complicated, it stands to reason that to relearn to have fun together again is going to take some time and some relearning. Such learning goes far beyond facing the barriers to double's diversions that can easily prevent them from getting started. As absurd as it sounds, it is not uncommon for one or both marriage partners to exclaim, "I don't even know how to have fun anymore."

Certainly it is necessary for both partners to commit themselves to the time needed to enjoy fun activities together. Not just once, but on a regular basis. And, you already know that it may take some experimenting to find an activity that you both will enjoy at this point in your lives. As you begin to spend this pleasurable time together, don't expect miracles. At first, it may be very difficult to let go. You

may feel like you're just going through the motions. As with anything, however, repetition helps and soon you will find yourselves
slipping into the leisure mode of relating quite easily.

The emphasis in having some fun together is to make leisure
time quality time. Here are a number of suggestions that will help you
to make that time the purest possible, that is, clear of distractions.
The result is that you will enjoy that time together much more.

1. PLAN ENOUGH REGULAR TIME. The fact is that if you
haven't relaxed together for a while, it is literally going to take some
time to psychologically let go. If you don't let yourself become
deeply absorbed in having fun, you'll be thinking of what you've got
to do next. In the beginning, at least an hour or two will be necessary. With practice, this time can be shortened to as little as thirty
or forty minutes as you learn to shift gears more quickly.

2. FOCUS ON THE PROCESS. Make it a point not to approach
leisure activities the same way as work. Good fun has no past and
no future; enjoy yourselves moment-by-moment just being together because that's the essence of relaxing and rejuvenating. Play
for fun and don't get upset if you don't win. Set no goals for the
experience. The best attitude is simple: Become involved in and enjoy the experience to the fullest.

3. BUILD IN SOME ADVENTURE. Remember way back when
you were young? There were new things to try and do all the time.
When you're re-creating recreation, some adventure helps. Trying
something new and different is stimulating and helps break you out
of routines, even leisure routines. As you face a new adventure
together, you are sharing a fresh experience. Such experiences are
bonding and give you something to talk about.

4. STICK WITH THE BASICS. Unless you are very sure of
yourselves, it is usually a mistake to invest a lot of money in the
purchase of the finest equipment or latest technology for your leisure
activities. Keeping your fun activities very basic and simple in the
beginning turns out best. Then, add needed equipment slowly and
only as your involvement in that activity dictates. Because fooling
around with fancy gadgets is often frustrating and distracting,
enjoyment is diminished.

5. KEEP IT LIGHT AND HUMOROUS. Thinking about work
and talking about problems are two common, but very bad habits
during leisure activities. Make it a point to consciously monitor
yourselves and eliminate such topics from your conversation. Instead,
relate to your partner in a very present-oriented way that is easy,

comfortable, and light. Humor and joking around helps you to let go and become free spirits for a short time.

6. KEEP WORK AWAY FROM THIS TIME. It's going to be very difficult to "disconnect" from work and psychologically get away from it all if your leisure time is contaminated with work. To counter this problem, do not carry a beeper. Never take work along on a recreational outing. Resist the urge to call home or the office to "check in." Actively discourage others from contacting you during your precious leisure time together.

7. PRACTICE TAKING SHORT "LEISURE BREAKS." Spontaneous minibreaks for a spot of fun on weekends or evenings help couples enjoy themselves. For example, on a moment's notice go out for an ice cream cone together. Or, decide to share a cup of coffee on the deck. Such activities don't take much time and break the routines of the day and evening. However, to make them work you've both got to be willing to break away and go *right now.*

8. DEVELOP LEISURE RITUALS. Without getting too rigidly routine about it, top off your leisure time together with an enjoyable finale. After golf, go to a cafe for a light lunch. Or, after fishing for a morning, cap the time spent together with a soft drink and some small talk with others on the dock. These activities can be fun and, with repetition, often become traditions that are fondly remembered.

9. ACKNOWLEDGE THE GOOD FEELINGS. It is very important for marriage partners to directly and verbally tell one another how much they enjoyed a leisure activity and one another. Particularly important in the beginning, this kind of acknowledgment reinforces the positive aspects of the experience and deepens commitment to repeating it. Even if things didn't go well, find something positive to comment on.

Having Fun the Right Way

For couples who work hard at home and in their careers, having fun makes it all worthwhile. It is unfortunate that many men and women don't recognize this reality until all of their leisure time together has been given up simply to get more done or meet personal responsibilities. The result is that the emotional rejuvenation that stems from getting away from it all to have some fun together disappears. In its place grow resentment, marital distance, and high levels of stress. It is only when double's diversions are recreated in a marriage that many couples realize just how estranged they have become from one another and from the good things in life.

True, many men and women do hold onto their own recreational outlets and find time to pursue them at least occasionally. The problem is that their leisure time is spent without a spouse to share it with. While this may be better than no leisure time all, it still has the undesirable effect of further separating a husband and wife. This leads to even more distance between them in a marriage where both spouses have already begun to live separate lives under the same roof. To put it succinctly, having your personal leisure outlet is no problem as long as it does not become a substitute for recreation time spent as a couple having fun together regularly.

One often-asked question focuses on whether there are cues that indicate whether a couple is using precious leisure time in the best way possible. Indeed, several signals indicate whether leisure time spent together is beneficial. If two or more of these are absent, look long and hard at what is going on between you during recreation time.

1. THE EXPERIENCE IS PLEASURABLE. At its best, recreational time is stimulating because it is pleasurable—with no goal-setting or delayed gratification. The pleasure is the experience of the moment because it frees you from the past and from the future. You are both together experiencing fun in the moment and, for a period of time, nothing else.

2. YOU FEEL EMOTIONALLY REJUVENATED. Although you may feel physically tired after active leisure time spent together, at the same time you feel emotionally invigorated. The emotional fatigue of all the mental work you do each day has eased. The reason is that you have shifted for a period of time out of your mental "work mode" to experience moment-by-moment.

3. YOU BECOME ABSORBED IN THE EXPERIENCE. An excellent sign of quality leisure time is deep personal absorption in the experience. During your recreational time, you are having so much fun that you don't even think of work or responsibilities. With practice, you will find that you are able to mentally "let go" to the point where you even lose track of time.

4. YOU FEEL CLOSER TO YOUR SPOUSE. Quality leisure time together is actually an often-forgotten form of intimacy between marital partners. As you share fun times together, a closeness develops. With repetition, you become pals and good friends, just having some fun together. When regular leisure experiences are shared, it's then easier to stay close when the chips are down.

5. YOU LOOK FORWARD TO DOING IT MORE. The fact is that whatever your age, fun times grow on you. One of the best signs of quality leisure time is simply wanting to do it more. You think that "This is the way it should be." As this need for fun times together grows, you make a commitment to them, and such times become a priority in your lives.

One more point. At the risk of sounding like a broken record, do keep in mind that time for leisure and fun is not a bonus anymore for work well done or for being all caught up on everything. It's a health mandate necessary to rejuvenate and to make your marriage relationship more meaningful. Not only do fun times make all the hard work worthwhile, but fun is good for the spirit: it keeps you feeling young and active. In sum, don't forget Mark Twain's astute comment about fun: "A good and wholesome thing is a little harmless fun in this world; it tones up a body and keeps him human and prevents him from souring." Her, too! Now, if you've found one another "going sour" lately, you've got the remedy.

Chapter 17

Resolving Career Crises: Finding Fulfillment in Your Life's Work

At best, a person's chosen life's work is a continuing source of personal fulfillment. Why? Because it has been developed over the years as an important part of personal identity. It is a growing, interesting, learning, creative, expressive, and emotionally important part of what defines a man or woman. Many years (and sometimes decades) are spent gaining the skills and experience that permit an individual to become established and to economically "make it" in a particular line of work. Early in a career, a young man or woman usually sets out with great enthusiasm to prove personal competence and establish some level of security in the tough "real world."

Such a personally meaningful career orientation to a life's work stands in stark contrast to those who psychologically have only an "occupation." Often developing early in life, an occupational orientation to work carries little or no personal identity investment. As a result, a man or woman with an occupation works only because it must be done and because there are financial obligations to meet. As such, work is approached as nothing more than one big pain with little personal satisfaction gained from it. Needless to say, because of this perception of work, the motivational level of individuals with occupational orientations often leaves something to be desired.

However, an important third category of men and women emerges when their relationship to a life's work is examined. These are individuals who begin their working lives with a very strong career orientation. Typically, they have proven themselves and are experienced and successful in the work they do. However, at some point a distressing change in their relationship to work begins to grow. Slowly, a successful career becomes a focal point for great personal unhappiness and dissatisfaction. In a nutshell, such an individual has moved from a career orientation to an occupational relationship to work. A career crisis is often the primary reason why this shift occurs.

To deal in positive ways with a career crisis requires first some personal understanding of this distressing psychological event. Typically, over a period of time, a pattern of negative feelings and perceptions about the workplace and the people in it develops. However, because the individual is highly responsible, productivity and quality of work typically remain quite adequate. Inside, however, emotional turmoil is growing in intensity. Here are the various emotional characteristics that together signal the onset of a career crisis.

1. A SENSE OF "GOING THROUGH THE MOTIONS." Early in a career, an individual gets a paycheck and also gains significant personal and emotional fulfillment from work. Years later, though the paycheck is better, personal satisfaction from work has all but vanished. It is replaced by a strong sense of just "going through the motions" or of daily struggling to keep up with overwhelming work responsibilities. Work that is accomplished now seems to require much more energy than in the past.

2. QUESTIONING PERSONAL MOTIVATION. Typically, within the individual, a nagging question begins to pop out at odd times. There is no clear or easy answer to this disturbing question, but it is there and becomes ever more insistent as time passes. The question is as simple as it is deeply distressing: "Why am I continuing to do this? I must be crazy." Some men and women openly express and discuss these feelings to a spouse or a good friend. Others keep them completely bottled up inside.

3. ANGER AND RESENTMENT BECOME MANIFEST. Because so little personal satisfaction is now being gained from a career, negativity and resentment begin to build. This growing anger and resentment may be directed toward work itself, the company, responsibilities, coworkers, a boss, or all of the above. Because of a strong sense of personal accountability and professionalism, this anger is usually controlled in the workplace, but either emerges at home or is internalized to create depressive symptoms.

4. SIGNS OF STRESS BEGIN TO DEVELOP. As personal dissatisfaction at work slowly grows stronger, the continuing pressures there begin to impact more heavily on the individual. One consequence is that physical and emotional signals of stress overload begin to emerge. In addition, unhealthy habits like smoking, drinking, and overeating are often exacerbated. Over time, these symptomatic stress-related responses begin to negatively affect relationships with a spouse and children.

5. ESCAPE FANTASIES. With personal doubts and emotional distress about work steadily deepening, fantasies of running away from everything frequently develop. Escape fantasies are often tinged with anger and usually take the form of beginning a new life alone somewhere else (*e.g.*, living in a shack at the beach or in a cabin deep in the woods) under an assumed name and leaving everything and everyone behind. These fantasies reflect a growing need for a life that is simpler and more fulfilling.

6. LOOKING AT OTHERS WITH ENVY. This is the "grass is always greener" problem, and it slowly but surely begins to bloom in the midst of a career crisis. Because of personal unhappiness at work, one's friends, relatives, and acquaintances are often perceived to "have it made" and are looked upon with envy. From a perspective biased by unhappy feelings, they are seen to have money, time, and little stress in their lives. This perception, although usually unwarranted, serves to worsen personal dissatisfaction.

7. QUESTIONING ORIGINAL CAREER CHOICES. Often accompanying this envy of others comes an internal questioning of a personal career choice. Individuals in the midst of career crises often go back to their college days, or to the circumstances of first employment, and begin to question the wisdom of that choice. Their thoughts are characteristic: " I thought I was suited for this kind of work and that it would be a fulfilling career choice. Now I wonder if that's true because I'm so unhappy at work."

The fact is that the great majority of men and women who are career-oriented are going to experience a career crisis at some point during their working lives. In fact, career crises are at once both very common and very serious life events. And, they are not only frightening, but also have far-reaching implications for the well-being of the individual and the family, not to mention ability to live the good life. If a career crisis is resolved well, personal and professional growth occurs, and the individual involved moves forward in personally meaningful directions. Conversely, if the crisis is not dealt with in healthy ways, personal distress and financial disaster can very well be the end result.

Parameters for Resolution

When a career crisis occurs, it goes without saying that many negative emotions well up inside. Sometimes, these emotions are confusing and may even conflict with one another. These myriad feelings usually grow in intensity over time. Again, because this kind of problem typically occurs in a highly-responsible person, that man or woman continues to go to work. And, at work, that individual does what needs to be done and does it well. Initially at least, productivity and quality of work remain at quite acceptable levels. However, because of constant emotional turmoil, continuing to maintain high standards at work becomes increasingly difficult.

One other result is that the man or woman experiencing a career crisis begins to respond in emotionally distorted ways to the perceived source of distress. As this occurs, a broader and more objective perspective on the problem is often lost. And, with such changes, the ability to clearly "see" the problem and to actively work toward positive resolution may become immensely more difficult, or even impossible. It is very helpful for any individual in the midst of a career crisis to express feelings and perceptions through ongoing discussions to someone who is trusted. In the best of circumstances, that trusted someone is a supportive and caring husband or wife. Such discussions are perhaps the best possible way to preserve an objective perspective on the issues that must be confronted and to define viable options for resolving them.

Although a career crisis is at one level a personal issue, at another it is a couple's problem as well. Why? Because it affects all family members during its course. Further, how it is resolved may involve lifestyle changes for the entire family. Again, the major source of support and objectivity required for resolving the problem in healthy ways ideally should come from a spouse. Ongoing conversations about the future and what living the good life is all about should be as much a focus for dialogue as the specifics of the work problem. In fact, both areas are often intimately related. "What do *we* want out of life and how are *we* going to get there *together*?" should be the theme.

To help an individual or a couple to gain even more perspective on what a career crisis is all about, clarifying some of the basic characteristics of career crises is the next step. These understandings help create reasonable and realistic expectations for dealing effectively with the issues at hand. Here are ten ideas that together define a basic framework within which to work toward resolution of a career crisis.

1. CAREER CRISES TYPICALLY BUILD SLOWLY FOR SEVERAL YEARS BEFORE BECOMING INTOLERABLE. Rarely do intense questioning of and lack of fulfillment in a life's work occur overnight. More typically, by the time it reaches a serious level, these feelings have been slowly building for several years. When they first start, uncomfortable feelings may be easily dismissed as transitory and negative thoughts are just pushed away. With time, jaded perceptions of work become constant and more dominant.

2. LATE THIRTIES OR EARLY FORTIES IS PRIME TIME FOR CAREER CRISES. While a career crisis can occur at virtually any point during an individual's working life, the most frequent time occurs after about ten to fifteen years of experience. The individual has proven himself or herself on the job. In addition, some of the material ingredients of the American Dream such as a car, a home, and a few extras have been purchased. Then comes an awareness that life is half over and more of the same just isn't bringing happiness.

3. INTERNAL OR EXTERNAL EVENTS CAN TRIGGER A CAREER CRISIS. Sometimes a work-related crisis is set in motion by a specific external event: for example, a reorganization, a promotion (or demotion), or getting a new boss. In other cases, no specific external precipitant is evident. For some men and women, reaching a key age may be a trigger (a 40th birthday is a big one!). Or, an initially vague but ever stronger disenchantment with work just begins to grow although externally things are going well.

4. PEOPLE OFTEN KNOW MORE ABOUT WHAT THEY DON'T WANT THAN WHAT THEY DESIRE. The vast majority of men and women who are experiencing career crises can easily define specifics of what they do not want. However, when asked what is desired or what would create personal fulfillment at this point in life, the answers become vague and nebulous. The reason is simple. Past work experience provides a negative frame of reference, but gives much less usable information about what is wanted and what will bring personal satisfaction.

5. CAREER CRISES MAY TAKE TWO OR THREE YEARS TO RESOLVE. Because a career crisis usually takes several years to become acute and emotionally painful, it is not typically resolved in a week or two or even several months. In fact, healthy resolution may involve consideration of a number of significant issues: income, impact on the family, changes in personal needs (or definition of success), and ego. Because of its emotional complexity, many career crises require two or three years before optimal resolution occurs.

6. A CAREER CRISIS IS A DEVELOPMENTAL EVENT. Every individual is different. And, every man and woman is constantly changing with age and experience. Because of this, it stands to reason that what is wanted and needed at one point in life may not be at all valid five or ten years later. It is very easy to blame oneself or others when a career crisis occurs. However, work crises should not be perceived as personal failures, but rather as positive signals that personal needs have now changed.

7. MAKING TWO OR MORE "FALSE STARTS" IS PART OF THE DISCOVERY PROCESS. Because more is known about what is not wanted when a career crisis develops, finding out what is fulfilling at a particular point in life often requires some experimentation and a number of false starts. Granted, false starts do take time and they are certainly frustrating when they don't work out. However, they are much easier to accept if seen as providing useful information and, as such, essential to the process of personal discovery.

8. IT IS IMPORTANT NOT TO CREATE PERSONAL VULNERABILITY. The emotional turmoil and personal unhappiness caused by a career crisis make a precipitous career move (or running away) an extremely tempting option. However, drastic and impulsive changes are often risky financially, and the consequence may be even more serious problems for the individual and for the family. To prevent expensive false starts and consequent financial vulnerability, a well-conceived plan and careful preparation are an absolute necessity.

9. TREAT WORK CRISES AS A COUPLE'S PROBLEM. When a man or woman experiencing a work crisis is married, resolving it together is certainly the best way of proceeding. It is helpful simply because a career change significantly affects a couple's life together, not to mention its potential impact on the children. Ongoing discussions about what is wanted (and what is not), exploring possible options together, and deciding what "we want" out of life right now and for the future clarify possible directions that will be most fruitful.

10. RESOLVING WORK CRISES OFTEN REQUIRES PERSONAL OR FINANCIAL SACRIFICE. To bring personal fulfillment closer, the status quo is by necessity disrupted during a career crisis. To resolve it, tradeoffs must be accepted: for example, less money for more time together, relocating but leaving good friends, temporarily working harder to start a new business. With a partner's support and involvement, moving forward is easier because necessary sacrifices are accepted as part of attaining mutually defined goals.

Options for Resolution

No matter what your line of work or your life circumstances, career crises are virtually always resolvable. The reason is simple: No individual is ever without choices. However, because of the many strong negative feelings associated with career crises, individuals may feel that they have no available options. Or, they make impulsive and unreasoned choices. The net result is that additional problems are created or a bad situation is made even worse. It is more difficult, but often a much sounder choice, to stay in a present position (if circumstances permit) and begin to carefully and systematically explore all available alternatives. Then, begin to make the necessary preparations for moving toward the one that seems most viable.

By virtue of deciding to move ahead (even though temporarily remaining in one's present position), personal control over the situation is being reestablished. And, because there is a clear direction with a defined endpoint, the daily discomfort of a present position becomes much easier to handle emotionally. Each particular individual needs to consider all options as means to resolve a career crisis. When exploring available directions for resolving a work problem, be as creative as possible. Sometimes elements of several alternatives can be blended as the best solution for a particular individual or couple.

During the process of finding the direction needed to resolve a work crisis, don't neglect to give strong consideration to factors that contribute to emotional well-being and living the good life together. Make it a point to give them at least equal weight to purely economic considerations. Keep in the forefront the fact that quality of life is just as important as your standard of living. In fact, at this point in your life, it may be even more so. Further, it is entirely possible that focusing too much on raising your standard of living for years may have contributed heavily to the development of your current work problems.

Here are eleven of the most common avenues for resolving career crises. Some of these solutions are obvious while others are not. Interestingly, some solutions do not require leaving a present position. As you sort through them, do keep in mind that decisions based only on strong negative emotions tend to have a higher probability of failure. The reason is that the focus may be on getting rid of uncomfortable feelings instead of carefully planning what will work optimally in the long run for you and your spouse. Instead, although it may be difficult, take your time. Choosing a personal direction on the basis of ongoing discussions, on personal thought and introspection, and on objective considerations of the impact of a particular choice on your marriage and on the family seems to work best.

1. RESOLVE HOME LIFE ISSUES. A man or woman who lives in a stressful work environment every day needs some modicum of relief after work in order to emotionally survive. When things are not going well at home, when there is so much work to do around the house that there is virtually no relaxation time, or when a husband and wife are constantly meeting the many demands of the kids, but don't do anything fun together anymore, a work crisis may be precipitated. One of the very best beginning steps for any man or woman experiencing a career crisis is to begin to re-create quality of life after work. When there is regular after-work relief, the job may not seem as difficult, personal fulfillment increases, and life begins to become enjoyable again.

2. REGRESS TO WHAT YOU LIKE TO DO. It is interesting how many men and women, very competent in their work, allow themselves to be promoted into positions where they are either not skilled or not equipped to deal with new kinds of stresses. Usually, such positions are accepted (or actively sought!) solely for the money or the status, but emotionally that individual may not be suited for the work. The eventual result may be intense emotional distress and a resulting career crisis. Ironically, many men and women may perform well in a position for which they are not suited, but at an extremely high emotional cost. It takes a strong and personally secure man or woman to decide that the money just isn't worth the aggravation and to then "step back" to enjoyable work.

3. DEVELOP A FULFILLING HOBBY OR AVOCATION. Many men and women who confront career crises simply cannot afford to leave their present positions. They may not be financially able to do so. Or, so much time may be accrued toward retirement that it would be a mistake to leave except under the most dire circumstances. On the other hand, no possibility of advancement exists, and thus there is no way out of the monotonous routine of work. In such situations, developing an interesting avocational outlet is often a helpful remedy. Such activity provides stimulation, may help to make a little extra money, and increases tolerance for the routines of work because of an interesting and personally-meaningful activity to look forward to after work.

4. BEGIN YOUR OWN BUSINESS. Given the instability and insecurity of many workplaces these days, an increasing number of men and women are thinking about beginning their own businesses. However, with this option, very careful preparations must be made. One must have an "inside" familiarity with a planned business, any necessary financial backing must be arranged, and one's personality must be such that the long hours and self-discipline required can be tolerated. Impulsively quitting a job to begin a new business without laying solid groundwork is often a prescription for great emotional distress and financial disaster. Testing a market, starting very small (often as a sideline after work), and then "jumping off" into the business full-time once it is established is one viable way of making this dream come true.

5. CHANGE YOUR SPENDING HABITS. It is surprising how many couples live beyond their means despite entirely adequate incomes. However, a time may come when a debt load accumulated from years of excessive spending begins to trap them and even precipitate a career crisis. Work becomes less fulfilling and even resented when it can't be stopped or cut back because creditors are always insistently waiting with hands out. However, some work crises can be prevented and others resolved simply by modifying spending habits. Make it a point to begin to systematically reduce your debts. Stop buying so many things. Move into more affordable housing. For some necessities, purchase good second-hand items. As a couple, grow beyond need for status items and the "bigger, better, more" philosophy of materialistic living. Then, life will become simpler and work more satisfying.

6. MAKE A LATERAL MOVE. For some men and women who cannot afford to leave an organization or who don't desire to do so, making a lateral move within the company may create new work stimulation. In some instances, this may mean moving to another department with new people and new ways of doing things. Or, an interesting personal project at work can sometimes be arranged. For some individuals, a lateral shift may mean a move to a new locale with a brand-new living and working environment. To a surprising degree for at least some men and women, a lateral move can be accomplished by refocusing basic skills in a new direction to stimulate professional growth and interest. For example, a tax accountant may start doing estate planning.

7. ARRANGE FOR EARLY RETIREMENT. These days, because of reorganizations, buy outs, or reductions in force, it is becoming increasingly common for organizations to offer early retirement packages to many middle and senior managers. Or, a man or woman may be in a financial position to make an independent decision to retire early with reduced benefits. However, while this sounds easy, early retirement as an option does require more than financial preparation. The individual needs something personally meaningful to do with time. More often than not, it is necessary to have an available and viable option to supplement income in order to meet financial responsibilities. In spite of many pitfalls, early retirement, if planned well, can be wonderful for a couple ready to live the good life.

8. DECIDE TO BECOME A ONE-CAREER FAMILY. When both husband and wife work full-time, the additional income can purchase extras. However, a two-career lifestyle also brings new problems: less time for one another (or the kids), home maintenance chores always looming in the evenings and on weekends, stresses brought home from work, couples vulnerable to growing apart while living together, constant irritability, and chronic fatigue. For some families, deciding that the financial extras aren't worth the emotional toll on the family is a choice they are willing to make. However, for this choice to work, spending patterns must be modified and debt load reduced. After deciding how this will be done, either a husband or wife interrupts a career to stay at home or only works part-time.

9. TAKE A LEAVE OF ABSENCE. At least some organizations these days recognize the need for their employees to completely get away from the workplace for a period of time. For example, most educational institutions and some corporations offer experienced employees paid (or reduced pay) sabbaticals after a specific number of years on the job. Or, with preparation, some men and women can arrange for an unpaid leave of absence from their place of employment. When a career crisis looms, this option often proves very helpful. Given needed physical and psychological distance from work, a person can regain a more objective perspective on life directions, pursue a personally interesting project, or complete needed education.

10. DON'T DO AS MUCH OF YOUR WORK. This option is so obvious and so simple that it is often completely missed by men and women in the middle of a career crisis. The fact is that a career or work crisis can easily result simply from doing too much of the same kind of work without needed relief and a chance to rejuvenate emotionally. While there is sometimes little choice about the hours being spent working, more often the man or woman involved has allowed (or even inadvertently encouraged) a work overload to occur. For this problem, a sound adage should be kept in mind: "To feel good about your life's work over the long term, three qualities must be present: First, you must have an aptitude for it. Second, you must experience success in it. Third, you must not do too much of it!" The remedy here is to make it a point to leave the office (or the business) earlier or to take an afternoon off each week for recreation. Teach others not to call you on weekends or the evening. Sometimes delegating more is helpful. This very basic strategy can work wonders for work crises.

11. CHANGE ORGANIZATIONS. Not infrequently, a given man or woman is quite content working in a particular setting. Then, for any number of reasons, the work environment changes in a negative direction. For example, a new boss arrives who places tremendous pressure on the personnel of a particular department, or an administrator arrives who has poorly developed managerial skills. Often, in a reorganization, a whole new management philosophy is put into place with a radically changed set of priorities or values that are difficult to accept. An individual in this uncomfortable position must first clearly define what is valued in a work setting (and what has been lost). Then, armed with this knowledge, that man or woman must begin to search for new opportunities in organizations that reflect these important personal needs.

Working Toward Fulfillment

At best, a life's work can be source of continuing emotional fulfillment and a focal point for personal growth and development. At worst, it can create neverending stress and seriously erode quality of life for decades despite a good income and many material possessions. No question about it, problems are part of every job. That just goes with the territory. However, attitude makes all the difference in the world. The difficulty is that with the incessant pressures of today's busy lifestyles, maintaining the positive attitude and perspective needed to resolve a career crisis is certainly easier said than done.

For those many men and women who are seriously questioning their work directions, it is helpful to think about a career crisis within the context of several contemporary realities. First, evidence is accumulating that an entire career spent in one company or organization is rapidly becoming a relic of the past. In fact, it is increasingly accepted that a given individual these days may have several distinctly different "careers" during a forty-year working life. This necessitates coping with changes, making adjustments in personal directions, and facing the emotional turmoil of at least one and perhaps several career crises. The bottom line is that because of these changes in the workplace, the question is not whether a given individual will experience a career crisis. A better question is: "How many will I have and when will they occur?"

Second, this reality is certainly made more serious by the fact that security on the job is and has been rapidly eroding in recent years. Reorganizations, leveraged buy outs, reductions in force, and new technology which requires fewer people all add to the probability that at some point a given individual may become unnecessary to the organization. And, the days when organizations consistently bent over backward to keep good people on the payroll sadly seem to be over. As employer-employee loyalty has diminished, the result may be a pink slip coming right out of the blue with little or no warning.

What these facts mean is that while many career crises grow primarily within the individual, many others may be precipitously imposed through major changes in the organization. Is there a message in all of this to individuals and couples? Yes, indeed, and it can be reduced to just three words: anticipate and prepare. Do yourself a favor and protect yourself because a problem may occur at any time and often without warning. To do a good job of preparing for the eventuality of a career crisis, any couple who wants to live the good life should definitely begin taking a number of sound steps right now.

1. PSYCHOLOGICALLY BEGIN TO WORK FOR YOURSELF. This first step in establishing personal control requires a shift in your perception of yourself as a career professional. Begin to think of your work in terms of your own skill development and movement toward fulfilling personal goals. The fact that your paycheck comes from the company is only incidental because in every way except the superficial, you treat yourself psychologically as a self-employed man or woman with your own goals and directions.

2. CREATE A POSITION OF STRENGTH. This is your safety net and, psychologically, your ace in the hole in case anything happens. There are a number of ways to construct this crisis buffer: make it a point to get cross-training in a related area, create a nest egg as security for career emergencies, develop an avocation that could someday economically sustain you. Be sure to establish your safety net when things are going well; it's extremely difficult and often virtually impossible during a career crisis.

3. STAY OUT OF A "VICTIM" POSTURE. Because of the negative feelings involved, those in the midst of career crises frequently feel—often validly—like victims. And, with a victim come oppressors: a boss, the company, the economy, even a spouse or children. The fact is that no one is going to resolve a career crisis except you. By staying out of a victim's posture regardless of the circumstances and by remaining firmly in control from within, you can gain support from loved ones and begin to move in personally productive directions.

4. DEVELOP A REALISTIC FIVE-YEAR PLAN. One of the very best ways to stay on a personally positive career track is to have a five year plan that is updated annually. In other words, always have a fairly well-developed perspective on where you want to be five years from the present. It also helps to have a contingency plan in case unexpected events occur. Your plan should include lifestyle considerations, meeting personal and family needs, as well as definition of career direction. Keep your plan updated by redefining or modifying it annually through discussions with your spouse.

5. ELIMINATE UNHEALTHY EXTREMES FROM YOUR LIFESTYLE. Many sources of personal or family vulnerability reduce the number of available options when a career crisis occurs. Some of the most common ones are drinking too much, constantly overspending and going deeper in debt, and bending work rules too much or even engaging in unethical behavior. In fact, some of these very factors actively contribute to a work crisis. As such personal problems are eliminated, a healthier lifestyle develops and career crises that do occur become far easier to resolve.

6. SOLIDIFY YOUR MARRIAGE RELATIONSHIP. A husband and wife who are already estranged from one another when a career crisis occurs often find themselves in double trouble. While crises bring some couples together, more often the emotional turmoil involved drives them further apart. By taking necessary steps to solidify your marriage relationship, you are gaining several benefits: 1) you feel better about yourself, 2) you have a source of support when a career crisis occurs, and 3) you are closer to living the good life together.

It goes without saying that a career crisis is absolutely no fun at all. And, unfortunately, the reality is that most men and women are going to experience at least one episode of intense personal questioning about work and of directions for personal fulfillment during their working lifetimes. For some individuals, comparatively, the discovery process of resolving a career crisis is relatively painless. For others, it creates an extreme sense of vulnerability, personal confusion, and excruciating emotional pain like nothing ever before experienced.

Regardless of severity, if handled well, a career crisis can be a strengthening event. Approached with understanding and wisdom, a work crisis can become a springboard to deeper personal awareness, to an emotionally-closer and more intimate marriage relationship, to stronger coping skills, and to definite movement toward all the satisfactions of living the good life together. In other words, a career crisis, like many other life events, can be a powerful learning experience if it is approached as such with an open and inquiring mind.

The bottom line is that learning from an emotionally intense experience like a career crisis, even though not much fun, is immensely more helpful in the long run than blindly reacting only to the pain. And, it's entirely up to the individual involved to make sure that personal awareness and wisdom are plucked from such an emotionally tumultuous experience. Otherwise, you may not have grown either personally or professionally. In point of fact, you don't have to learn anything at all from a career crisis. If that happens, you may become more vulnerable to additional career crises in the future.

Finally, for an important tip on how to approach a career crisis, or any crisis for that matter, keep in mind Mark Twain's wry comment about the cat that accidentally sat on a hot stove: "She will never sit down on a hot stove lid again—and that is well; but also she will never sit down on a cold one anymore." What has such a cat learned from the experience? Think about it. It's really not very much because that cat never figured out what was important about that particular painful experience. Too many adults do exactly the same.

Chapter 18

Creating Contentment: Settling Down Inside and Finding Peace Within Yourself

If you ask young couples why they are willing to work so hard when they first begin their lives together, the answer comes easily: "So that we can enjoy life later." Living the good life later on becomes the primary justification for hard work, sacrifice, and gritting one's teeth to do what needs to be done right now. And, every day, the dream is out there, dangling like a carrot. It's seen as a time of life with fewer demands, more time, and just a little extra money to do some fun things. Couples remind one another, "When we get to that point in our lives, we'll really enjoy life. We'll be content!"

Little do these couples realize that they have fallen into the "someday" fantasy. The fallacy in their thinking is that personal contentment is out there waiting for them and that it will automatically be theirs when they reach particular life goals. Take a look at these two couples.

Jason is a self-made man and has all the money he will ever need. He and his wife Samantha (Sam for short) live in a luxurious home and know everyone worth knowing in their small city. No question at all that he and his wife are well-respected. They travel extensively and have all the possessions anyone could ask for. Jason and Sam have worked hard and sacrificed their entire lives to get where they are; they believe they are on the verge of the good life.

On the other side of town live Jack and Sally. About the same age as Jason and Sam, they both work and live in a nice home that is well-furnished. They like to fish and have a small motorboat that is now almost ten years old. Rather than buy a new one, they have kept the one they have in good shape. Some months, financially, it's difficult to make ends meet now that the kids are getting older. Somehow, they manage as they always have.

Now, the question: Which of these couples is really content? By comparing the economic and social status of these two couples, Jason and Sam are the easy winners. But, do hard work and material wealth equate to personal contentment? Not by a long shot. The fact is that there is simply not enough information given in the two descriptions to really assess contentment. To get at the real aspects of living that create contentment, we must look at the "rest of the story" for each of these two couples.

With all the material success they have experienced, it is unfortunate that Jason and Sam are miserable and have been for years. Although economically well-off, they tend to live right at the edge of their financial means. They do not have a close-knit family, and good times together have all but disappeared. Within the home, even the children have adopted a very materialistic orientation to life. The tension in the home keeps everyone constantly irritable.

In stark contrast, Jack and Sally do enjoy life as a couple and as a family. They are very close to their children and spend as much time as possible doing fun things with them. They are well-liked in their neighborhood and have a few couples that they socialize with regularly. They love to fish and do so often. Aunts, uncles, cousins, and parents visit often and are always welcomed. For Jack and Sally, life is good and they know it.

The bottom line is that Jack and Sally have found a sense of peace and contentment in their lives, but Jason and Sam have not. The difference between these two couples lies not in possessions, income, social status, or prestige. In point of fact, many quite affluent families are very content, and other couples who live quite modestly are not happy at all. The factors that create personal contentment lie in the deeper values and priorities that guide their lives. Perhaps at this point, it would be helpful to define personal contentment.

CONTENTMENT: *A deep emotionally settled feeling accompanied by regular experiences of personal satisfaction derived from activities that reflect healthy life priorities.*

In other words, personal contentment is manifested in a deep knowledge and regular feelings like: "I'm complete. I am loved. I have most everything I need. Life is good and this is the way it should be." Do note that personal contentment does not mean the absence of problems, glitches, setbacks, hassles, or disappointments. These frustrating experiences are part of every station in life and every age. And, these minor problems do not detract from contentment because the man or woman who is content puts them in clear perspective in the greater scheme of one's life.

Nor is the feeling of contentment present every minute of every day. Rather, it is a deep feeling within the individual that regularly moves into conscious awareness. But, even at those times when it is not on the surface, it is always there deep down inside. In those men and women who are content, the feelings are ongoing, and as such, are a source of life fulfillment. They reflect an individual who has learned what life is really all about and what is truly important in living life each day. Some ask about the relationship of happiness and contentment. The answer is quite simple. Happiness is nothing more than the conscious experience of deep contentment.

Those who have not found much deep peace and personal fulfillment in their lives wonder how contentment comes about. The answer to this question requires several basic understandings. First, and make no mistake about it, personal contentment is possible for virtually everyone regardless of present life circumstances and past problems. And, it is possible to find personal contentment right now. It typically does not come automatically at a particular age nor at some preconceived point in the future.

The bottom line is simple. Personal contentment is usually found by those who actively seek it and who are not afraid of taking the necessary steps to create it. Often, contentment is easier to find when a husband and wife (and by extension, their children) seek it together. In other words, at best, creating contentment is a family-based "do it yourself" project. It's a wonderful feeling that "We've got the world by the tail." And, once this feeling is established and nurtured, life just gets better and better.

Looking in the Right Places

It is ironic that almost everyone wants contentment and virtually all young men and women seek it throughout their lives. At the same time, it is also remarkable how few men and women, living in a very frenetic and materialistic society, ever seem to find true contentment within themselves these days. And, unfortunately, many of those who do find it do so only very late in their lives. As a result, they've missed many good years of enjoying some of the very best things that life has to offer. The time to begin creating contentment is right now—today—but it helps to have some ideas about how to start.

Someone once wrote a song about looking for love in all the wrong places. Most certainly, there is a parallel to seeking contentment. Predominant but superficial social values, fueled by a very materialistic orientation to life and the constant pressure of life responsibilities, lead many men and women to completely miss the boat in seeking personal contentment. Tremendous amounts of energy, time, and money are spent fruitlessly seeking contentment in places where it simply cannot be found.

In order to begin creating contentment for yourself and your loved ones, you must first of all know where *not* to look. There are five dead-end streets to eliminate right away. Why? Because all of these dead ends make contentment conditional on external factors. True contentment is found within, right now, and does not depend much at all on external conditions.

MISTAKE #1: FOCUSING ON GOAL ATTAINMENT. Here, contentment is contingent on reaching some predetermined goal— paying off the mortgage, waiting until the kids are gone, having more money in the bank. Contentment is perceived to be possible only when these external conditions are present, but they are always in the future. Therefore, contentment is *not possible right now!* The net result is an individual or couple who is always waiting for contentment, but never experiencing it right now—today. In reality, personal contentment is possible anytime that you decide to create it in your life regardless of whether you have attained important goals.

MISTAKE #2: LOOKING FOR SENSORY STIMULATION. Many men and women mistake sensory stimulation for contentment. In reality, sensory stimulation provides pleasure, but not deep personal satisfaction and fulfillment in life. However, as a result of this mistake, such individuals or couples spend their lives seeking new sensory "highs," sometimes in dangerous forms—drugs, alcohol, unsafe sex, or constant partying. While such activities are certainly stimulating, the "highs" never last and then must be repeated. Real contentment does not come from sensory stimulation, but rather is a deep peace with inner origins.

MISTAKE #3: ACCUMULATING POSSESSIONS. In a very materialistic society, this mistake in seeking contentment is extremely common. Once an individual or couple begins to define personal adequacy and fulfillment through what they own, there is no end to it. That is, what one already possesses loses its ability to satisfy, spurring a reach for "more, better, and bigger" possessions that become increasingly expensive. For many, part of the satisfaction comes from impressing others: "Look. See how successful we are!" In truth, contentment is not found in things, but rather in being satisfied and enjoying the basics life has to offer right now.

MISTAKE #4: SEEKING NEW ENVIRONMENTS. Sometimes called the infatuation mistake, this strategy involves looking for contentment in new people and places. Reflecting a restlessness or wanderlust, a man or woman keeps trying new relationships and new locales. But, no place or person is ever satisfactory for long. Newness and novelty are mistaken for contentment. And, as soon as the infatuation of a person or place wears off, it's time to begin the search for "contentment" anew. Real contentment, however, comes only after infatuation ends, and deep companionship in relationships and caring involvement in a community grow.

MISTAKE #5: WANTING NO RESPONSIBILITIES. Far too often, men and women believe contentment will come only with retirement. They envision a life with adequate money and no responsibilities. Too many people with this belief finally do retire and then sit in a paid-off home with an adequate pension watching television all day feeling unhappy and depressed, just waiting out their days. Basically, to feel good, individuals must find personal meaning in their lives. This is what excites that man or woman and provides the motivation to get up in the morning. Simplifying life right now and focusing on developing deeper meanings in daily activities is an excellent way to start finding contentment.

The Components of Contentment

Content men and women can be defined not only by what they do, but also by what they know about life and about themselves. As a result, these individuals experience life each day very differently than those who are not content. While from a distance it is often difficult to tell who is content and who is not, merely talking to an individual often communicates that characteristic settled feeling that is almost always associated with personal contentment. At its base, this settled feeling reflects a core of self-knowledge and healthy life values that enhance life each day and that consequently bring personal fulfillment with them.

On the other hand, contentment cannot be manufactured overnight. Rather, it is the end result of a process of personal evolution and change that requires effort and focus. One other point is worth making here. It's that creating personal contentment is one of the most cost effective and economical endeavors possible. It costs virtually no money at all—it's a mistake to try to find contentment through expenditures. In no way, shape, or form can contentment be purchased. Ironically, at the same time, finding contentment within brings personal riches and rewards that last a lifetime. In fact, you will never know how powerful personal contentment is until you change the underlying values that guide your life each day, thereby enabling yourself to experience contentment.

There are a number of very fertile areas in which to begin the change process. And, although a husband and wife can search for contentment together, in the end it must be created for oneself. Seven of these are outlined along with specific suggestions. Some of these areas may have little personal relevance because you are already doing the right things. Other areas may define gaps where making changes will remove significant barriers to building personal contentment.

I. Demonstrating Spontaneous Good Will

It is an unfortunate reality that simple human kindness seems to be disappearing in our society. With a faster pace and more pressure, little time remains for spontaneous acts of kindness toward others, including family members. Instead, people focus on getting done what needs to be done, moving as quickly as possible from Point A to Point B, and irritably confronting all the frustrations that must be faced each day. As it evolves, this life orientation brings a self-centered "I need to get this done, so get out of my way!" style of living. Sadly, the end result is diminished sensitivity to others, even loved ones, and as a consequence, the milk of human kindness begins to diminish. What "I want right now" and what "I need to get done" take precedence over everything else.

To their credit, the men and women who make up our society are very generous in financially supporting worthy causes. However, developing spontaneous human kindness is not the same. It does not necessitate much in the way of financial giving. Rather, an important part of contentment lies in giving small gifts of oneself that, most of the time, cost very little or nothing. What it does require is awareness of others and their needs and the willingness to give a little time or to make small personal sacrifices to meet those needs.

Spontaneous acts of kindness can be practiced every single day. What does it cost an individual to offer one's seat on a subway or bus to an elderly person or a pregnant woman? Just a small sacrifice of personal comfort. What is the price of waving another car through an intersection when you have the right of way? Just a few seconds time. Such small and spontaneous acts of kindness produce many benefits. Another person in need is made more comfortable. Kindness is modeled for everyone else. And, perhaps most wonderful of all, a warm personal feeling, an inner glow, develops (sometimes called the "helper's high").

No doubt about it, regularly reaching out with courtesy, kindness, and small acts of love to other people helps your personal contentment to develop. Further, these responses make you emotionally deeper and more aware than many of those around you. Nothing is expected in return except good feelings. With time, a self-image begins to change in positive ways and, although not the reason for being kind, these acts let others see you in more complimentary ways as well.

Here are some examples of human kindness as these men and women generously "reach out and touch someone." There are similar acts of spontaneous good will going on every day in every community. Look around you and find your own quiet ways to join these good people in your neighborhood.

• Carl, living in a small rural community, cooks a bit extra and makes it a point now and then to share dinner and good conversation with an elderly neighbor who lives alone and who has few living relatives.

• Eve, a busy and successful attorney, works at lunch one day a week at a local mission that focuses on meeting the needs of homeless people. She cooks and serves men and women less fortunate.

• Joe, semiretired and living near the coast, loves to take the children of a divorced neighbor crabbing in the inlet. After they get home, they cook the crabs and share a meal as Mom gets a few hours for herself.

• Gayle's after-work hobby is making (and occasionally selling) stained glass panels. However, she also regularly makes suncatchers and, at the hospital, gives them away to sick children who need cheering up.

II. Appreciating Natural Beauty

It's a simple fact that beauty must be seen to be appreciated. It's also a fact that beauty surrounds every person every day regardless of the locale in which they live. The question is not whether beauty is present, but rather whether the viewer can see it and thereby gain the many benefits that the experience of beauty can provide. In a world filled with unfulfilling distractions (like television), heavy demands on time and energy, and a very fast pace, the beauty of the world often takes a back seat. It's there, but it's no longer seen except perhaps occasionally on vacation and sometimes not even then.

There are several important requisites to really appreciate beauty. First, it is necessary to slow down, or stop, long enough to see the beauty in a particular object or environment. In other words, it is difficult to see beauty when you are moving, literally and figuratively, at ninety miles an hour. Second, a man or woman must be looking for that beauty. Many individuals can view some of the wonderful objects and beautiful vistas square in the face and never see the beauty in them. Third, it is necessary to mentally open oneself to experience the beauty that is present. That is, to learn to deeply and emotionally savor the sensory experiences that are the essence of beauty.

Further, every person is not able to appreciate all forms of beauty. Finding a form or source of beauty that can be appreciated as part of your life may require some experimentation. However, once a personal source of beauty is found, a number of positive and influential benefits accrue. Granted, many of these rewards are subtle. At the same time, they contribute significantly to contentment and are almost immediately missed when time for the personal experience of beauty is neglected.

A. RENEWAL. Even short periods of time away from the hustle-bustle and demands of daily life are emotionally rejuvenating. The regular absorption of oneself in beauty produces a tremendous healing effect on the psyche and the soul.

B. CENTERING. Regularly removing oneself from external demands in the midst of beauty helps keep life priorities healthy. These moments help keep alive and in the forefront of awareness what is really important, deep, and enduring in life.

C. EMOTIONAL AWARENESS. For many men and women, regularly immersing themselves in beauty helps keep them in touch with their positive and tender emotions. In a fast-paced world, positive emotions (but not negative ones) are often suppressed.

D. WONDERMENT. Often, those who take time to experience beauty report that they gradually come to see themselves as part of a larger whole. And, as a result of this awareness, they come to accept themselves and their place in the world.

Although it can be argued that there are many "manmade" forms of beauty (for example, beautiful artwork, operas, or symphonies), perhaps the most fundamental form of beauty lies in the natural environment. For men and women out of touch with the beauty around them, experiencing it in its natural forms is often the best place to start. Regular exposure is important because this kind of appreciation slowly grows in importance internally. In other words, the many positive effects that beauty brings definitely do not come from a "quickie, one-shot" kind of experience tightly sandwiched between pressing responsibilities.

Sometimes, the appreciation of beauty is best as a solo experience, but it can also be experienced with a spouse, even children. However, if with a spouse, it is important not to contaminate the experience with discussions of current problems and other irrelevancies. One further suggestion. It is not necessary to travel to places of great acknowledged beauty (for example, the Grand Canyon or Yellowstone National Park) to get in touch with these deeper parts of yourself. Rather, beauty can always be found locally, even in your own back yard. Here is where some men and women have found it.

• Ken, living on the edge of town near a small woods, takes regular slow and easy walks through it. What he really enjoys is seeing the woods gradually change with each coming season.

• Anne has been a gardener since she was a child. It keeps her in touch with a deeper part of herself to plant her annual garden, nurture it, and watch her fruits and vegetables grow.

• Al and Suzy live on a small lake. Regularly, they spend time in the evenings quietly sitting together on their porch watching the fish jump as a beautiful sunset forms across the sky.

• John has a favorite spot on a hill near where he lives. It's where he often goes for a while just to let himself settle down. It's especially helpful when life begins to overwhelm him.

III. Developing a Sense of Belonging

To feel a sense of acceptance by others, that is, to belong, is a truly wonderful feeling. It is also a personal knowledge that contributes significantly both to mental health and to the capacity to live the good life. The awareness of deep personal acceptance is actually double-edged in a positive way. On one hand, in the presence of truly accepting others, it is a feeling that "I can relax and really be me." On the other hand, there is also the knowledge that "They like and accept me for being me." Such experiences are truly rejuvenating because there is no need to impress, perform, or prove anything to others. You can just be yourself: no roles, no competitiveness, no defensiveness.

At the same time that this is a truly fulfilling feeling, many men and women simply do not experience nearly enough of it these days.

One major problem encountered by many men and women is that in a very mobile society, it is now more difficult to establish a sense of belonging—that is, to really feel part of a community. People move frequently, sometimes as the result of company transfers. They leave childhood friends in their hometowns. And, in a society that is increasingly fragmented and competitive, finding a relaxed and accepting group to "belong to" is simply not as easy as it was in years past.

Of course, family members powerfully contribute to this feeling of belonging, but for maximum positive effect, the awareness of personal acceptance must extend beyond an immediate family to a network of friends. These experiences with friends are also important to give an individual or couple something to look forward to together. Such positive anticipation helps break the impact of deadening routines that are so much a part of busy and pressured lifestyles these days.

As friendships are neglected, busy men and women often find themselves isolated, although they live and work each day in the midst of many people. Many also find maladaptive ways to meet their needs for community, acceptance, and belonging. For example, a physician or attorney may gain some sense of acceptance from the positive feedback of patients or clients. Or, a sales person can join a country club to develop a network of contacts who can provide sales leads. A teacher may socialize only with other teachers and then talk about the problems of teaching with one another. In each of these instances, the individual is not presenting himself or herself outside of work roles as a person to be liked, loved, and accepted. The result is that the feeling of truly belonging and being accepted is compromised and diminished. The bottom line is that role acceptance is no real substitute for complete acceptance as a person by good friends.

It should also be noted that there are two ways to be excluded from a group that could otherwise provide a sense of belonging. The first is obvious: for whatever reason, a group does not truly accept a man or woman, but merely tolerates that individual. This type of exclusion is easily felt. The other type of exclusion is more insidious because it is internal. That is, an individual is part of an accepting group, but will not let himself or herself be open enough to relax and become part of it! This internal defensive reaction is the result of personal insecurity about acceptance by others. It is resolved only by taking the risk of being open with others; only then will their acceptance be truly felt.

To develop a sense of belonging, or of being part of a community, other people—especially good friends—are needed. Regular, but not necessarily long periods of time, need to be spent with that group. Optimally, the ambience is that of relaxed openness and camaraderie. It can be either a formally or an informally organized group. However, the best affiliation groups always maintain a primary interest in the individual, with little emphasis on work or its problems as the focus of interaction. Many men and women join and find friends in established groups to gain this important sense of belonging and acceptance. Others create their own groups. Here's how some men and women found ways to meet their needs for belonging through friendship.

• Kent and Barbara have become close to other members of a small volunteer organization that solicits and then fixes toys for needy children. All good friends, they meet regularly and have a ball when they're together.

• Linda loves being a homemaker, but felt isolated until she started a "readers' club" of neighborhood women. Each week they read a particular article and then get together to discuss it over coffee.

• Jeff, in the retail business, starts his day having breakfast at a small local breakfast house. Every morning "the gang" meets there to rib one another and tell the latest jokes.

• Jan and Tim have always liked to cook. They get together once a month with an informal "Gourmet Supper Club" they started. They take turns cooking interesting meals for the group in their homes.

IV. Reconciling Wants and Needs

Everyone has heard of Henry David Thoreau who sought the quiet, contemplative life living beside Walden Pond. There, he found inner peace and contentment. To this day, Thoreau's time at Walden Pond serves as a vision for those who seek to escape the endless frustrations of everyday life. It is to our good fortune that, while at Walden Pond, Thoreau articulated many thoughts that contemporary men and women find highly relevant to their lives, even today. He is perhaps best known for his statement that most men lead lives of "quiet desperation." How true. However, one of Thoreau's comments about material things is at least equally worthy of some thought by anyone seeking the good life: "I make myself rich by making my wants few."

There is no question that contemporary society is materialistically rich by any standard. And, technological advances and material goods have certainly been instrumental in making life easier. Up to a point, that is. It is truly distressing that so many men and women who live in such a society eventually find themselves living a lifestyle driven by a basic fallacy. This undesirable motivation is usually learned early in childhood, particularly if parents modeled it, and it is massively reinforced throughout all of adult life. It goes like this: *"I must work harder so I can buy more things so that I can be happy and feel good about myself."*

When this internalized drive is really thought through and a little information is added, its faulty basis becomes readily apparent. To see the problem, it is first necessary to make a fundamental distinction between needs and wants. Your material *needs* are defined primarily by that item's *functional* value—that is, whether a car reliably takes you from Point A to Point B no matter what year it was made. Conversely, *wants* are strongly determined by a linkage between that item and personal adequacy ("I'm acceptable to my peers because I have this label on my blouse/shirt"), by competitive needs ("I'm more successful because I've got a bigger house than you do"), or by the desire to impress others ("Look at my car; it turns heads wherever I go").

For the most part, it seems to be consistently true that once an individual or couple has secured the basics (*i.e.*, enough food and adequate shelter), little relationship can be noted between income and possessions and one's personal contentment. In fact, a case can easily be made that the more money and possessions one has accumulated, the more complicated and stressful life tends to become. Why? Because with possessions come secondary require-ments, that is, additional time, money, and energy needed to maintain them. More possessions then simply become part of the externally-oriented focus ("What do I need to do/buy/fix next") that begins to erode satisfaction in life.

This reality brings to the forefront another theme found in Thoreau's experiences: the search for simplicity. Although it is probably not practical for most couples to leave everything behind and live beside their own Walden Ponds, everyone can begin to simplify life. How do you do that? It's simplicity itself! Keeping their functional value in mind, purchase only those items you really need. Don't replace items that are in good working order. By doing so, you will eventually reduce the number and complexity of your possessions.

As a result, your "cost of living" will begin to go down, thereby reducing financial pressure. The result will be greater personal contentment and perhaps even a bit of extra money for a nest egg. Here are some men and women who have found ways to do just that.

• All her life, Annette accumulated possessions to prove to others she wasn't from the "wrong side of the tracks." The day she decided she was just fine, she stopped buying and began to enjoy life.

• Jeff is a highly successful contractor who doesn't need to prove anything to anybody. He habitually drives a beat-up pickup truck and comfortably joins his laborers each day for lunch.

• Both hard working, Dave and Melinda concluded they had many possessions they didn't need. Their contentment grew after moving to a smaller and more affordable home and eliminating some extraneous possessions they didn't use.

• Don and Tammy decided that peer pressure at work was pushing them to live far beyond their means. They made it a point to develop friendships with other couples who were not materialistically competitive and who accepted them as people.

V. Struggling to Define Personal Meanings

There comes a time in virtually every person's adult development when a struggle to find answers to life's big questions begins. More often than not these questions reflect a turning inward toward consideration of some of the deeper aspects of what life is really all about. These questions are also spurred by the need to develop more personal fulfillment in life after years of stressfully focusing only on work and other responsibilities that must be met each day.

The core questions may be somewhat different for each person or couple. Sometimes these questions grow gradually within husbands and wives as they become economically successful, but find life less fulfilling. At other times, the search for deeper meanings in life is triggered by an awareness of personal mortality: a good friend or a parent passes away or the realization comes that life is half (or more) over. For still others, it takes a personal crisis (serious health problems, loss of a job) to trigger the need for contemplation of the important questions.

Regardless of your age or the present circumstances of your life, it is important that you take regular time to try to find answers to deeper life issues. In the end, each man or woman must make basic decisions about these important questions for himself or herself. At the same time, it is often immensely helpful to talk about these kinds of questions with a spouse or a good friend (or couple) who cares. The perspectives of others aid in defining yourself, but remember you must ultimately define for yourself what you stand for in life. Although these questions have no easy or pat answers, thinking about them and putting the answers you find into practice certainly is an important step in finding personal contentment and direction for attaining the good life.

This age-old (if somewhat trite) question is often at the core of the struggle to redefine oneself in different and more positive ways: "What is the meaning of life (in twenty-five words or less)?" However, to make this core question more personally relevant, it must be changed only slightly to: "What are the important personal beliefs that will now guide my life from this point onward?" This general question can then be broken down into a series of other questions that are well worth pondering. Here are some examples.

"What is a good person and am I a good person?"

"What is the ultimate purpose of my life's work?"

"What is living 'the good life' really all about?"

"What is enduring and lasting in this short life we live?"

"What role should money and possessions play in my life?"

"What qualities are found in every fulfilling marriage?"

"What is most important for me to give to my children?"

"What is love and am I a loving person?"

"How is real success in life defined?"

"How do I want other people to remember me?"

It is important for every person to take regular time to think about these questions and struggle to answer them in personally-meaningful ways. Most of the time, the answers don't come easily. Nor are there single set answers to each of these questions. Further, the answers you find may change as you yourself change with age and more maturity, but that's all right as long as you keep thinking about them. Taking regular time for contemplating these important questions helps keep your priorities healthy and your life headed in a positive direction. And, the values your answers to these questions represent become guides to help make both big and small decisions every day.

However, if your attempts to define healthy personal meanings in your life are not translated into how you respond to loved ones, to other people, and to daily situations, the intent of this search is lost. At best, all your struggle means is that you talk a good line. Or, at worst, that you are a hypocrite who blithely says one thing and does another. While there are always disparities between your behavior and what is good and enduring, it is the consistent attempt to close this gap that ultimately redefines you in positive ways. And, striving to bring personal responses into congruence with healthy and deep beliefs about what is really important in life will surely bring you closer to personal contentment.

Here is how some people go about finding answers to important life questions and defining personal meanings for themselves.

• Sophie likes to walk on the beach year round. For her, it is a nourishing spiritual experience that brings her closer to God and helps keep what is important to her in clear perspective.

• Irv took a course that taught him how to meditate and now makes it part of his day for about twenty minutes. Not only does he feel better, but he is kinder and less hurried since he began.

• Jack and Helen are part of a small group of married couples who meet regularly to discuss important life questions. It has not only brought them close friends, but also a more intimate marital relationship.

• Janice and her husband, K. O., have taken to reading to one another from important books and discussing the issues reflected in them. When they get stuck, they sometimes go to their minister for consultation.

VI. Accepting a Personal History

At first glance, the suggestion to accept a personal history may seem an odd component of personal contentment. Actually, however, it is one of the most important. It is truly amazing how many successful and otherwise reasonably well-adjusted men and women alienate themselves from their past, deny their history (or ignore it), or otherwise minimize its impact on how life is lived right now. To a great extent, we are all a product of our past experiences—these cannot be forgotten. However, to the extent that the past represents unresolved conflicts, personal hurt or rejection, or deep resentments that are kept alive and well emotionally, such men and women are held back from their own development toward the good life.

To put this principle into perspective, a rule of thumb that holds surprisingly true and that might be called the *Potential Principle* nicely makes this point. Here it is stated simply and to the point:

THE POTENTIAL PRINCIPLE: *Adult men and women are*

*never completely free to develop to their fullest potential until
they have forgiven both those who hurt them while growing up
and their parents for how they were raised.*

To be more specific, with old resentments alive and well, it is
more difficult to cope with present frustrations or setbacks. Further,
relationships with loved ones or friends may be impaired and real
success in life may eventually be seriously compromised. Last, but
certainly not least, until personal conflicts are resolved, it is difficult
to really feel comfortable with oneself. Doubts and insecurities and
anger are barriers to experiencing the good life. Those who must be
forgiven in order to put a personal past to rest might include parents,
childhood or adolescent friends, or even an entire community where
rejection has been felt.

Once forgiveness occurs, that is, emotionally "letting go" of old
hurts and insecurities, a man or woman is ready for the second part
of accepting a personal history. This involves reconnecting to the
past in new ways. It is often accomplished simultaneously with the
forgiveness process. Essentially, the individual begins to redefine
himself or herself in terms of the past and, in so doing, frees himself
or herself from negative ties to personal development. Replacing
negative feelings about the past are positive ties (or at least neutral
feelings) to developmental experiences.

This process, although it takes time and involves personal risk,
is well worthwhile because it creates in the past an emotional anchor
for the individual. When the process is successful, old insecurities
are replaced with a sense of personal well-being. Resentments and
deep anger dissipate to free energy for the present and future. New
relationships that are personally fulfilling and that add to a solid
sense of personal identity are forged. In short, a man or woman has
made a tremendous step by emotionally coming to the point of feeling
that "I'm really okay." As a result, more closeness is possible in a
marital relationship and the good life has come closer.

To clarify the process of reconciling their personal histories, here
is how some men and women have gone about it.

• After growing up feeling like an outsider, Jason and his wife,
Elaine, went to his twenty-fifth high school reunion. There, he felt
very accepted as he rediscovered old friends and made some new
ones.

• Jessica felt emotionally neglected during her growing years as
parents focused on her sister who had problems. She finally risked
disclosing her feelings to her parents. From that starting point, a new

closeness to them developed.

• Now married and a successful career woman, Angela loves to travel. On vacations and business trips, she began to look up and spend time with childhood friends she had neglected for many years.

• Andrew's parents, now deceased, were of Scottish heritage. During his childhood, it never meant much to him. But as an adult, he finds great fulfillment in attending Highland Games and family clan meetings each year as he has ethnically defined himself.

VII. Finding Joy in Small Acts

Children tend to have lots of fun every day. Busy adults often look back with fond feelings of times when life was simpler and the experience of joy was part of every day. In some respects, it is truly unfortunate that so much shallow external stimulation like television, video games, and loud music abounds these days. While these aspects of contemporary life aren't bad in moderation, the ease with which they can provide massive external stimulation for adults and children does have a potentially serious and detrimental impact.

This availability and the growth of jobs that require mental, rather than physical, work make escape from disturbing thoughts of daily demands and responsibilities ever more difficult. Add to this situation the necessity to do everything faster ("hurry sickness") in order to get everything done each day, and the resultant problem is as pervasive as it is distressing. Many men and women begin to use strong sources of external stimulation like television, video games, and loud music (sometimes combined with alcohol or drugs) simply to get away from the mental work that goes on between their ears all day every day.

The fundamental problem here has several facets. First, consistent use of massive external stimulation to escape, particularly when used habitually, is neither ultimately relaxing nor emotionally rejuvenating. Second, these passive activities substitute for healthier and more active pastimes outside the home. Men and women with very sendentary and mentally stressful careers need some physical activity to remain healthy and to feel good about themselves. Finally, these kinds of habitual "escape" activities sabotage the wonderful and rejuvenating experiences that can be found by taking just a bit of time to enjoy life's simple pleasures.

Many varied kinds of activities can be placed in the category of simple joys. But the experiences that bring these good feelings for one person may not do so for the next. For those men and women who have lost touch with their innate ability to find joy in simple acts, some experimentation may be necessary. These suggestions will help you rediscover this kind of experience within yourself. A word of warning, however. Because they're so pleasant, such experiences can be highly addictive!

A. SCHEDULE ENOUGH TIME. You're not going to experience much joy if you're hurried because of an impending deadline, pressing obligations, or a looming need to be somewhere else.

B. GET OUTSIDE THE HOUSE. This is very important in the beginning. It's easier to enjoy a simple experience when you can't look around and see work you should be doing.

C. DO NOT SPEND MONEY. In fact, spending money is part of the problem. These kinds of very simple and fulfilling experiences typically cost very little money, if any at all.

D. GO "LOW TECH." Beware of too much technology or fancy gadgets. Such instrumentation typically requires attention and is frustrating when things go wrong. Stick with the basics.

E. LET YOURSELF GO. That is, let yourself become totally absorbed in the experience for its own sake. Don't try to make anything happen. Set no goals. Instead, just go with the flow.

It is quite characteristic that as an individual or couple engages in such experiences, very telling thoughts surface: "You know, it just doesn't get any better than this" "This is what life is really about" or "Right now, at this moment, I'm really content." Although these thoughts are often fleeting, the experiences are not. They help to make everything else worthwhile. They become fond memories. And, they become a source of stability, an anchor in a fast-moving life.

The bottom line is that when you give up life's simple joys just to get more done, you will feel it subtly but powerfully as vague discontent, as a discouragement with life in general, or as resentment toward all you have to do and get done. Now, let's take a look at how a few men and women have found ways to experience simple joys for themselves.

• On Saturday mornings, Fran frequently takes her godchild, Roy, out for a leisurely walk around the golf course. They mosey around and leisurely look for golf balls that have been lost.

• In the summertime, Eleanor and Will love to go to a local stream to spread out a blanket and read together. Conversing little, sometimes they just stretch out, hold hands, and watch the clouds drift by.

• Tim and Josey are fortunate enough to live on a small lake in the South. Sometimes alone, sometimes together, they go out on their small dock to fish and leisurely watch the world go by.

• A very special time for Al is inviting his neighbor over on the spur of the moment just to enjoy a cup of coffee together on the back porch and spend some time just "shooting the bull."

Going for the Deeper Feelings

Now you know that the process of creating contentment is really developing an awareness and enjoyment of your inner self. In a very real sense, it is really enhancing your spiritual side. It is most interesting how many men and women associate enjoying this part of oneself with the years after retirement. To do so is a serious and very common mistake. The misperception is that developing this side of oneself takes time and that time is not available during the busy years with children, home maintenance, a busy career, and community involvements.

The reality is that all the richness and perspective that your inner life can give to you should never have been neglected in the first place. The sad result is that those men and women who find this kind of personal satisfaction and contentment only during their retirement years have probably missed several decades when they could have been enjoying life together. What has usually happened is that a myriad of responsibilities, pressing incessantly in very part of life, began to slowly redirect the attention of such men and women, all day every day, toward external demands. As this change slowly insidiously took place, the personal contentment that was once part of daily life began to wither and die.

Rediscovering this part of yourself once again brings with it a new way of living, a new way of experiencing life each day. While creating contentment involves steps that individuals must take, the benefits definitely go beyond that person to a more fulfilling marital relationship. However, much of the time these benefits often do not show up in an immediate and blatantly obvious form. Rather, they create a series of subtle changes that can be seen clearly only when viewed from the perspective of a year or so after beginning the process of creating contentment. While sometimes hard to clearly define, a more settled feeling grows within the individual that shows up in a number of ways. Here's what happens.

1. **MORE ATTENTION IS GIVEN TO RELATIONSHIPS.** As an

emotionally-deeper side of oneself is nurtured, an awareness of the importance of people also grows. The result is that relationships improve because loved ones, friends and relatives, colleagues, and even strangers become more important. As such, they are the recipients of more time, attention, and positive caring.

2. THE "DRIVEN" QUALITY DECREASES. This is the achieving part of oneself that must prove something to the world or that is obsessed with being so responsible that life accelerates to high speed every day. As this responsibility–oriented and driven quality diminishes, a deeper and better perspective on what is really important in life grows stronger.

3. MATERIALISTIC NEEDS ARE REDUCED. This important change reflects more acceptance of what is already possessed as "just fine." Then, without the need to accumulate more material things, an individual or couple can begin to enjoy life with what they have right now. This change stands in contrast to orienting life solely around "wants" and how to find the money to purchase them.

4. A SELF-ACCEPTANCE DEVELOPS. This is a growing sense that "I know who I am and I like who I am." Once this self-trust develops, there is no need to waste energy trying to gain acceptance by others or to impress them. In its place grows an inner confidence that permits more relaxation with others, including family members. Relationships begin to blossom.

5. PERSONAL HEALTH IMPROVES. When life perspective changes in the direction of deeper and more fulfilling priorities, it is almost a sure bet that personal stress will correspondingly decrease. There is more personal security which results in healthier and more adaptive coping. The end result is that the individual feels better as mental and physical health improves.

6. LIFE BECOMES MUCH MORE ENJOYABLE. An individual who spends every day speeding through life "getting things done" or simply making more money to buy things usually isn't enjoying life. When that same man or woman begins to focus on meeting healthy emotional needs and strives for personal fulfillment right now, life each day becomes much more enjoyable.

7. THE ABILITY TO LOVE IS ENHANCED. More often than not, as personal contentment grows, the pace of life begins to slow. As a consequence, important feelings that have been consciously suppressed or emotionally buried begin to reemerge. Emotions that reflect deep caring, unconditional love, even passion (including libido) pop into awareness and can be expressed openly.

It's undoubtedly true that life can never again be as simple and as uncomplicated as when you were young. But, it's just as true that life can get even better than that because now you're wiser and know more about what's really important. Rather than expending energy lamenting the "good old days" that are now gone, begin making those changes necessary to create contentment for you and your spouse right now. Besides, at this point in your life you've paid your dues and you deserve more out of life than you're giving yourself. You know, after all, that living the good life and getting better together can begin right now. As the saying goes:

> "If not you . . . who?
> If not now . . . when?"

Epilogue

Carpe Diem and the New American Dream

One of the worst habits of responsible men, women, and couples is putting off enjoying life in general and one another in particular until "later." That's what *carpe diem* is all about. Simply put, the translation from Latin is "Seize the day." In other words, learning to value and enjoy each day to its fullest right now is mighty good advice. Actually, the full Latin quotation is taken from *Odes* written by Horace many centuries ago: *Carpe diem, quam minimum credula postero.* In other words, enjoy each day and trust tomorrow as little as possible. That's an even better suggestion.

At its core, it's a serious mistake to neglect living the good life—today—simply because you have so much to do. Getting more done every day isn't what you're going to remember late in your life. Living the good life certainly doesn't necessitate neglecting the future; that would be foolish and irresponsible. Besides, setting healthy and reasonable goals that define your life's direction brings its own rewards. Living life in a fulfilling way today while maintaining a healthy direction for your life is not only possible, but highly desirable. It's also how you start getting better together. And, in fact, many more men and women are doing just that—for their marriages, for themselves as men and women, and for their children.

It is interesting that definition of the good life has shifted to one that reflects healthier priorities. In the past, amassing wealth, accumulating possessions, gaining influence and status, and getting on the fast track to the top were all key ingredients. However, as many men and women have found to their chagrin, this orientation to life led to a lifestyle with highly superficial values and an emotionally shallow existence. All the deeper and more meaningful parts of life were ignored. In the process, some important lessons were painfully learned.

One positive result of these distressing lessons is that many more savvy men and women are looking inward to find what is deep, enduring, and meaningful in their lives. What they are discovering is that Quality of Life is quite different from Standard of Living once the basics of food and shelter are attained. Emerging in importance is hard work balanced by having time to enjoy life, by being in a close and fulfilling relationship with a husband or wife, by nurturing children, by having good friends, by developing a sense of community, and by living life ethically with a sound sense of personal values. These are the defining elements of the New American Dream.

In a very real way, these kinds of experiences are what loving one another is all about. Antoine de Saint-Exupéry believed that "love does not consist in gazing at each other, but in looking outward together in the same direction." On reflection, however, to get better together perhaps you must do both. As you've stepped back and looked at your life as a couple, you realize that for years you and your spouse have been moving in different directions while living together. It's time that you both stopped cold, gazed into one another's eyes and made a deeply felt commitment to one another:

"We've neglected one another for too long. We've lost all the really good things in life and in each other. Let's get back to the way it should be and the way we always wanted it to be. Let's do it for us right now. Life's too short to continue living this way."

When you make this commitment—gazing into one another's eyes—and really mean it, then you will be looking together in the same direction. And, you'll walk the same path toward a fulfilling life together—holding hands.

Goals of the Good Life

No matter what your life's work, how much you have achieved, where you live, or your other particular circumstances, the good life is within your grasp. It need not be impeded by the past. Nor should it wait for the future. The key to the good life lies within you right now. And, again, it's a fallacy to think that the good life costs a lot of money. It doesn't. It's composed of some of the best things in life and they're virtually free for the taking. When you and your partner make a decision to pursue these "freebies" together, your entire family will begin to live life fully and richly in a way never possible before.

In a nutshell, the good life has as its foundation five goals that, when reached, will redefine you as a person and keep you on a clear path toward fulfillment for yourself and your marriage. Each one of them requires that you make a decision that these goals are important and that they are worth attaining. And, each of these goals is reached through many small decisions and actions made every day.

PERSONAL GOAL #1: DEVELOPING A BEST-FRIEND MAR-ITAL RELATIONSHIP. *Definition: A marital best friend is a husband or wife with whom regular positive experiences are shared and in whom emotional trust is so complete that anything can be discussed without fear of abandonment or retribution.*

Your spouse was once your best friend, but as the years rolled by and life became more hectic, that marital friendship slowly began to erode. Now it's only a shell of what it was in the past. You've become more distant and share fewer good times these days. It's time to make a personal decision to redevelop a solid friendship with your spouse, your partner in life. Then, reach out to other people you both enjoy and develop friendships with them.

PERSONAL GOAL #2: REDEFINING SUCCESS IN YOUR LIFE. *Definition: Real success is arranging your life in such a way that you are able to do more of what is deeply fulfilling and less of what is not satisfying in ways that reflect healthy life priorities.*

When you and your partner first started out in life, you both pushed to accumulate all the material things necessary for a solid middle-class lifestyle. You also sought to prove yourselves at work to gain promotions and professional security. As you did so, fun times you once regularly shared began to fade. Now it's time to make a decision to back away from simply making more money and accumulating possessions. It's time to experience real success by doing more of what is deeply satisfying for both of you at work and at home.

PERSONAL GOAL #3: STRENGTHENING YOUR CAPACITY TO LOVE. *Definition: Marital love is a deep personal decision to remain emotionally close to a husband or wife combined with a willingness to consistently give of oneself to that partner even when the desire to do so isn't present.*

Giving of yourself is the essence of love. It was there every day when you were young and deeply in love with your spouse. Then, as life slowly filled up with responsibilities, a slow but subtle change occurred that was emotionally destructive to you both. You shifted into providing *for* your spouse and children in lieu of sharing and giving *of* yourself *to* them. It's well past time to make the decision to love your spouse and children more deeply by caring and sharing yourself with them every day.

PERSONAL GOAL #4: CREATING PERSONAL CONTENT-

MENT FROM WITHIN. *Definition: A deep emotionally settled feeling accompanied by regular experiences of deep personal satisfaction (happiness) derived from activities that reflect emotionally-healthy priorities.*

When you were young and life was simple, it was relatively easy to be happy. It was a natural part of life. Now, getting through each day has not only become very complicated, but persistent feelings of discouragement, personal discontent, and unhappiness with life have set in. With more years of experience behind you, it's well past time for you both to decide to examine your life priorities to find contentment in what is emotionally deep, personally fulfilling, and enduring in life.

PERSONAL GOAL #5: DEVELOPING A SENSE OF CLASS. *Definition: Your ability to relate with unshakable dignity and respect toward other people manifested in consistently courteous responses no matter how personally distressing the situation.*

Looking back, it is easy to see that early on, your life was balanced between working hard and enjoying life together. As your stress level has gone up, you find that you're often not such a nice person anymore. Impatient, irritable, and discourteous responses occur far too frequently and you feel bad about them. The fact is that you've lost a lot of class. You've realized it's now time to recover that easygoing, kind, and generous person you once were. In so doing, you'll become a class act once again.

Relationship Trust Will Grow

It is almost axiomatic that as a marriage relationship becomes strained, the implicit trust that a husband and wife once had in one another begins to evaporate. And without trust, no true partnership or deep emotional intimacy can be sustained. Because of the way things have been, you've both become wary of one another—always vigilant for anticipated irritability, emotional betrayal, or personal hurt. To protect yourself, you have slowly closed yourself off and, as a result, your relationship has become superficial and emotionally shallow. You're lonely and unhappy within. That's the bad news.

Because you now understand what has happened, and you know how to fix it, you're already starting to make needed changes. You have redefined the good life that you both want for yourselves. As you work together to get better together, there will certainly be bumps in the road that you both will experience. But, with time and focused effort, a level of trust that hasn't been there for years will slowly begin to reemerge. You may not even realize how unhappy and emotionally malnourished you've been until the closeness that you've both lost begins to reappear.

As trust begins to build in your relationship, you will find that you can relax and enjoy one another more easily. This will free more energy within you both to live the good life. That's the good news. In fact, there are four kinds of trust that together create the environment for true intimacy to develop once again. Rebuild all of them.

1. THE TRUST OF PREDICTABILITY. This simplest type of trust lies in a husband's or wife's ability to know how a spouse will respond in a given situation. Many minor events serve to destroy the trust of predictability. One afternoon you get a warm hello after work, and the next day a growling bear greets you at the door. In the face of emotional inconsistency or erratic behavior, there is a strong tendency to keep your distance from that person because you never know what will happen. But as trust reappears, true warmth and responsiveness becomes easier. You can become more open because you know what to expect.

2. THE TRUST OF CONTINUITY. One surefire way to create emotional distance in a marriage is to threaten to leave or seek a divorce whenever there is anger or conflict. Whether intended or not, statements threatening to end the relationship are demoralizing. They slowly but surely kill motivation to make things work because a partner is constantly verbalizing lack of commitment in no uncertain words. But as these destructive statements disappear, a strong foundation of personal commitment will reappear. This builds trust that the relationship will continue and that any problem can be worked out.

3. THE TRUST OF SHARING. This important form of trust is the core of healthy intimacy. It is a trust that your spouse will allow you into his or her world, intellectually and emotionally, by sharing what is going on inside. It is letting your partner know how you feel and experience life each day. Such sharing is in lieu of hiding thoughts, feelings, and actions from one another. It is surprising how many men and women continue to shield significant parts of themselves from a partner of many years. As personal growth occurs and a marital relationship begins to improve, sharing from the inside develops and a fulfilling intimacy grows.

4. THE TRUST OF VULNERABILITY. One major reason why the trust of sharing disappears in a relationship lies in emotional betrayal. Personal sensitivities or deep feelings are used as a weapon by a partner in the heat of anger. As a result, men and women quickly learn not to trust a partner who uses personal vulnerabilities in destructive ways. This kind of betrayal is extremely easy to fall into in times of emotional upset, but if a relationship is characterized by deep caring and love, a partner's vulnerabilities are *always* respected. In short, if you want your spouse to trust you enough to share emotionally, never betray what is shared.

Three Positive Principles

Three principles of human behavior form the foundation for all the suggestions contained in *Getting Better Together*. These principles are not only necessary for accurate self-assessment, but they also form the basis for the forward movement that will be necessary to attain the good life. To understand each of these principles and how the neglect of them has adversely affected your life is the beginning of personal growth. Carefully memorize these guiding principles and never forget them. In whatever you do, respect them and they will serve you well for a lifetime.

PRINCIPLE #1: HEALTHY EMOTIONAL NEEDS NEVER CHANGE. In other words, while cultural values and societies evolve, basic human needs do not. These needs—for caring acceptance, love, security in a relationship, sharing with loved ones, and time for leisure to "get away from it all" for brief periods—have always been important to self-esteem and to personal life satisfaction. Couples and individuals must not only respect these key human needs, but also find ways to meet them despite the stresses and strains of contemporary life.

PRINCIPLE #2: YOUR BEHAVIOR ALWAYS TELLS THE TRUTH. It's a fact that most men and women are experts at rationalizing their behavior. And, while most individuals say all the right things to themselves and to others, the truth is found by examining behavioral responses made every day. The level of your personal hypocrisy is found in the disparity between what you state as your life priorities and how you live each day. To determine what important changes you may need to make, objectively assess your behavior, not your statements.

PRINCIPLE #3: ALL NEGATIVE RESPONSES STEM FROM POSITIVE TRAITS CARRIED TOO FAR. Virtually all problematic responses have some positive basis. It is when fundamentally good attributes become too strong or when they are used in inappropriate settings that they become dysfunctional. For example, to have very high or perfectionistic standards may be essential to performing surgery, building a home, or doing accounting work. However, when such perfectionistic standards are applied to nonessential tasks at home, everyone may be unfairly criticized for failing to meet them. It is important to keep the positive core of problematic responses. At the same time, it is equally important to moderate them and to use them only in settings where they are beneficial. This means personally choosing when to use them and when to turn them off.

Three Negative Beliefs

At the other end of the spectrum, a surprising number of men and women allow negative beliefs to guide their lives. As already noted, these become evident not in what is said, but in what is done. Remember, behavior tells the truth! Many of these beliefs are manifested in rather subtle ways. Others are quite obvious. However, to the extent that they are held, they become major impediments to making progress toward the good life. Each one of these beliefs has in common a way to avoid or escape personal responsibility for issues that must be addressed if the good life is to be yours.

In addition, a core dimension in each one of these beliefs leads couples (or individuals, for that matter!), to perceive that they have no viable choices. In other words, these beliefs reinforce the uncomfortable feeling of being trapped by circumstance. The bottom line is that no matter what your situation, you are always responsible for your life and lifestyle, and you *always* have choices. To begin making significant progress toward creating the good life for you and those you love the most, you must begin removing barriers from the past, the present, and your future.

NEGATIVE BELIEF #1: THE EFFECTS OF MY PAST CAN NEVER BE OVERCOME. This is the blaming "prisoner of the past" myth. Who you are as a person is not set in stone. When persistent efforts are made, based on a personal choice to improve one's life and relationships, positive results will always be forthcoming. Major changes may not occur overnight, but with persistence they will surely come with time. The past can't be forgotten, but that's different from letting your history short-circuit your progress toward the good life. By emotionally forgiving the past, you strengthen your ability to make positive changes right now.

NEGATIVE BELIEF #2: WHAT EVERYBODY ELSE IS DOING RIGHT NOW HAS GOT TO BE RIGHT. This is the mindless "going along with the crowd" cop out. An old saying suggests that "what is right is not always popular and what is popular is not always right." Nowhere is that more true than in contemporary society. Buying into the commercial culture and superficial values that are so rampant today does not lead to personal fulfillment and good relationships. Couples must cut straight through the shallow and the superficial to find what is deeply fulfilling for them *despite* what everyone else is doing.

NEGATIVE BELIEF #3: IT WILL ALL COME TOGETHER SOMEDAY AND WE WILL LIVE HAPPILY EVER AFTER. This is the "someday over the rainbow" myth. The fact is that waiting for some point in the future to begin enjoying yourselves is not a sound strategy for living the good life. And, it's certainly not a good idea to assume that the good life will happen automatically. To get better together, you must decide that the future begins today. And, couples must decide to make the good life happen for them, beginning right now. Only then will it come true. There is no magic age. There is no ideal time. Life circumstances will never be perfect. The right time is whenever you and your spouse make the commitment to get started.

The Gift of the Good Life

One final note. Never forget that the good life is something that you give to yourselves. It may take some energy and some refocusing, but you know you can do it because you're both committed to *Getting Better Together.* The satisfaction that it brings to you both each day is a wonderful gift to yourselves and to one another. You deserve it. It's healthy. And, it reflects a deeper and more caring part of you that has long been pushed to the sidelines. The good life is also a gift to your children who will grow up in a loving home and see—every day— what a close and fulfilling marriage is all about. Then, because of your gift, they'll know exactly how to do it when they marry.

Perhaps it is only in retrospect that you realize that your lives have become excessively fast-paced, constricted to work and meeting responsibilities, and superficial in values. You're breaking out of old habits and thinking about life in a new way. While change isn't always easy, these changes are stimulating and adventuresome. New meanings and a whole new way of living are emerging. Together, you're changing your life and your style. To stay on track to the good life as you begin *Getting Better Together*, keep this counsel as your guide.

"*Your lifestyle* . . .

. . . *slow it down,*
round it out,
go for deep feelings
and simple joys."

B. A. Baldwin

GLOSSARY

ACQUISITION COMPULSION: A persistent emotional need to purchase or upgrade material possessions to support self-esteem and validate personal adequacy.

BEST FRIEND: An individual with whom regular positive experiences are shared and in whom emotional trust is so deep that anything can be discussed without fear of abandonment or retribution.

CLASS: Your ability to relate with unshakable dignity and respect toward other people, manifested in consistently courteous responses no matter how personally distressing the situation.

CONTENTMENT: A deep, emotionally settled feeling accompanied by regular experiences of personal satisfaction from activities that reflect healthy life priorities.

COUPLES MENTALITY: A husband and wife who automatically think in terms of one another and "us" because at a deep level they are partners and emotionally together.

"DREAD" EMOTIONS: An acronym describing a constellation of feelings that result from chronic stress and the systematic neglect of emotional needs: *D*efensiveness, *R*esentment, *E*scape, *A*nxiety, *D*epression.

HAPPINESS: The conscious awareness and acknowledgement of contentment.

HAPPY-HEALTHY COMMITMENT: "I commit myself to maintain my home in such a way that it is clean enough to be healthy and dirty enough to be happy."

HAVING SEX: Engaging in sexual acts for personal physical release or doing so primarily in response to a partner's needs.

HOME: An emotionally comfortable and fulfilling living environment where family members consistently relax, enjoy one another, and regularly share positive experiences.

HOUSE: An emotionally barren domicile filled with personal possessions where family members eat, sleep, and coordinate their schedules.

HUMANE TIME MANAGEMENT: The process of creativity balancing personal organization and productivity with the skills required to insure emotional well-being and to preserve quality of life.

LOVE: A deep, personal decision to remain emotionally close to a husband or wife, combined with a willingness to consistently give of oneself to that partner even when the desire to do so isn't present.

MAKING LOVE: A sensual union in which caring partners together experience an emotional closeness that is deepened and made more meaningful through physical sharing.

MARITAL MIDLIFE CRISIS: A developmental point of transition, marked by deep unhappiness in a husband, wife, or both, where previous lifestyle values and priorities have become unfulfilling and new ways of relating must be found to recreate personal contentment and life satisfaction.

MATERIALISTIC DEPENDENCY: A state of ongoing emotional vulnerability that exists when self-esteem and personal adequacy are excessively linked to ownership of status-oriented items.

META-FEELING: A feeling that is derived from and has as its root another emotion (*e.g.*, fear is transformed into anger).

PATTERN PRINCIPLE: Consistent daily decisions to complete tasks and to be highly responsible become, over time, long-term patterns of emotional neglect of loved ones and oneself.

PLEASURE: Sensory stimulation experienced in a positive way.

POTENTIAL PRINCIPLE: Adult men and women are never completely free to develop to their fullest potential until they have forgiven both those who have hurt them while growing up and their parents for how they were raised.

QUALITY OF LIFE: A measure of life success using emotionally-based criteria such as satisfying work, adequate time for leisure, enjoying positive family relationships, feeling fit and healthy, and experiencing personal contentment.

RELAXATION: The ability to allow oneself to become deeply and pleasantly absorbed in any activity that is valued primarily for the pleasure of the experience.

ROMANCE: When a man and a woman are simultaneously experiencing one another in an open and intimate way that affirms their emotional bond and the physical attraction between them. Sometimes referred to as lightly eroticized intimacy.

SELF-AFFIRMATION: Positive statements made out loud or silently to oneself about oneself to internally reinforce self-esteem, enhance healthy motivation, or facilitate personal goal attainment.

STANDARD OF LIVING: An economically-based measure of life success using materialistic criteria such as income, professional perks, size of home, and number and quality of possessions.

SUCCESS: Arranging your life in such a way that you are able to do more of what is deeply fulfilling and less of what is not satisfying in ways that reflect healthy life priorities.

TACT: The art of communicating without offending.

TRADITIONAL TIME MANAGEMENT: A philosophy of organizing oneself more tightly and enhancing personal efficiency to increase productive output from a given amount of time.

INDEX

Getting Better Together

LIVING THE GOOD LIFE WITH SOMEONE YOU LOVE
by Bruce A. Baldwin, Ph.D.

Would Another Copy Of
GETTING BETTER TOGETHER
Be Helpful?

Consider these uses for this remarkable book:

▶ As a caring gift from one FRIEND to another.

▶ For a HUSBAND or WIFE (or RELATIVE) who is encountering difficult times.

▶ As a resource for MARRIAGE COUNSELORS or their clients.

▶ For TEACHERS use as a text to help students understand today's complex lifestyles.

▶ For CLERGY to help individuals and couples experiencing marital distress.

▶ As a gift from PARENTS to their adult children and for ADULT CHILDREN to give to their parents.

▶ As a guide for CHURCH DISCUSSION GROUPS and ADULT SUNDAY SCHOOL CLASSES.

▶ For MENTAL HEALTH PROFESSIONALS to use as an adjunct to couple's counseling and individual psychotherapy.

▶ For CORPORATE GIFT-GIVING to reflect an organization's emphasis on healthy and fulfilling lifestyles.

▶ For PHYSICIANS to suggest to their patients who are experiencing marital or life stresses.

▶ For ANYONE interested in living the good life and "getting better together."

GETTING BETTER TOGETHER
$10.95
ISBN 0-933583-20-6
(SEE ORDER FORM)

(SEE ORDER FORM)

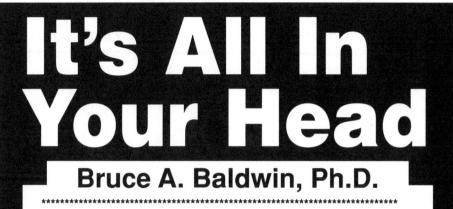
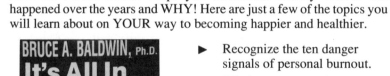

SEE WHY PEOPLE SAY . . .

ORDER FORM

QTY	ITEM	EACH	TOTAL
	GETTING BETTER TOGETHER	$10.95	$.
	IT'S ALL IN YOUR HEAD	10.95	.
	BEYOND THE CORNUCOPIA KIDS	10.95	.

SUBTOTAL	$.
N C RESIDENTS ADD 6% SALES TAX	$.
POSTAGE & HANDLING (SEE BELOW)	$.
AMOUNT ENCLOSED	$.

POSTAGE & HANDLING:
ADD $2.00 one book + **$.60 MORE** for each additional book.

CANADA: U.S. Currency. **ADD $3.00** for one book + **$1.00 MORE** for each additional book.

The **DIRECTION DYNAMICS** catalog is packed with additional information about other materials by **Dr. Bruce A. Baldwin**. Send for a free copy today.

‡ Call for details on bulk order discounts (6 or more books) and postage.

MAIL ORDER TO:	SEND MY ORDER IMMEDIATELY TO:
DIRECTION DYNAMICS 309 Honeycutt Dr. Wilmington, NC 28412-7171 Telephone: (910) 799-6544	Name: _____ Address: _____ _____ City: _____ State: _____ Zip Code: _____ Telephone: (___)_____